The Encyclopedia of
GERMAN MILITARY AIRCRAFT

The Encyclopedia of
GERMAN MILITARY AIRCRAFT

Bryan Philpott

Arms and Armour Press

A Bison Book

First published in 1980 by
Arms and Armour Press Limited
Lionel Leventhal Limited
2–6 Hampstead High Street, London NW3 1PR

Copyright © 1980 by Bison Books Limited

Produced by Bison Books Limited,
4 Cromwell Place, London SW7

British Library Cataloguing in Publication Data
ISBN 0 85368 427 8

Printed in Singapore

Designer: David Eldred
Editor: Anthony Robinson
Indexer: Penny Murphy

Page 1: the streamlined lines of the Pfalz D IIIa
are shown to advantage in this photograph.
Pages 2–3: the Bundesmarine's Panavia
Tornados will be armed with Kormoran
antishipping missiles.
Below: this Focke-Wulf Fw 190A-4 fighter is
parked on an airfield in France in 1943.

Contents

Introd

uction

Above: in Luftwaffe service the Panavia Tornado will be armed with the unique, belly-mounted MBB MW-1 dispenser for antitank bomblets.

During the early years of aviation Germany, like many other nations, took a guarded interest in the military use of the airplane. As early as 1884 a unit had been established to evaluate the use of balloons as observation platforms, resulting three years later in the formation of an independent body known as Luftshiffer Abteilung (Lighter-than-air Unit) which by 1901 had blossomed into two companies. The next logical step was the use of airships which gave considerably more flexibility than their tethered cousins. As Ferdinand von Zeppelin is generally considered to be the doyen of controllable, free-moving balloons (dirigibles), it is perhaps not surprising that of the 26 such craft existing in the world in 1910, 14 were German. The use of the airship for aerial reconnaissance was very much favored by both the German Navy and Army who, understandably, could not envision the heavier-than-air machines then beginning to appear as likely replacements. However, in 1908 the General Staff decided to watch closely the developments of technologies closely allied to military fields, including radio and aviation both of which were to play a vital part in future wars. The Technical Section soon concluded that aircraft would play an increasingly important role in military strategy; a view supported by two officers who acted as aeronautical advisors to the War Ministry. One of these men, Hauptmann de le Roi, had for the previous two years been pressing not only for financial support for the embryo German aircraft industry, but also help in the training of pilots. His continual efforts resulted in some success for, although the Ministry was not prepared to provide large sums of money, it did encourage officers to learn to fly at private schools and gave small amounts of money toward aircraft and the training of personnel.

Continuing efforts by those farsighted enough to appreciate the importance of aviation resulted in the purchase of seven aircraft for the German Army during 1910. This led to a certain amount of reorganization to accommodate the machines within the laid down military parameters. The following year more money was allocated for the purchase of aircraft, with the result that by the year's end not only had the army acquired 37 machines, but also their potential had been assessed in military maneuvers.

Despite the views of high-ranking officers, who still thought in terms of infantry, artillery and cavalry when it came to waging war, the experience of those who had participated in the 1911 exercises engendered enthusiasm for the airplane as a weapon. However at this stage the concept of air power was still a long way off. Initial progress was made in establishing a training program for pilots and observers, who undertook their basic training at civilian flying schools, and then moved on to military controlled *Fliegerstationen* (Air Stations) set up at Strassburg and Metz.

Right: this Albatros D V carries the personal markings of the German ace Hauptman Ritter von Schleich, who flew with Jasta 32.
Below: two unusually-marked Albatros D Vs in a group photograph.

Right: this Fokker Dr I Triplane is a replica which is preserved at Old Rhinebeck Aerodrome in New York state.
Far right: two views of an Albatros D V undergoing restoration for the Smithsonian Institution's National Air and Space Museum.
Below: the Albatros D V was planned as a counter to the British SE 5, but it proved to be no great improvement over the D III.

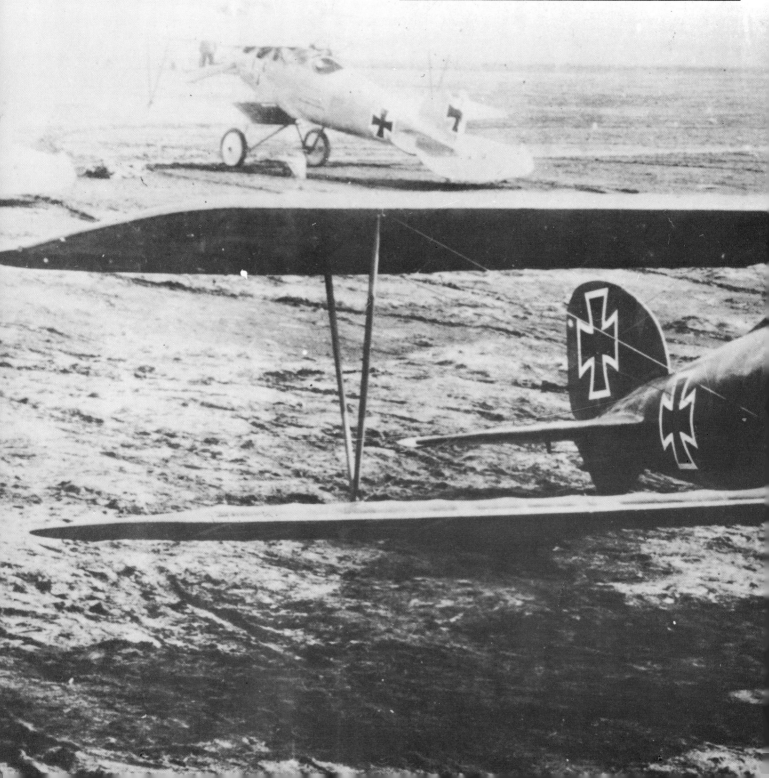

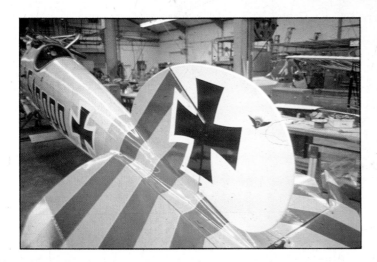

12

Training aside, consideration had to be given to the establishment and deployment of the fledgling air arm, which was still considered to be an extension of the army. Generaloberst Helmuth von Moltke, the Chief of the General Staff, proposed that each army command should include two or three aviation units, supported by a supply and communications unit. This organization could be expanded to provide every corps with an attached aviation unit in the event of war. His recommendations also included the provision of an artillery-cooperation unit for every corps, as well as a proposal – not very popularly received – that the air units be divorced from overall command of the *Verkehrstruppen*, with their own inspectorate. Although these far reaching proposals were not generally approved by the War Ministry or General Staff, who could see in them too great a measure of independence for an untried arm, they were gradually infiltrated and by the autumn of 1912 von Moltke's suggestions formed the basis of reorganization. *Flieger Kommando* Döberitz, where the first 10 army officers had been trained to fly,

joined Strassburg and Metz as a third *Fliegerstation*, and a *Fliegertruppe* comprising 21 officers and 306 men was attached to the Guards Corps. Another significant move in 1912 was the General Staff's decision to replace airships with airplanes in the tactical-reconnaissance role, although airships used for bombing and strategic reconnaissance were retained and their future seemingly assured by a planned expansion program.

The trend toward integrating flying units into army corps continued throughout 1913 and on 1 October an *Inspektion der Fliegertruppen* (*Idflieg*) came into existence, with Oberst von Eberhardt as *Inspekteur der Fliegertruppen* at its head. Flying units were still very much subservient to the army who directed their operational usage. Their role was still considered to be primarily artillery spotting and reconnaissance, although experimental work in the fitting of guns and bomb sights was being carried out with, at this time, inconclusive results.

Twelve companies forming four *Flieger Bataillone* were established at 11 airfields located at, Döberitz, Grossenhain,

Posen, Graudenz, Königsberg, Cologne, Hanover, Darmstadt, Strassburg, Metz and Freiburg, with the semiindependent Bavarian Army adding a two-company unit at Schleissheim. This impressive start formed part of an overall plan to provide 57 *Feldfliegerabteilungen (Flt Abt)* by April 1916, with another 46, forming artillery spotting units, to follow. However, the General Staff realized that this expansion was rather grandiose in view of the resources available, and settled for the formation of four *Fl Abt* from each of the 12 *Flieger Kompagnie* by 1 April 1914. The last few months of peace saw priority being given to training and the refinement of reconnaissance methods, with special emphasis being placed on artillery spotting and methods of communication between the ground and air.

On the outbreak of war in August 1914, the total strength available to the Military Aviation Service was 246 aircraft, 254 pilots and 271 observers, distributed among 34 *Fl Abt* and seven *Festungsfliegerabteilungen* whose task was the defense of the fortress towns of Metz, Strassburg, Cologne, Posen, Königsberg, Graudenz and Lotzen. The single and two-seat Taube accounted for about half the aircraft, the rest being parasol monoplanes or Albatros and Aviatik B-type biplanes. Six aircraft were allotted to each of the *Fl Abt* and four to the *Festungfl Abt*. Early operations quickly revealed the shortcomings of the Taube, but the B-types proved their worth in reconnaissance flights, although some army commanders still regarded the information they obtained with some suspicion.

Others tended to regard reports too literally without considering their necessary limitations. A notable example of this occurred early in the war when General Alexander von Kluck, commanding the 1st Army, attempted to outflank the retreating Allies during the retreat from Mons. In moving north and west to outflank the British Army he opened a dangerous gap between his forces and those of General Karl von Bülow's 2nd Army. Eventually von Kluck decided to make use of aerial reconnaissance, although his faith in this was somewhat guarded. Eventually a report reached him which stated that all the roads through the Forêt de Mormal were clear of troops. He interpreted this to mean that there were no enemy troops in the area. What he failed to appreciate was that on hearing the approach of the aircraft, the infantry had taken cover, so although the reconnaissance was factual in that the roads were in fact clear, it did not reveal that the troops had taken the countermeasure of concealment. Assuming that the retreat was in full swing, von Kluck ignored the gap his advance had created, thus leaving the way open for a counterattack through the gap, which brought the German advance to a halt. The truth of the matter was that the use of the airplane was still very much in its infancy and no one had yet appreciated that there was a vast potential in both its defensive and offensive use.

Times however were to change quickly and October 1914 brought with it an astute move by the Germans that in the long term was to bring about some of the first efforts at strategic bombing. On the 19 October Major Wilhelm Siegert joined the

Below: this replica represents the Fokker D VII, which was widely considered to be the finest fighter aircraft of World War I and was the only aircraft to be named in the peace treaty.

Oberste Heeresleitung (OHL) or German High Command, as adviser on military aviation. He was given command of a small unit whose task was to be the bombing of English targets from Calais. Unfortunately for Siegert, Calais did not fall as predicted so he had to operate from his original base at Ostende – which was out of range of English targets – and content himself with the bombing of French ports, including his proposed center of operations at Calais! However, the failure to reach this initial objective acted as a spur, rather than dampening enthusiasm for long-range bombing. The need for a *Grosskampfflugzeug* (G type bomber) to carry out strategic bombing, brought several design proposals from aircraft manufacturers. Gotha eventually produced the greatest quantity of such aircraft, but the failure to adopt one particular type resulted in some six different designs being present in the German air arm in 1915.

Apart from long-range bombers, developments in tactical roles were already afoot. The nuisance of reconnaissance aircraft quickly led to measures being taken to afford them some protection as they undertook their tasks. Reconnaissance crews had taken to arming themselves with pistols and carbines, initially for self-protection in the event of being forced down but it was not long before these weapons were turned, perhaps somewhat ineffectively, at other aircraft when they were encountered. This was only one step away from the mounting of machine guns on aircraft and, inevitably, air-to-air combat.

By the end of October 1914 the land fighting had become static and the importance of accurate reconnaissance took on a new dimension, but reorganization was necessary, especially to coordinate the efforts of the independently operating air units. A major move in this direction came with the appointment of Major Hermann von der Lieth-Thomsen to the position of *Feld-flugchef* (Chief of Field Aviation), responsible only to the OHL for military air operations. This was followed by the appointment within each army headquarters of a Staff Officer responsible for aviation. Thus a sound foundation for the integrated operations of all *Fl Abt* was laid.

The problems of coordinating several independent units into a single fighting force were beginning to be resolved, and progress was made in the fitting of armament to aircraft. Early difficulties were encountered in finding a suitable point of installation for machine guns, which had to be light, air-cooled weapons. Another problem was preventing the rather fragile aircraft then available from suffering some form of structural failure from the recoil when the weapon was fired. Ideally it was necessary to mount the observer in a position where he had a 360-degree field of fire. The British favored a front-mounted gun with a pusher propeller, whereas the Germans usually adopted heavier caliber guns mounted in rear cockpits. Aircraft thus equipped began to venture deeper into enemy territory and it was not long before weapons began to be used for offensive purposes, with some of the more adventurous crews seeking to use their machines to intercept other aircraft. The breakthrough came in April 1915 when the French ace Roland Garros had the fuel pipe of his Morane-Saulnier Type L fractured by rifle fire from the ground and was forced to land in German-held territory. He was unable to destroy his aircraft before capture, and the Germans discovered that the propeller was fitted with metal deflector plates which afforded it protection from bullets fired by a machine gun aimed through its arc.

At this time a Dutchman, Anthony Fokker, had his M5 monoplane undergoing military trials by the Germans, and no time was wasted in bringing Garros' Morane to his attention. Fokker's

engineers designed an interrupter mechanism for the M5 and the Fokker El was born. It immediately gave the German air arm an extremely effective fighter. It is interesting to reflect that Fokker's design was based on the Morane-Saulnier which itself had been fitted with interrupter gear but had been removed because of its unreliability, the deflector plates being considered an improvement. Fokker is often credited with inventing the synchronization/interrupter gear, but in fact several patents had been lodged and examples built before his encounter with Garros' aircraft. In fact it is very likely that a design by the Swiss engineer Schneider had been used on an LVG E VI as early as December 1914.

The Fokker El soon began to account for large numbers of Allied aircraft, and with it emerged some of the pilots whose names were to become household words, including Max Immelmann and Oswald Boelcke. The Fokker El enabled the Germans to redress the balance of air power which had been growing in favor of the Allies, whose bombers and reconnaissance aircraft had been taking a heavy toll of German targets. Such was the impact of the new fighter that questions were asked in the British House of Commons as to the measures being taken to counter what had become known as the 'Fokker Scourge.'

At this time aircraft used by the *Fl Abt* were not classified into groups by function, and initially single E types were allocated to *Fl Abt*. However, the formation of specialized units was already in gestation and the Bavarians had formed three single-seat fighter units by the summer of 1915, by which time categories into which aircraft types fell were becoming evident. The classes into which aircraft were divided were designated as follows:

B. Single-engined unarmed biplane
E. Single-engined armed monoplane
C. Single-engined armed biplane
CL. Light C type
J. Two-seat armed biplane for infantry support
D. Single-engined, single-seat armed biplane
Dr. Single-engined, single-seat armed triplane
G. Multiengined armed biplane
R. Three- to six-engined armed biplane

By the spring of 1915 the unarmed A type monoplanes and B type reconnaissance biplanes were being replaced by more powerful machines. Since the outbreak of war the German aircraft industry had been drawing on the experience of automobile manufacturers, whose experience in the production of racing engines enabled them gradually to improve the power output of engines. The early 80-100 hp engines had been developed into overhead-valve, water-cooled six-cylinder in-line units with outputs claimed up to 180 hp. The first generation of C type aircraft such as the Albatros CI, Rumpler CI and Aviatik CI, were fitted with 150-160 hp engines, giving them improved all-round performance in speed, climb rate, and service ceiling. They were also armed with a Parabellum MG 14 lightweight machine gun operated by the observer. The Rumpler and Albatros were more successful than the Aviatik, mainly because the observer was located in the rear cockpit and therefore had a better firing arc than his opposite number in the Aviatik who sat in the front cockpit, where he was somewhat hampered by the location of the wings and their bracing. Oswald Boelcke developed the basic principles of air fighting while flying the Albatros, which is probably the best-known and is generally regarded as the most successful C type of the period. The development of improved aircraft and armament increased the efficiency of the air arm, which although still suspect in some

Below: the L.F.G. Roland C II was nicknamed the Walfisch (whale) because of its rotund fuselage. Several hundred of this reliable two-seat reconnaissance aircraft saw service.

quarters was growing into a sizable force, boasting 72 *Flt Ab*, 18 Aircraft Parks, 11 Flying Training Units and 2 *Festung Abt* by June 1915.

The increasing effectiveness of antiaircraft weapons resulted in a search for greater altitude. This in turn led to improved C types, which in many cases introduced standard fittings carrying forward-firing Spandau machine guns operated by the pilot, a feature added to some of the early C type machines. As need arose, the C type continued to be improved and those used for aerial observation and artillery spotting carried radio equipment and cameras operated by the observer. This equipment added some 220 lb to the overall weight, consequently by 1917 260 hp engines were being introduced on such machines as the Albatros C X and Rumpler C VII.

While the development of aircraft proceeded, moves were also afoot to carry out further reorganization of the fighting units to bring about greater efficiency and better coordinated control. Major Thomsen's scheme for amalgamating all flying units into a self-governing third service did not find favor with the army commanders and was therefore rejected by the Commander in Chief, General Erich von Falkenhayn. Undeterred by this setback, Thomsen concentrated on strengthening his existing organization by the addition of a seventh *Kampfgeschwader der Obersten Heeresleitung* (Army High Command Battle Wing, or *Kagohl*) which came into being in August 1916. The same month also saw the introduction of *Jagdstaffeln* (Fighter Squadrons) which had long been advocated by Boelcke, who took command of one of these units, *Jasta 2*.

The fragmented organization and lack of an authoritative overall control of the flying services produced many unsatisfactory situations. The need for an officer of some seniority, which had been evident to many for a long time, was realized in October 1916 when Generalleutnant Ernst von Hoeppner was appointed to the newly created post of General Commanding the Air Services. Thomsen, who was now an Oberstleutnant, became his Chief of Staff and saw his long campaign for a separate air service take a step toward realization, for although it was still under the

control of the army, von Hoeppner held the reins. More centralized organization quickly followed. Most of the old designations disappeared, the *Feldflieger Abteilung* became the *Flieger Abteilung* and artillery-cooperation units were designated *Flieger Abteilungen (A)*. Kagohls were reduced to three and their task became purely offensive, emphasis being placed on equipping them with G type machines. Some units within the *Kagohls* were renamed *Schutzstaffeln*. Their task was to escort two-seater reconnaissance aircraft, although they also had a brief to attack front-line targets whenever possible. Jastas were not affected, as their primary task was to gain aerial superiority over allied fighters.

Reorganization was not only aimed at the flying units. Those responsible for control of the air services, supply, intelligence interpretation, as well as the many other functions necessary for efficient operation, were also subjected to a complete overhaul.

Throughout 1916 the Allies had gained air superiority, not only through the availability of better aircraft but also because of better lines of supply and greater numbers. In 1917 the Germans retrieved the situation by the introduction of new aircraft operating in more clearly defined roles, but the basic problem still facing them was the supply of both equipment and manpower. The planned expansion implemented in 1916 created a severe drain on raw materials which had not been resolved by the time the United States entered the war in 1917. The huge resources of this new enemy presented many problems for the Germans, because although it would take some time to mobilize American forces, there was ultimately no way in which they could be countered. Thus the situation in late 1917 was not unlike that which was to face Germany some 25 years later.

Organization and politics aside, the air arm, with its new-found freedom, began to assert its authority on the battles raging in Europe. The crews of the staid reconnaissance aircraft carried out a difficult task with great courage and fortitude, their contribution to the German war effort was probably greater and more effective than that of the more publicized fighter pilots. The task of these crews made them prime targets, consequently the casualty rate was very high, which does not mean that they were always 'easy meat.' As aircraft improved, so too did their armament and agility and many a fighter pilot found to his cost that what appeared to be a lowly reconnaissance machine was quite

Below: typical of the early C-type armed two seaters was the Albatros C I. A captured aircraft is pictured on exhibition in London. Note the side mounted radiators.

capable of giving a good account of itself. The C types used for this work were supplemented by the CL machines which came into use in the autumn of 1917. These aircraft, initially the Halberstadt CL II and Hannover CL II and III, were lighter versions of the C types and their prime task was to act as escorts. In this role they formed the basis of the equipment of the *Schutzstaffeln* and were also used in the attack role when they carried out offensive duties under the auspices of Battle Flights and Squadrons. Their contribution to the air war cannot be overemphasized since they played a far more offensive role than any other part of the German Air Force.

The improved antiaircraft weapons of the Allies forced the reconnaissance aircraft to seek the sanctuary of higher operating levels, this led to the improved C types already mentioned. The search for greater altitude curtailed troop harassment which the C types had carried out, albeit with very small bomb loads. Operation at low level, with its inherent dangers from ground fire, was essential to enable aerial support to be given to the infantry. Until such time as armored aircraft were available, several C types were modified to carry out this task. D.F.Ws and L.V.Gs were fitted with protective armor around the crews' seats and fuel tanks and these were followed into service by the specifically designed J types. The Albatros J 1 was a modified version of the C XII and its contemporary, the A.E.G. J 1, was a similarly modified C 1V. However, the most successful aircraft in this category was the Junkers J 1 which began to equip the *Infanterieflieger* units in 1917. The aircraft had a completely armored nose section and was able to withstand a tremendous amount of punishment from ground fire. Ground-attack aircraft were used extensively in this specialized role for the first time during the Battle of Verdun in 1916. They continued to carry out their tasks most effectively until the introduction of the CL types, which greatly increased the scope of this type of operation.

During the summer of 1915 aircraft with the sole purpose of air-to-air combat were introduced in small quantities to *Fl Abt* to afford some form of protection for two-seat reconnaissance machines. These aircraft, which were mainly Fokker and Pfalz monoplanes, were the forerunners of the fighter squadrons which began to be formed in 1916. Losses during the Somme campaign brought about recognition of the need for greater protection for the vulnerable reconnaissance 'workhorses' of the flying service and from this need grew the *Jagdstaffeln*. The initial aim was to form 37 *Jastas*, and training of the first unit began during the summer of 1916. Operations began in September 1916, by which time the first of the Albatros D Is had become available and were in the hands of Boelcke's *Jasta 2*. Just over a month later, this German ace who had been instrumental in the formation of the fighter squadrons was dead, but his expertise did not die with him. Many of the pilots who formed the nucleus of his unit went on to command their own Jastas, among them being perhaps the most famous of all World War I German fighter pilots, Baron Manfred von Richthofen.

The Albatros D III began to appear in 1917 and formed the major equipment of the 37 *Jastas* which had been formed by April. Their primary role was defense. Their tactics centered on laying in wait for the Allied two seaters to cross the line whereupon they attacked, usually from the sun, with devastating success. The mounting losses led to this time being named 'Bloody April.' This was a period of great success for the single-seat fighters, but it was short-lived for by May 1917 the British and French had introduced the redoubtable Sopwith Camel and SPAD Scout which balanced the scales. Improved versions of the Albatros, the D V and D Va, were introduced but it was not until 1918 when the formidable Fokker D VII began to appear that the *Jastas* again enjoyed aerial superiority.

In an attempt to bring a satisfactory end to the war before the might of American production and manpower resources could take effect, the Germans planned major offensives for the spring of 1918. Naturally the air force featured prominently in these and the task of gaining air superiority fell to the Jastas, which had been reorganized into *Jagdgeschwadern* in July 1917. The idea behind this was to group several *Jastas* into a self-contained wing which could be sent to any part of the front where the

achievement of air superiority was necessary. The first to be formed was *Jagdgeschwader 1*, comprising *Jastas* 4, 6, 10 and 11, which came into being on 26 July 1917 under the command of von Richthofen. It was followed by numbers 2 and 3 on 1 February 1918. The fourth wing, which encompassed all the Bavarian *Jastas*, was formed on 14 October 1918, just one month before the end of the war. The movement of these wings along the front during 1918 resulted in the coining of the now-famous appellation 'Flying Circus' which gradually became applied to all fighter units whether or not they formed part of a *Geschwader*. The use of these large wings virtually brought an end to the individualist fighter pilot who operated alone looking for targets of opportunity, for they brought about large-scale air battles between massed formations of fighters.

In March 1918 the strength of the *Luftstreitkräfte*, as it was then known, had reached a total of 81 *Jagdstaffeln*, 153 *Flt Abt*, 38 *Schlachtstaffeln* and eight *Bombengeschwader*, a formidable force by any reckoning and one which fought with determination and distinction against growing Allied superiority.

It is necessary to generalize in this brief summary of the development of the German Air Force. The prime use of the airplane was tactical, however it would be grossly unfair to overlook the strategic role carried out by the German bomber force. On Christmas Eve 1914 a German airplane dropped a single bomb on England. It fell harmlessly in London but was the first sign of how the new dimension in warfare could extend to involve civilian targets. Although military installations were considered to be prime objectives, particularly those on the East Coast and the Thames Estuary, airships of the German Imperial Navy carried out ineffective sorties over most of southern England. In May 1915 London was bombed by an Army airship and in the ensuing months similar raids took place in other areas. The damage caused by these raids was minimal but it led to the strengthening of air defenses which took an increasing toll of the lighter-than-air raiders. The cost effectiveness of such raids was soon considered unacceptable and thoughts had to be turned toward the use of aircraft.

Siegert's early moves to establish a strategic bombing force in 1915 now paid dividends and the bomber force, which had comprised mainly of twin-engined biplanes, began to take shape. The formation of *Kampfgeschwadern* (KG) started in earnest in 1916. Six Staffeln, each with six aircraft, formed a unit. KG 3 worked at its primary role of attacking targets in England and on 25 May 1917 carried out its first raid. The target was London but as it was found to be obscured by cloud the aircraft returned, dropping their bombs on Folkestone on the way back. Eleven days later the German bombers returned, this time their target was the naval dockyard at Sheerness, but little damage was inflicted. A week later London was again the target for the Gothas and this time their bombs killed 162 people, including 16 school children. The public outcry was enormous and led to the recall of two fighter squadrons from the Western Front for home-defense duties.

The Gotha G IV and Zeppelin-Staaken R VI carried out most of the raids over England. They caused a total of over £3,000,000 worth of damage and took the lives of 1413 civilians. Apart from the 52 bombing raids made over England, the force also operated over Italy and Bulgaria.

Taken within the total context of the war effort the results of strategic bombing appear to be insignificant, nonetheless they did bring about disruptions in production with consequent small, but at the time significant, delays in supplies to the front. The crews also learned a great deal about long-range air operations, night navigation and defensive tactics, lessons that were to prove valuable later on. Another result of the German bombing raids over England was the decision to form the Royal Air Force; this move was certainly not a direct result of the raids, but there can be no doubt that they influenced the committee responsible for its formation. It is interesting to reflect that the German air force's early attempts at strategic bombing helped to bring about the formation of a force that some 26 years later was to mount a similar, but very much larger offensive, against the German homeland.

18

By August 1918 the German offensive had been halted and the Allied push began to take its toll. The German air force continued to make its presence felt wherever it could, but its operations were more in the nature of harassment and did nothing to change the inevitable outcome of the final Allied victory. When the Armistice was signed, the German air force was disbanded and some 2000 aircraft, of which the majority had been in first-line service, were handed to the victors. From the days of its tentative beginnings all its units and personnel had fought with honor and distinction; 15,562 men had been killed, wounded or taken prisoner, and 3182 aircraft had been lost. The bitter pill of defeat proved hard to swallow, some took it philosophically but others did not; they knew that the war had seen a new weapon forged and in it they saw a potential not only for civilian use but as a means of waging perhaps a more profitable war in the future.

The Treaty of Versailles, signed on 28 June 1919, called for a considerable reduction in the size of Germany's army and navy as well as placing a total ban on military flying and the production of military aircraft. There was also a clause which prevented the importation of aero engines, aircraft or components for a period of six months. The provisions of the Treaty covering aeronautical matters, therefore appear to have been quite definite in their intentions. This was not in fact so, for only limitations – mainly concerned with engine power – were placed on the development of civil aircraft.

In 1922 the Allies placed a limit on the size and quantity of civilian aircraft which the Germans could build as well as limiting the numbers employed in the aircraft industry. These, and other restrictions were removed by the Paris Air Agreement of 1926 but even before this, under the guise of the development of commercial and private civil aviation, moves were afoot to reestablish an effective air force. Hardly a month after the end of World War 1, the first German airline using converted military aircraft to initiate its schedules began operations. Two years later, in a bid to promote the Junkers F 13, the company formed its own airline, Junkers-Luftverkehr. On 6 January 1926 it joined forces with Deutscher Aero Lloyd – a successor of the first airline – to form Deutsche Luft Hansa (now Lufthansa). One of Deutsche Luft Hansa's directors was Erhard Milch; a man who was to feature prominently in the buildup of the new Luftwaffe.

It is clear that those responsible for the Treaty of Versailles had no way of foreseeing the subterfuge that would be used to develop military aircraft thinly disguised as genuine commercial machines, but initially some efforts were made to keep a close watch on such developments. In late 1919 the Inter-Allied Aeronautical Commission of Control confiscated six Junkers F 13 transport aircraft which had been sold to the United States, explaining that in their view the F 13 could be used in military roles. Less than a year later the decision was reversed, thus negating one of the major purposes of the Treaty and leaving the way open for its exploitation.

Slowly a small but effective aircraft industry was developed

to meet the demands for light sports aircraft and larger civil machines for commercial operators. This small but by no means prosperous industry included many of the names that were to produce famous World War II aircraft, and their formation during this period enabled them to keep abreast of technical developments in aeronautical fields. At the same time as the embryo industry was tentatively finding its feet, many of the ex-flyers of the German air force were themselves continuing to take an interest in aviation. They were well supported by General Hans von Seeckt who, as Chief of the General Staff, formed an aviation section at the Defense Ministry in Berlin in 1921.

The 1920s saw the German aircraft industry struggling against financial difficulties, but managing to produce aircraft and, perhaps more important as far as the visionaries of the new Luftwaffe were concerned, keeping together a team of experienced designers and workers which would form the nucleus around which an unrestricted industry could grow. Germany gradually became the most air-minded nation in the world, with over 50,000 members in the Deutscher Luftsportverband (DLV or German Aviation Sports Union) ostensibly a national aviation sports club. The DLV gave flying instruction to young men and women in gliders and light aircraft, thus laying the foundation for a core of personnel who had the necessary aptitude for flying training when the opportunity presented itself. Meanwhile, in 1923, mainly through the endeavors of von Seeckt, secret training schools were established in the Soviet Union and many

of the officers who reached senior rank in the Luftwaffe during World War II received their initial flying training at these schools.

With hindsight it seems that Germany's clandestine air armament programs should have been obvious. Thinly-disguised specifications for sporting single-seat aircraft, as well as long-range air taxis and mailplanes, were being issued to the manufacturers, and the civil flying schools were training pilots at a rate that could not possibly be absorbed by civilian operators. It is likely that some did appreciate the buildup that was taking place, but conveniently turned a blind eye, while others were far too trusting and accepted what they saw at face value.

One of the most remarkable examples of this general acceptance of the situation can be seen in the activities of Deutsche Luft Hansa. Milch, now chairman, ensured that the airline had the best available aircraft, a surfeit of personnel and numerous airfields throughout Germany. Training in all types of flying, including both day and night navigation and instrument flying, is the very backbone of military bombing and reconnaissance operations, yet no one seems to have taken more than a passing interest, even when the government changed a decision to halve the grant allowed to the airline after Milch became acquainted with Hermann Göring, then a relatively new member of the Reichstag.

Despite unheeded warnings and veiled hints progress continued to be made, with the result that when Adolf Hitler became German Chancellor on 30 January 1933, the groundwork for the

Below: this Albatros D III, flown by Leutnant Georg Simon of Jasta 11, was brought down by Captain G. Chapman of 29 Squadron RFC. It is shown at Dunkirk on 20 June 1917.

creation of an air force had been more or less completed. With the National Socialist Party in power the necessity for a strong air force was quickly realized and funds were made available for the expansion of the aircraft industry. Hermann Göring was appointed *Reichskommissar* for Air and Erhard Milch became his deputy. On 1 January 1934 Milch instituted an expansion program aimed at providing the still-secret air force with a strength of over 4000 aircraft by September 1935. This total included 1760 trainers which reflected the priority given to the training of new personnel. This program was modified later in the year to place the emphasis on combat aircraft in order to counter any threats to Hitler's new and aggressive foreign policy. By January 1935 deliveries had fallen below the required rate of the original program, with an average output of 162 aircraft per month, but by the end of the year this had risen to 300. By this time there was no longer any need for secrecy as Germany's rearmament program was clear for all to see. The Führer's demands for increasing the number of new combat types and cutting down their development time so that they could reach production status sooner, was already causing Milch problems. He had based his estimates on those made by Göring which allowed for the Luftwaffe to reach its peak by 1943. Already the inconsistency in decision making and Göring's weaknesses in facing the Führer with reality, was becoming evident.

On 1 March 1935 the Luftwaffe was revealed to the world and units which had been masquerading as flying clubs were handed over to the military. At this time its total strength was over 1800 aircraft and 20,000 men, and was still expanding.

The Spanish Civil War, which started in 1936, gave the Luftwaffe an opportunity to try some of its aircraft and personnel under combat conditions. Junkers Ju 52s and Heinkel He 51s were dispatched to the aid of General Francisco Franco's Nationalist forces. In November 1936 the Condor Legion was formed and by the time it returned to Germany in 1939 had achieved a lot of success and gained useful experience in operating such types as the Messerschmitt Bf 109, Heinkel He 111 and the Junkers Ju 87.

When Germany invaded Poland on 1 September 1939, the Luftwaffe had a strength of over 4200 aircraft and looked to be superior to any other air force in the world. However, in many ways its strength was illusory, for it had few reserves and a number of its bomber and fighter units were below their planned numerical establishment. During the previous year the overall rise in operational strength had been about 25%, the majority of this being attributable to the increase in supply of transport aircraft, dive bombers and reconnaissance machines. This seems to indicate that Göring clearly saw the coming war as one in which the Luftwaffe would operate mainly in a tactical role, clearing the way for the army as well as maintaining supplies from the air once air and ground superiority had been achieved.

Göring's failure to expand fighter units to the same extent as the rest of the Luftwaffe appears to indicate that he felt his bombers would not need fighter protection in depth, and that there was no major requirement for them in defending the German homeland. The defense of Germany was in the hands of a few day fighter units, which were considered to be adequate to counter any enemy bombers foolish enough to enter German airspace, and a considerable number of antiaircraft guns supported by searchlights.

Göring's belief that the enemy air forces would be incapable of mounting a successful bomber offensive, is underlined by his often misquoted comment made during a tour of Rhineland defenses in July 1939: 'If an enemy bomber reaches German soil, my name is not Hermann Göring. You can call me Meier.'

It must be remembered, however, that at this time he had no idea that Germany would be faced with a war on the scale that it was to reach within two years. Nonetheless, it is hard to reconcile Göring's opinions. On one hand he believed that enemy

bombers would not penetrate German airspace, and on the other that there was no defense against the bomber, a view he is known to have shared with other air leaders of the period. The most likely explanation is that his own philosophy as far as air war was concerned, was that aircraft were intended for use in offensive and not defensive roles, and that the war Germany was about to embark on would be of short duration. He was also aware that a high proportion of the forces available to him would be called upon to support Hitler's ground offensives, thus reducing any air defense potential he might consider necessary.

On the outbreak of war the Luftwaffe was not equipped to wage a strategic campaign of the type launched by the RAF and USAAF in 1943–44. Its bomber squadrons *(Kampfgeschwader)* were equipped with what were called long-range twin-engined bombers which are better described as medium-range bombers, suited to carry out tactical operations. This, in fact, was their prime purpose as seen by Field Marshal Albert Kesselring, an army-trained officer who became the Luftwaffe's Chief of Staff in 1936. Together with Göring, he had been instrumental in cancelling the development of the four-engined Dornier Do 19 and Junkers Ju 89, in which his predecessor General Walther Wever – a firm advocate of strategic bombing – had placed great faith. It is often claimed that with Wever's death in June 1936 died all belief in the strategic bomber, but this is not so; it was simply given a lower priority since no immediate use for this warplane could be foreseen. Kesselring favored development of the so-

Above: this Junkers Ju 87B-1 Stuka of II/StG 2 'Immelmann' is typical of the dive-bombers which achieved such success during the Polish Campaign and the assault in the West.
Below: the Focke-Wulf Fw 190A-8/U1 conversion trainer was used to retrain Junkers Ju 87 ground attack pilots.

called Bomber A, to which specification Heinkel had proposed his *Projekt* 1041, eventually to become the He 177. It is possible that if Wever had not died the Luftwaffe may well have been equipped with some four-engined long-range bombers which may have proved their worth, especially on the Eastern Front, but this must remain as pure conjecture.

As it was, on 3 September 1939, the Luftwaffe had on strength 1270 twin-engined bombers capable of reaching England from German airfields. Of these 780 were Heinkel He 111s, 470 were Dornier Do 17s (mainly the Do 17Z variant) and 20 were Junkers Ju 88s. In addition there were some 280 Do 17 reconnaissance bombers and 335 Junkers Ju 87 dive bombers. The Ju 87's were purely for tactical support of the army, which in Kesselring's view was the main objective of the bomber force. At this time Hitler did not plan the widespread bombardment of the British Isles, as he still hoped that the two countries would not go to war with each other. If his intention had been to mount an aerial campaign from German bases, it is very unlikely that he would have achieved the rate of bombardment feared in England, since both the He 111 and Do 17 would have needed to have sacrificed at least half their designed bomb load if they were to carry sufficient fuel reserves to allow for variable weather, formation buildups, and diversions.

In the Polish campaign the Luftwaffe performed its intended tactical role with frightening efficiency, and repeated the performance in the assaults on Norway, the Low Countries and France. Indeed, during these campaigns, with the possible exception of that in France where RAF fighter squadrons were encountered for the first time, the Luftwaffe was virtually unopposed by modern aircraft and thus surrounded itself with an aura of invincibility. The occupation of the Low Countries and the collapse of France opened up bases from which the German bombers could strike against England, and enjoy some fighter protection. At this time military targets were still the main objectives and bombing of the civilian population was forbidden.

The stubborn resistance of the RAF which prevented the Luftwaffe from gaining the air superiority needed to enable an invasion of the British Isles to take place has been documented many times, and will therefore be familiar to most readers. There can be no doubt that the Luftwaffe crews fought valiantly against a force which could match them in equipment and outmatch them in leadership, since on several occasions the initiative could easily have gone the Luftwaffe's way if decisions to change tactics, points of attack and deployment of forces had not been made.

The campaigns in the Balkans and Middle East and the decision in 1941 to attack the Soviet Union, resulted in the Luftwaffe fighting a three-front war. Although this may have appeared viable in the short-term it was obvious that the longer the war lasted the more stretched resources would become. The entry of the United States into the war greatly increased these problems, since the vast resources of this nation could in no way be matched by the Germans. Germany was in no position to attempt an early end to the fighting, as they had tried to do for basically the same reasons in 1918.

By the end of 1942, although aircraft production had been increased considerably, mainly as a result of the inspiring work of Albert Speer who became Minister for Armaments and Munitions earlier in the year, the Luftwaffe was already going onto the defensive. The efficiency of the aircraft industry cannot be questioned, for it is reflected in stark facts. In 1939 production was running at 700 aircraft per month from a 40 hour shift. The working week was not increased until 1943–44 when it went up to 48 hours then to 60 hours, reaching a peak of 72 hours by the end of 1944. Continual attention from Allied bombers eventually forced it to disperse, but even when aircraft were being produced in component factories scattered all over Germany, production was still reaching high figures. Over 90,000 tons of bombs were dropped on aircraft factories but the industry's output continued from temporary factories hidden in woods, tunnelled

dugouts in mountain sides, and a variety of other unlikely places.

The aircraft built were mainly variants and developments of the types with which the Luftwaffe had been equipped in 1939. Replacement designs were trailing far behind and in some cases had low priority. It was not until 1943 that completely new aircraft were rolling off the production lines, their gestation having been protracted due to an atmosphere of complacency. The lesson of always having a replacement on the drawing board, however successful current designs might be, had been forgotten. This is something of an oversimplification, since the industry did, in fact, have improved aircraft planned, but efforts to get them into production at the right time were often frustrated until it was too late. Machines such as the Bf 109, Fw 190, Ju 88 and He 111, proved to be classics of their time, but they were modified and improved during their service life to a degree well beyond their originally planned design life.

The Allied bombing of fuel supplies and lines of communication sounded the death knell of the Luftwaffe as an effective force. Fuel was necessary not only to wage war but also carry out training of replacement crews. Losses in the Soviet Union reached horrific proportions, and although similar losses were inflicted in return, Soviet production facilities were located well beyond the reach of Luftwaffe bombers, and were able to replace their losses at a greater rate than they were occurring. It is possible that the possession of a good strategic bomber may have caused some disruption of production in the Soviet factories, but since German aircraft production was not brought to a standstill by Allied bombing, it is extremely unlikely that the eventual outcome of the war would have changed.

By late 1944 the Allies had total air supremacy and dwindling fuel reserves, coupled with decreasing numbers of experienced crews, allowed the Luftwaffe to offer only token resistance. The fact that the Luftwaffe failed to achieve the aims expected of it during the war years has been the subject of much analysis during the last 35 years. Hitler and Göring must accept responsibility for the ultimate debacle that resulted from their leadership, or to be more correct, lack of it. Göring in particular proved to be quite inadequate and was incapable of understanding even the simplest tactical and strategic use of air power, and was far too ready to agree with the whims of the Führer even when these left his own staff out on a limb. Every air force has its faults but after a war it is often the defeated who are subjected to public examination in detail, and in many respects supposed errors made by Luftwaffe staff have been magnified out of all proportion. However, it is certain that for at least $3\frac{1}{2}$ years the Luftwaffe had the aircraft and crews backed by technical knowledge to achieve more decisive results than they in fact did. Although there may well be question marks placed against both the aircraft and those who flew them, these are insignificant when compared with the major tactical blunders that were perpetuated.

So in 10 years the Luftwaffe emerged, Phoenix like, from the funeral pyre left by the Treaty of Versailles. It reached a peak in 1940 when it looked almost invincible, only to die in 1945 at the hands of an Allied air force which had not been shackled by indifferent leadership and which was in the end much better equipped.

There can be little doubt that the aircraft used by the Luftwaffe were, in most cases, equal in every respect to those of their adversaries. The fact that this balance had all but evaporated by the end of the war, is not the fault of the industry or designers. The latter had some revolutionary aircraft on their drawing boards when the war ended, many of which were captured in prototype form or in an advanced design stage. They were quickly analyzed by the victors and much German wartime technology was incorporated into postwar Soviet, British and American military aircraft.

Today the West German armed forces, the Bundeswehr, are a fully integrated and major component of the NATO Alliance. The achievement of this status has taken many years of deter-

Below: two Messerschmitt Bf 110G-2s are readied for action over the Eastern Front in April 1944. By that time most Bf 110s were serving as night fighters in defence of the Reich.

mined effort and has not been accomplished without overcoming many technical and political problems along the way. On two occasions following world wars, Germany has had to create its armed forces anew following lengthy bans on military involvement imposed by its former adversaries. However, the second creation in the 1950s was of a very different nature to that under Hitler's Third Reich. Germany was now divided and the creation of the modern West German armed forces was an entirely overt operation conducted with the full backing of Western governments and the NATO Alliance. Starting afresh does have certain advantages, for the whole operation can be planned and executed without many of the restrictions that established forces find inhibiting in times of major reequipment or reorganization. Also unlike Hitler's comparatively slow rearmament, the requirement in the 1950s was for instant armed forces.

In the years immediately following World War II the whole of Germany was controlled by the four-power agreements between the United States, Great Britain, France and the USSR, each of the powers operating its own armed forces in its own sectors. Any military forces or work associated with military hardware was banned. Indeed, the design and construction of light civil aircraft and the operation of any German airline was also prohibited. German nationals wishing to pursue their work in these fields were forced to do so abroad. On 23 May 1949 the three western sectors were integrated to form the Federal Republic of Germany, with a new capital in Bonn; Berlin, the traditional capital, was geographically isolated inside the Soviet sector, and itself split into four sectors under the controlling powers. The Soviet-occupied sector of Germany became the German Democratic Republic (GDR), but it did not receive

diplomatic recognition from the West. With West Germany's long-term economic and political stability assured, the Western powers relaxed some of the controls over military activities, and set about clearing the way for her to rearm as a partner within the proposed European Defense Community. In the event the EDC failed to materialize, and it was not until the ratification of the 1954 Treaty of Paris early in 1955 that West Germany could formally join NATO. By this time ambitious plans had been made for Germany's proposed armed forces. These were not entirely realistic, for when the time came to implement the plans considerable revision was needed.

The two essentials were to find suitable hardware and personnel with which to operate it. Finding the hardware was the lesser problem, since there was a host of countries willing to sell Germany armaments. In smaller nonindustrialized countries, the total armed forces can often be 'hired' as a package deal, coming complete with all the necessary organizational expertise and personnel to run them, but such options usually incur heavy financial and political problems. West Germany had, with massive aid, already reestablished itself as a major financial and industrial base, and self-interest dictated that much of the vast quantity of hardware needed should be built by German industry even if it was not of indigenous design. Apart from the immediate financial and employment gains, the long-term benefits of enabling German industry to regain its traditional role as a leader in the field of advanced technology were not only attractive but necessary.

In respect to aviation, many of the aircraft needed were purchased from abroad, especially older combat types approaching replacement or obsolescence in the massive arsenal

Below: the Dornier Do 31E was designed to meet NATO specification NMBR4, which called for a V/STOL transport aircraft. The prototype first flew in February 1967 and the second machine to fly, the Do 31E-3, is illustrated. The Do 31 was developed beyond the prototype stage.

of the United States. Such equipment would fill the gap during the formative years, but for the future large numbers of newer types would have to be obtained. Great Britain also supplied a number of new aircraft, these going mainly to the Navy's air arm, the Marineflieger. Meanwhile, most of the famous firms in German aviation whose names had been household words up to 1945 were still in existence; Messerschmitt, Focke-Wulf, Henschel, Heinkel and Daimler-Benz to name a few. These firms now engaged mainly in producing light motor vehicles and other earthbound products and most of them were only too pleased to reestablish themselves in aviation. The logical solution to the equipment problem was to make direct purchases abroad of those types needed only in small numbers or where the operational requirement could be seen as relatively short term. Then by organizing German aero industries into suitable groupings both internally and with partners abroad major programs could be tackled by Germany. Two subsequent and outstanding examples of this practice have been the NATO Starfighter program and the trinational Tornado program.

Manpower was to prove a more intractable problem, and large amounts of hardware without trained manpower to operate it does not deter aggressors or win wars. Although the Bundeswehr's assessment of equipment levels was realistic enough, its hopes that large numbers of ex-servicemen would respond to the invitation to resume their military careers, and so form a large nucleus of semitrained personnel, was sadly overoptimistic. After some 10 years out of the armed forces fewer men than hoped for were willing to give up new-found prosperity for a late start in another job. Also, in the intervening period the rate of technological progress had considerably

outdated much of the experience such recruits could offer. In particular, many experienced pilots or other aircrew from the war years would now be too old or unfit to start flying again in significantly more sophisticated aircraft than they had last encountered. For obvious reasons, the German public at large was apathetic toward anything military, added to which there was a significantly vocal section of the population totally opposed to any rearmament. The Luftwaffe's plans for some 80,000 administrative personnel and some 1300 former pilots to fly the similar number of aircraft planned had to be considerably revised. This could only be achieved by cutting the number of aircraft, and extending the period of buildup to allow sufficient time to train a correspondingly larger number of new, but in the main younger, recruits. Plans for the army and navy underwent similar revisions, but the date of 24 September 1956 was fixed as the official birth date of the new Luftwaffe, with much still to be accomplished.

Despite the aforementioned problems, the new Luftwaffe did have a nucleus of experienced leaders and former Luftwaffe personnel, led by Generalleutnant Josef Kammhuber as *Inspekteur der Luftwaffe*. Well-known pilots such as Adolf Galland and Colonels Johannes Steinhoff, Dieter Hrabak, and Werner Panitzki, and Majors Gerhard Barkhorn, Walter Krupinsky and Herbert Wehnelt rejoined the service. These people were also very influential as advisers on aircraft procurement, having had the opportunities to evaluate several types of interest to the new service. In 1954, the USAF in Europe set up Luftwaffe aircrew-training establishments at Landsberg and Furstenfeldbruck, but this plan suffered a political setback as such training could not start before ratification of the Treaty of Paris. It eventually got under way in 1955, with training commencing on Piper L-18C Cubs, progressing onto Canadian-built Harvards and finally onto the Lockheed T-33. In June and July 1956, the Cubs and Harvards were transferred to the Luftwaffe, although they lacked full military and national insignia until the official birth date some three months later. This ceremony duly took place at Furstenfeldbruck on 24 September, and was a modest affair during which three aircraft (one each of the three training types) were handed over, resplendant in the readopted World War I style crosses; the first 10 pilots, all ex-wartime aircrew, also received their new wings.

Army and naval aviation sections developed at a slightly slower pace than did the Luftwaffe, with the air arms of these two services respectively reaching operational status in 1957 and 1958. Aircrew for these two services were trained in Germany, the United States and, for the Bundesmarine, in Great Britain. By 1959, all three services were well established, if not at the levels originally intended, and looking forward to receiving newer types to carry them through the 1960s and beyond. One such type was to be the Lockheed F-104G Super Starfighter.

Among the more unlikely projects tested by the Luftwaffe in 1966 was Lockheed's 'ZELL' (ZEro Length Launch) system of launching aircraft, which Lockheed had developed in 1962 as a means of launching aircraft from dispersed sites and retrieving them by arrested landings. The system was unlikely to be a success because the aircraft being launched were F-104G Starfighters and, apart from the practical difficulties of operating such a system effectively, the Starfighter was already the subject of headline news, all of it bad. During the previous year a record number of machines had been lost, and since 1962 when the type entered service a considerable number of aircrew had died or received severe injuries. With a program as large as that of the F-104, which was in production for several NATO air forces with Germany operating the largest number, there were bound to be political repercussions following such losses. The irony of the situation is that even a modest percentage loss rate for a type of which many hundreds are in service naturally amounts to a noticeable number, whereas the much higher percentage loss rates for some other combat aircraft operated in comparatively limited numbers barely makes the news. Indeed, one or two other NATO air forces which operated exactly the same versions of the F-104 did suffer higher percentage loss rates than the Luftwaffe and Marineflieger. Nevertheless, German losses did to some extent result from the continued shortages of experienced pilots and maintenance personnel, as well as contributory factors such as comparatively crowded airspace over central Europe, difficult terrain and often bad weather conditions, especially in the south of Germany. Certain modifications were made to the machines, the main one being retrofitting with Martin Baker zero-zero ejection seats, and other steps were taken to improve flying training, so that after the mid-1960s the loss rates for the Starfighter fell sharply, and the type is still in widespread front-line service.

Details of the various aircraft and their service will be found in the following pages, and this brief account precludes a detailed appraisal of the three air arms since their inception in 1956. The

Luftwaffe currently has some 110,500 personnel and operates approximately 700 front-line aircraft, including two fighter wings with F-4F Phantoms; seven fighter-bomber wings with F-4Fs, F-104Gs and TF-104Gs and Alpha Jets (some of the wings have nuclear capability); two reconnaissance wings with RF-4E (with some of these being converted to the offensive role); and two light bomber and attack wings with Fiat G-91R-3s. The G-91s are currently being replaced by Alpha Jets, and a large number of the F-104s will be replaced by Tornados during the coming years. Much basic and advanced jet training is carried out in the better weather conditions of the United States, following initial pilot selection in Germany. Trainers operated are the Cessna T-37B and Northrop T-38A with the 80th Flying Training Wing at Sheppard AFB, Texas, followed by type conversion onto F-104s at Luke AFB, Arizona, or F-4s at George AFB, California. Although these machines have the outward appearance of belonging to the USAF they are paid for by Germany under the auspices of *Ausbildungskommando-USA*. Operational conversion onto the Alpha Jet and Fiat G91 is undertaken by *Waffenschule* 50 at Furstenfeldbruck. Other operational units include three transport wings operating Transalls and UH-1D helicopters, one utility helicopter wing with UH-1Ds, and the *Flugbereitschaftstaffel* (FBS) using a variety of types for VIP transport. Tactical elements of the Luftwaffe are assigned to the 2nd Allied Tactical Air Force (2 ATAF) and the Command of the Baltic Air Region (AIRBALTAP) in the north, and 4 ATAF in the south.

The Army is the largest of the three services in terms of manpower, having some 341,400 personnel, and is organized into three *Korps*, each one having its own aviation command. The Heeresflieger is equipped with some 550 helicopters, mainly Sikorsky CH-53Gs, Alouette IIs, UH-1Ds and MBB105s, used for transport, battlefield observation and attack, casualty evacuation (casevac), liaison and general communications duties. The three *Korps* headquarters are at Munster, Koblenz and Ulm, and cover six Army regions (*Wehrbereich* 1–6). Apart from the various aviation regiments directly attached to each *Korps*, various squadrons are attached at divisional levels (*Heeresfliegerstaffeln* 1–12). The helicopter-training center (HFS(L)) comprises operational training units equipped with all the types in use, and the weapons school (HFWS) at Buckeburg also uses most types.

The Navy is the smallest of the three services, with approximately 38,000 personnel, and a comparatively small air arm, the Marineflieger, which operates a front-line force of around 100 F-104Gs and TF-104Gs serving with two attack wings (*Marinefliegergeschwader* 1 and 2). Maritime reconnaissance, anti-submarine and electronic intelligence (Elint) duties are carried out by MFG3 equipped with Atlantics, while Skyservants and Sea Kings are operated by MFG5 for communications, SAR and general duties. The F-104s will shortly be replaced by Tornados.

Below: all Lockheed F-104G equipped units included a number of TF-104G two-seaters, this TF-104G serving with the Bundesmarine's MFG 1 at Schleswig. The naval Starfighters are scheduled to be replaced with Tornados from 1982, when Marinefliegergeschwader 1 will convert onto this aircraft.

Part One
1912

1918

Left: pilot and groundcrew pose with a Halberstadt D III fighter. It began to replace the Fokker Eindecker on the Western Front in the summer of 1916 and it proved to be a highly maneuverable and robust machine. However the Halberstadt D-types never achieved the popularity of the Albatros scouts.

A.E.G. C IV

Year: 1916.
Manufacturer: Allgemeine Elektrizitäts Gesellschaft and Fokker Flugzeugwerke G.mbH.
Type: reconnaissance/artillery observation.
Crew: 2 (pilot and observer/gunner).
Specification: A.E.G. C IV.
Power plant: one Mercedes D III six-cylinder water-cooled in-line engine developing 160 hp.
Dimensions: span, 44 ft 2 in; length, 23 ft 5.5 in; height, 10 ft 11⅞ in; wing area, 421.20 sq ft.
Weights: empty, 1760 lb; loaded, 2464 lb.
Performance: maximum speed, 98.75 mph; climb rate, 6 min to 3280 ft; endurance, 4 hours; service ceiling, 16,400 ft.
Armament: one Spandau machine gun firing forward and one Parabellum machine gun on Schneider ring in rear cockpit; bomb load, approximately 200 lb in observer's cockpit.

Some 658 of all C type aircraft were built. The most successful of the A.E.G. C type, the C IV, entered service in 1916 to meet the need for a reliable reconnaissance aircraft. The C IV was similar to the C II but had a larger wing span. It was extremely well constructed and could absorb considerable punishment. The Mercedes engine had exposed cylinders and the exhaust was rather like a rhinoceros horn protruding from the manifold and carrying the gases over the top wing. This model was the most produced of the C series and some were still serving in 1918.

A.E.G. G IV

Year: 1916.
Manufacturer: Allgemeine Elektrizitäts Gesellschaft.
Type: bomber/reconnaissance.
Crew: three (pilot, observer, gunner, an additional crew member could be carried).
Specification: A.E.G. G IV.
Power plant: two Mercedes D IVa six-cylinder water-cooled in-line engines, each developing 260 hp.
Dimensions: span, 60 ft 5 in; length, 31 ft 10 in; height, 12 ft 9.625 in; wing area, 673.36 sq ft.
Weights: empty, 5280 lb; loaded, 7986 lb.
Performance: maximum speed, 103 mph; climb rate, 5 min to 3280 ft; endurance, up to 5 hours; service ceiling, 14,760 ft.
Armament: two Parabellum machine guns, one on ring mount in front cockpit, one on rail mounting in rear cockpit; bomb load, 880 lb.

Although using the same power units as the Gotha and Friedrichshafen bombers, the G IV could not compare with either in terms of range and lifting capability. It was the most widely produced of the A.E.G. G types but because of its shortcomings it was used in a tactical role for short-range bombing. With extra fuel tanks replacing its bomb load, the aircraft was used for long-range reconnaissance and aerial-photography missions. This rather staid performer was built in some quantity and remained in use until the end of hostilities. The G IVb was an extended span version with three bay wings, and the G IVk was an experimental version with a 20 mm Becker cannon in the nose.

Top right: the distinctive rhinoceros horn shape of the A.E.G. C IV's exhaust can be clearly seen in this view.
Right: the A.E.G. G I twin-engined bomber/reconnaissance aircraft of 1915 led to the widely-used A.E.G. G IV.
Far right: the Albatros C III general purpose aircraft became the most produced of all Albatros two-seaters.

A.E.G. J I and J II

Year: 1917.
Manufacturer: Allgemeine Elektrizitäts Gesellschaft.
Type: infantry patrol aircraft.
Crew: two (pilot and observer/gunner).
Specification: A.E.G. J I
Power plant: Benz Bz IV six-cylinder water-cooled in-line engine developing 200 hp.
Dimensions: span, 44 ft 2 in; length, 23 ft 7 in; height, 10 ft 11 in; wing area, 358.40 sq ft.
Weights: empty, 3201 lb; loaded, 3828 lb.
Performance: maximum speed, 93.75 mph; climb rate, 6 min to 3280 ft; endurance, 2.5 hr; service ceiling, 14,760 ft.
Armament: three machine guns, one Parabellum for defense and two Spandaus fixed to fire downward.

Basically a reengined C IV with an armored fuselage, the J I was allocated to the newly formed *Infanterie-Flieger* units pending the delivery of aircraft specifically designed for the infantry-support role. Some 609 J types were produced, the J II appearing in 1918. This

machine had redesigned control surfaces and a larger area fin. Experiments were carried out in which the aircraft was operated as a single-seater, the pilot operating up to six Spandau machine guns by remote control.

Albatros C Series

Year: 1915.
Manufacturer: Albatros Flugzeugwerke G.mbH and various other subcontractors including D.F.W., L.V.G. and Siemens-Schuckert.
Type: reconnaissance/light bomber/ general purpose.
Crew: two (pilot and observer).
Specification: Albatros C III
Power plant: Benz Bz III or Mercedes D III six cylinder water-cooled engine developing 160 hp. The Bz III developed 150 hp.
Dimensions: span, 38 ft 5 in; length, 26 ft 3 in; height, 10 ft 2 in; wing area, 399 sq ft.
Weights: empty, 1872 lb; loaded, 2976 lb.
Performance: maximum speed, 87.5 mph; climb rate, 9 min to 3280 ft; endurance, 4 hr; service ceiling, 11,000 ft.
Armament: one Parabellum machine gun on ring in rear cockpit and one Spandau machine gun on starboard side of engine firing forward.

Recognizing the need to add defensive armament to reconnaissance aircraft, which in the opening months of World War I had often carried nothing more lethal than the crews' pistols or at best a rifle, the Germans introduced

the C type armed reconnaissance biplane. One of the first type to appear in this category was the Albatros C I, which was basically a B II with a more powerful engine and a ring-mounted machine gun. It was also realized that a much better arc of defensive fire could be achieved by reversing the crew positions, hence the observer and his machine gun were moved to the rear cockpit.

The C I entered service in the spring of 1915 and served in substantial numbers. Its performance was such that it was able to carry out light-bombing tasks and aerial photography in addition to its originally intended role.

The C Ia, with repositioned radiators, was built in small quantities and the C Ib was a dual-controlled trainer which appeared in 1917.

The C II was an experimental aircraft with a 150 hp Benz Bz III engine in the 'pusher' configuration but did not go into production.

The C III followed the C I in production and was largely based on the earlier B III, retaining the same design empennage, albeit slightly modified. This gave the machine exceptional longitudinal stability and a good combat- maneuverability envelope. It was a compact and sturdy aircraft which carried out its tasks well and continued to serve in secondary roles after its withdrawal in 1917.

The C IV was essentially a C III airframe with revised wing but only one was built. Another

Top: the A.E.G. J I was modified from the C IV for ground attack duties. A more powerful engine was fitted to compensate for the weight of the armored protection.

Above: the Albatros C XV, developed from the Albatros C XIV, was the final production variant of the Albatros C series. Only a few were built before the Armistice.

singleton was the W 2, a floatplane version of the C III.

The C V was a complete redesign with a more streamlined fuselage and a more powerful engine. It proved to be difficult to handle and the engine gave constant problems, but despite this some 400 were built.

The C VII followed, which was an interim design utilizing many C V components. It was more successful than its predecessor and stayed in service until 1917.

Final major versions were the C X and C XII. The C X used a 260 hp Mercedes C IVa engine and entered service in 1917. Some 300 examples were built.

The C XII retained the same engine but had a completely new, streamlined fuselage which gave it an extremely pleasing appearance. It was by far the highest-performance version of the whole Albatros C series and came into widespread use in 1918.

Albatros D Series

Year: 1916.
Manufacturer: Albatros Werke G.mbH, LVG and Oesterreichische Flugzeugfabrik A.G.
Type: fighter/scout.
Crew: one.
Specification: Albatros D I.
Power plant: Mercedes D III six-cylinder water-cooled in-line engine developing 160 hp. Some models were fitted with the Benz Bz III 150 hp.
Dimensions: span, 27 ft 11 in; length, 24 ft 3 in; height, 9 ft 6 in; wing area, 247 sq ft.
Weights: empty, 1423 lb; loaded, 1976 lb.
Performance: maximum speed, 109.4 mph; climb rate, 6 min to 3280 ft; endurance, 1.5 hr; service ceiling, 17,000 ft.
Armament: two Spandau machine guns synchronized to fire through propeller.
Year: 1917.
Manufacturer: Albatros Werke G.mbH, O.A.W. and Oesterreichische Flugzeugfabrik A.G.
Type: fighter/scout.
Crew: one.
Specification: Albatros D III.
Power plant: Mercedes D IIIa six-cylinder water-cooled in-line engine developing 160 hp.
Dimensions: span, 29 ft 9 in; length, 24 ft 1 in; height, 9 ft 10 in; wing area, 221 sq ft.
Weights: empty, 1454 lb; loaded, 1949 lb.
Performance: maximum speed, 102 mph; climb rate, 4 min to 3280 ft; endurance, 2 hr; service ceiling, 18,000 ft.
Armament: two Spandau machine guns synchronized to fire through propeller.
Year: 1917.
Manufacturer: Albatros Werke G.mbH and O.A.W.
Type: fighter/scout.
Crew: one.
Specification: Albatros D V.
Power plant: Mercedes D IIIa six-cylinder water-cooled in-line engine developing 180 hp, basically a high-compression 160 hp engine.
Dimensions: span, 29 ft 9 in; length, 24 ft 1 in; height, 8 ft 11 in; wing area, 229 sq ft.
Weights: empty, 1511 lb; loaded, 2061 lb.
Performance: maximum speed, 116 mph; climb rate, 4 min to 3280 ft; endurance, 2 hr; service ceiling, 20,000 ft.
Armament: two Spandau machine guns synchronized to fire through the propeller.

The need for a single-seat twin-gunned fighter to restore the early air supremacy wrested from the Germans by the D.H. 2 and Nieuport was met by the Albatros design team under the guidance of Dipl Ing Thelen and Schubert with their D I Scout. The Fokker and Halberstadt D types had suffered a performance penalty when a second machine gun was added, but this was not the case with the D I which began to reach the newly organized *Jagdstaffeln* during August 1916.

By December 1916 50 D Is had been delivered and were being replaced on the production line with the D II with improved forward vision.

In January 1917 the D III began to replace the earlier Scouts and by November a total of 446

Right: the Albatros D II flown by Leutnant Max Bohme of Jasta 5 was forced down over the British lines in March 1917.
Above right: the Albatros D III, which introduced the distinctive 'V' interplane struts, played a major part in establishing German air superiority over the air forces of the Allies in early 1917.
Left: the revised rudder shape of the Albatros D V can be clearly seen, when compared with the more angular rudder of the D III (above left).

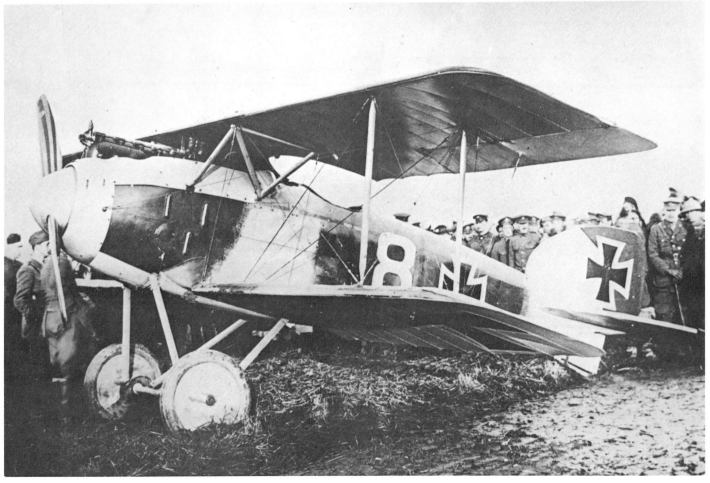

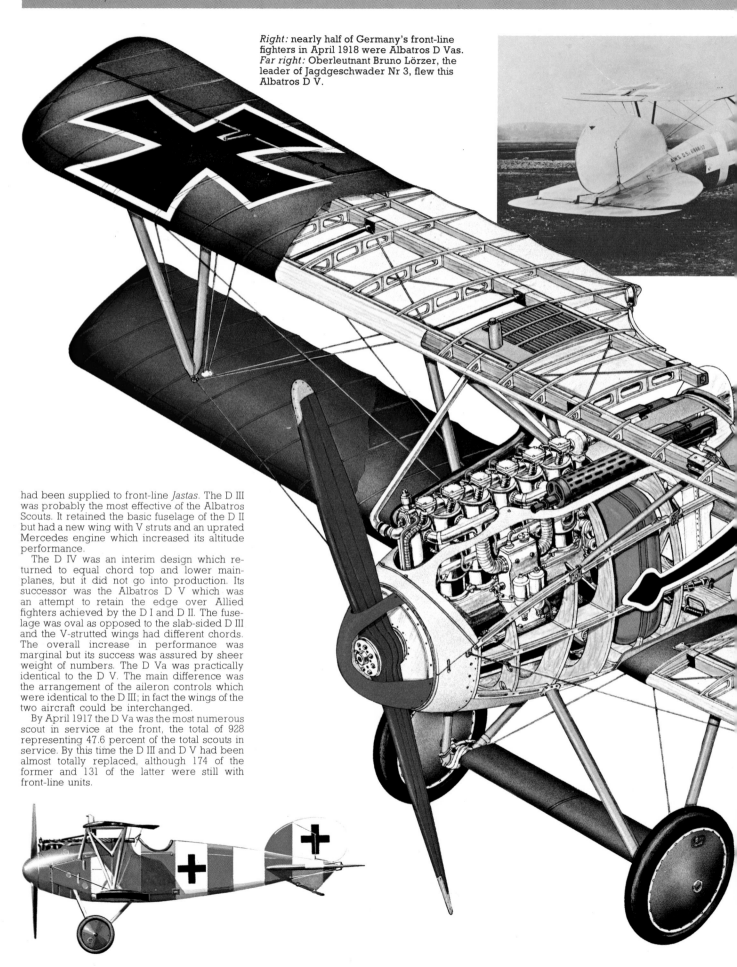

Right: nearly half of Germany's front-line fighters in April 1918 were Albatros D Vas. *Far right:* Oberleutnant Bruno Lörzer, the leader of Jagdgeschwader Nr 3, flew this Albatros D V.

had been supplied to front-line *Jastas*. The D III was probably the most effective of the Albatros Scouts. It retained the basic fuselage of the D II but had a new wing with V struts and an uprated Mercedes engine which increased its altitude performance.

The D IV was an interim design which returned to equal chord top and lower mainplanes, but it did not go into production. Its successor was the Albatros D V which was an attempt to retain the edge over Allied fighters achieved by the D I and D II. The fuselage was oval as opposed to the slab-sided D III and the V-strutted wings had different chords. The overall increase in performance was marginal but its success was assured by sheer weight of numbers. The D Va was practically identical to the D V. The main difference was the arrangement of the aileron controls which were identical to the D III; in fact the wings of the two aircraft could be interchanged.

By April 1917 the D Va was the most numerous scout in service at the front, the total of 928 representing 47.6 percent of the total scouts in service. By this time the D III and D V had been almost totally replaced, although 174 of the former and 131 of the latter were still with front-line units.

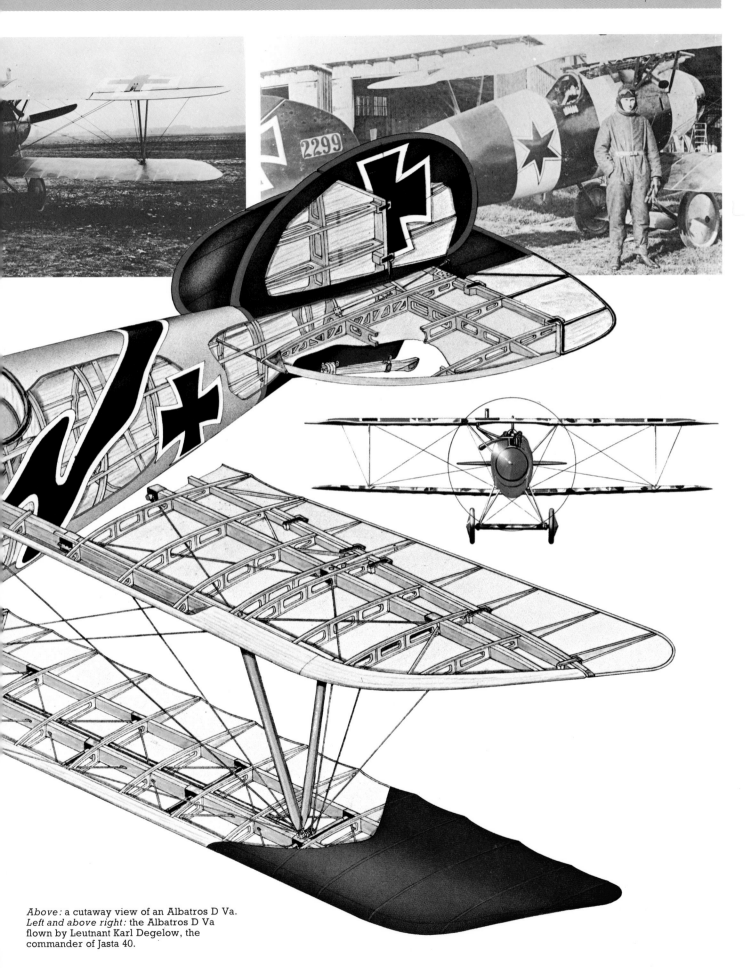

Above: a cutaway view of an Albatros D Va.
Left and above right: the Albatros D Va
flown by Leutnant Karl Degelow, the
commander of Jasta 40.

Albatros J I and J II

Year: 1917.
Manufacturer: Albatros Werke G.mbH.
Type: close support.
Crew: two (pilot, observer/gunner).
Specification: Albatros J I.
Power plant: Benz Bz IV six-cylinder water-cooled in-line engine developing 200 hp.
Dimensions: span, 46 ft 4 in; length, 29 ft; height, 11 ft 1 in; wing area, 462.45 sq ft.
Weights: empty, 3075 lb; loaded, 3978 lb.
Performance: maximum speed, 87 mph; climb rate, 11.4 min to 3280 ft; endurance, 2.5 hr; service ceiling, 10,000 ft.
Armament: one Parabellum on ring mount in rear cockpit and two Spandau machine guns fixed to fire downward at an angle of 45 degrees.

Like the A.E.G. J I, the Albatros, produced to perform the same duties, was also something of a hybrid. The wings of a C XII were attached to a armored fuselage which severly curtailed its climbing ability, but as the machine was required for close support this was not considered serious. The J I operated from 1917 and caused considerable havoc among ground troops.

The J II was an improved version with increased armor protection for the engine, but only a handful were built.

Aviatik C I and C III

Year: 1915.
Manufacturer: Automobil und Aviatik A.G.; Hannoversche Waggonfabrik A.G.
Type: reconnaissance/escort.
Crew: two (pilot and observer/gunner).
Specification: Aviatik C I.
Power plant: Mercedes D III six-cylinder water-cooled in-line engine developing 160 hp.
Dimensions: span, 41 ft; length, 26 ft; height, 9 ft 8 in; wing area, 465.40 sq ft.
Weights: empty, 1650 lb; loaded, 2732 lb.
Performance: maximum speed, 88.75 mph; climb rate, 12 min to 3280 ft; endurance, 55 min; service ceiling, 11,480 ft.
Armament: two Parabellum machine guns mounted on rails either side of front (observer's) cockpit.

Above: the Brandenburg W 20 single seat flying boat was intended to operate from U-boats, in the event only three examples were built.
Below: the Aviatik C I carried the observer in the front cockpit with the pilot seated behind him.

A conventional wood/canvas structure with unequal span mainplanes, the C I was developed from the unarmed B I and B II. It suffered from a restricted field of fire due to the observer occupying the front cockpit. This arrangement was changed on the C Ia but increased performance came only with the introduction of the C II and C III which were little more than refined designs of the CI. The CII and CIII were produced in some quantity and served in the reconnaissance and light-bomber roles on the Western Front. They had a more powerful Mercedes engine, giving an increased top speed, a streamlined spinner and modified exhaust and fuel systems.

Brandenburg K.D.W.

Year: 1916.
Manufacturer: Hansa und Brandenburgische Flugzeugwerke G.mbH.
Type: seaplane fighter/scout.
Crew: pilot only.
Specification: Brandenburg K.D.W.
Power plant: Benz Bz III or Maybach Mb III six-cylinder water-cooled in-line engine developing 150 and 160 hp respectively.
Dimensions: span, 30 ft 4 in; length, 26 ft 3 in; height, 11 ft; wing area, 216 sq ft.
Weights: empty, 2068 lb; loaded, 2662 lb.
Performance: maximum speed, 106.25 mph; climb rate, 5.9 min to 3280 ft; endurance, 2.5 hr; service ceiling, 11,500 ft.
Armament: one Spandau machine gun on starboard side of nose; later two Spandaus.

This aircraft was designed by Ernst Heinkel for defense of seaplane bases. A total of 146 was built and they served until they were replaced by Brandenburg W 12s.

Brandenburg W 19

Year: 1917.
Manufacturer: Hansa Brandenburgische Flugzeugwerke G.mbH.
Type: patrol seaplane.
Crew: two (pilot and observer/gunner).
Specification: Brandenburg W 19.
Power plant: Maybach Mb IV six-cylinder water-cooled in-line engine developing 260 hp.
Dimensions: span, 45 ft 4 in; length, 34 ft 11 in; height, 13 ft 6 in; wing area, 624.25 sq ft.
Weights: empty, 3157 lb; loaded, 4411 lb.
Performance: maximum speed, 94 mph; climb rate, 6.4 min to 3280 ft; endurance, 5 hr; service ceiling, 16,400 ft.
Armament: two Spandau machine guns fixed to fire forward and one Parabellum machine gun manually operated from rear cockpit.

Similar to the W 12 but much larger, the W 19 had a fairly long patrol time and often worked in liaison with the W 12 which would stay on the water until advised by the patrolling W 19 that a suitable target had been spotted. A total of 58 machines was delivered and some were used on early air-sea-rescue tasks.

Brandenburg W 29

Year: 1918.
Manufacturer: Hansa Bradenburgische Flugzeugwerke G.mbH.
Type: fighter/scout.
Crew: two (pilot and observer/gunner).
Specification: Brandenburg W 29.
Power plant: Benz Bz III six-cylinder water-cooled in-line engine developing 150 hp.
Dimensions: span, 44 ft 4 in; length, 30 ft 9 in; height, 9 ft 10 in; wing area, 347.75 sq ft.
Weights: empty, 2200 lb; loaded, 1494 lb.
Performance: maximum speed, 110 mph; climb rate, 6 min to 3280 ft; endurance, 4 hr; service ceiling, 16,400 ft.
Armament: one or two fixed Spandau machine guns firing forward and one Parabellum machine gun manually operated from rear cockpit.

Heinkel's most notable design to come from the Brandenburg works, the W 29 was a large monoplane twin-float fighter which entered service in April 1918. It proved to be a capable machine and was used effectively to harass enemy shipping.

D.F.W. C V

Year: 1916.
Manufacturer: Deutsche Flugzeugwerke G.mbH; subcontracted to Automobil und Aviatik, Halberstädt and L.V.G.
Type: reconnaissance/artillery spotter/aerial photography.
Crew: two (pilot and observer/gunner).
Specification: D.F.W. C V.
Power plant: Benz Bz IV six-cylinder water-cooled in-line engine developing 200 hp.
Dimensions: span, 43 ft 7 in; length, 25 ft 10 in; height, 10 ft 8 in; wing area, not known.
Weights: empty, 2143 lb; loaded, 3146 lb.
Performance: maximum speed, 97 mph; climb rate, 4 min to 3280 ft; endurance, 3.5 hr; service ceiling, 16,400 ft.
Armament: one Spandau machine gun fixed to fire forward and one Parabellum machine gun in rear cockpit.

Generally regarded as one of the finest two-seat C type airplanes to see service in World War I, the D.F.W. C V was produced in considerable quantity and over 600 were still in service at the time of the Armistice. Handling was exceptional and in the hands of an experienced pilot it was able to outmaneuver the most modern Allied fighters. On 17 June 1919 a D.F.W. C V established a world altitude record for an aircraft of its class by climbing to 31,561 ft.

Brandenburg W 12

Year: 1917.
Manufacturer: Hansa und Brandenburgische Flugzeugwerke G.mbH.
Type: seaplane fighter/scout.
Crew: two (pilot and observer).
Specification: Brandenburg W 12.
Power plant: Benz Bz III or Mercedes D III six-cylinder water-cooled in-line engine developing 150 hp or 160 hp respectively.
Dimensions: span, 36 ft 9 in; length, 31 ft 6 in; height, 10 ft 10 in; wing area, 381.25 sq ft.
Weights: empty, 2193 lb; loaded, 3198 lb.
Performance: maximum speed, 100 mph; climb rate, 7 min to 3280 ft; endurance, 3.5 hr; service ceiling, 16,400 ft.
Armament: either one or two fixed Spandau machine guns in nose and one manually operated Parabellum machine gun in rear cockpit.

This was a large two-seat biplane which could hold its own against many single seat scouts. Although primarily designed to defend seaplane bases, the W 12 was also used on reconnaissance duties when one of its forward guns was removed and replaced by radio equipment.

Right: the D.F.W. C V was considered to be one of the finest German two-seater aircraft of World War I. This example was forced down in Allied territory by British fighters in September 1917.
Above right: this D.F.W. C V is fitted with a fully cowled engine, but in service the panels over the cylinders were often removed. The engine was a 200 hp Benz Bz IV.

Above: this Taube monoplane was built by Germania Flugzeugwerke of Leipzig during 1914.

Etrich Taube

Year: 1912.
Manufacturer: Rumpler Flugzeugwerke G.mbH.
Type: reconnaissance.
Crew: two (pilot and observer).
Specification: Etrich Taube.
Power plant: Mercedes or Argus six-cylinder water-cooled in-line engines developing 100 hp.
Dimensions: span, 45 ft 11 in; length, 33 ft 10 in; height, 10 ft 4 in; wing area, 344 sq ft.
Weights: empty, not known; loaded, 1910 lb.
Performance: maximum speed, 59 mph; endurance, 4 hr; service ceiling, 9800 ft.
Armament: none.

Designed by Austrian engineer Dr Igo Etrich, the Taube monoplane was built in various configurations. Rumpler was responsible for most of those built in Germany and used by the Imperial Military Aviation Service. Entering service in 1914, it proved its worth as a reconnaissance machine but by the spring of 1915 it had been rendered obsolete by more-advanced types and was gradually phased out of front-line service and used for training.

Fokker E Series

Year: 1914.
Manufacturer: Fokker Flugzeugwerke G.mbH.
Type: fighter/scout.
Crew: pilot only.
Specification: Fokker E III.
Power plant: Oberursel U 1 nine-cylinder rotary engine developing 100 hp.
Dimensions: span, 31 ft 4 in; length, 23 ft 7 in; height, 9 ft 2 in; wing area, 172.80 sq ft.
Weights: empty, 878 lb; loaded, 1342 lb.
Performance: maximum speed, 81.25 mph; climb rate, 5 min to 3280 ft; endurance, 1.5 hr; service ceiling, 11,500 ft.
Armament: one Spandau machine gun, some fitted with two, synchronized to fire through propeller.

The E series of monoplanes brought Germany the first taste of air superiority and during 1915/16 achieved a 'kill' rate that earned them the epithet the 'Fokker Scourge.' The success they enjoyed was in no small measure owing to the Fokker-designed interrupter gear which synchronized the fire rate of the aircraft's machine gun to the gaps between the rotating propeller blades. The French found this particularly aggravating since not only was the airframe design based on the Morane-Salnier Type L, but the firing gear was developed after Fokker studied the primitive system used by the French ace Roland Garros, who was shot down on 19 April 1915.

The Fokker E I was developed from the M5 which was first flown in 1913, it was powered by an 80 hp Oberursel seven-cylinder rotary

Below: Leutnant Max Immelmann pictured in the cockpit of his Fokker E I.
Right: in an attempt to prolong the useful life of his Eindecker series, Fokker produced the E IV powered by an 160 hp Oberursel U III engine.

Above: the Fokker E III, which was produced in greater numbers than the other Eindecker variants, is represented here by a replica.

engine and had a wing span of 28 ft. Fokker, a Dutchman, had originally offered his early designs to Britain, but a distrust of monoplanes brought about early rejection although the official reason given was that the aircraft were poorly made.

The M5L (long-span) and M5K (short span) saw some military service with the Austro-Hungarian air arm before the basic design was changed to accommodate a fuselage-mounted Spandau and emerged as the E I. This model was quickly followed by the E II which had its span reduced to about 28 ft and its power increased by the installation of a 100 hp Oberursel rotary engine. Delivery of this version began in 1915.

The most numerous Eindecker was the E III which had increased span over both the E.I and E.II but retained the 100 hp engine. It is believed that approximately 260 of this model

were used by the Germans and their allies. Some E.IIIs were fitted with twin Spandaus but the weight penalty brought about severe performance restrictions. The E IV was an attempt to produce a viable twin-gun scout and made its debut in November 1915. Powered by a 14-cylinder twin-row rotary engine developing 160 hp and with an increased wing span of 32 ft 9.75 in, the aircraft proved to be faster but was less maneuverable, which offset the additional fire power. Max Immelmann, the famous German ace, flew Fokkers and in fact fitted three guns to his E IV for a very short period; he was killed flying a Fokker on 18 June 1916.

By mid-1916 the Fokker monoplanes had enjoyed their heyday and began to fade from the scene as more capable Allied machines began to reach the front.

Below: the Fokker E I monoplane was fitted with a 08 LMG Spandau machine gun firing forward through the propeller arc, thanks to its interrupter gear. The Allies described its period of dominance as the 'Fokker Scourge.'

Fokker D 1 to D IV

Year: 1916.
Manufacturer: Fokker Flugzeugwerke G.mbH.
Type: fighter/scout.
Crew: pilot only.
Specification: Fokker D III.
Power plant: Oberursel U III 14-cylinder two-row rotary engine developing 160 hp.
Dimensions: span, 29 ft 8 in; length, 20 ft 8 in; height, 7 ft 5 in; wing area, 216 sq ft.
Weights: empty, 994.4 lb; loaded, 1562 lb.
Performance: maximum speed, 100 mph; climb rate, 3 min to 3280 ft; endurance, 1.5 hr; service ceiling, 15,500 ft.
Armament: one or two Spandau machine guns synchronized to fire through propeller.

Evolved from a series of prototypes designed by Martin Kreutzer, the D I was an attempt to produce a successor to the E III. The production version was a twin-bay 30 ft wing span biplane grossly underpowered by a 120 hp Mercedes D II engine. Some 25 were produced but they

were soon found wanting when they went into service in the summer of 1916 and were quickly relegated to other duties.

The D II, which was in fact developed from an earlier MK design (the M17z), was similar to the D I but had shorter span wings and a longer fuselage. It was powered by a 100 hp Oberursel rotary but because of its lighter weight it had a better performance and was more maneuverable than the D I.

The DIII was fitted with a 160 hp Oberursel rotary engine which was accommodated in a strengthened fuselage mated to D I wings. Problems with the engine resulted in early termination of the D II and D III in their designed roles and they were also relegated to training duties. A total of 291 of both types was produced.

The D IV was also something of a failure, being an improved version of the D I powered by a 160 hp Mercedes D III engine and having slightly increased overall dimensions.

Fokker D V

Year: 1916.
Manufacturer: Fokker Flugzeugwerke G.mbH.
Type: fighter/scout.
Crew: pilot only.
Specification: Fokker D V.
Power plant: Oberursel U 1 nine-cylinder rotary engine developing 100 hp.
Dimensions: span, 29 ft 1 in; length, 19 ft 10 in; height, 7 ft 7 in; wing area, 167.4 sq ft.
Weights: empty, 797 lb; loaded, 1245 lb.
Performance: maximum speed, 106.25 mph; climb rate, 19 min to 9840 ft; endurance, 1.5 hr; service ceiling, 13,120 ft.
Armament: one Spandau machine gun firing forward.

The D V was basically an improved D III whose improved lines gave it a better overall performance. Last in the line of the M series thin-wing Fokkers it was a contemporary of the Albatros D I and D II which were very much superior. Most of the 216 built were used in training roles although it is believed that a few did serve with *Jasta* 6.

Fokker Dr I

Year: 1917.
Manufacturer: Fokker Flugzeugwerke G.mbH.
Type: fighter/scout.
Crew: pilot only.
Specification: Fokker Dr I.
Power plant: Oberursel UR II 110 hp nine-cylinder rotary or captured Le Rhône rotary; Oberursel UR III, Goebel III and Siemens-Halske Sh-3 also used.
Dimensions: span, 23 ft 7 in; length, 18 ft 11 in; height, 9 ft 8 in; wing area, 201.5 sq ft.
Weights: empty, 893.2 lb; loaded, 1289.2 lb.
Performance: maximum speed, 103 mph; climb rate, 2.9 min to 3280 ft; endurance, 1.5 hr; service ceiling, 20,000 ft.
Armament: two Spandau machine guns synchronized to fire through propeller. Each could be fired independently.

The legend which has grown around the Fokker Triplane owes a great deal to its use by Manfred von Richthofen and his death while flying Nr 425/17 on 21 April 1918. The facts are somewhat different, in that while there is no doubt that the Dr 1 was a fine fighting machine in the hands of an expert, it was unforgiving to the less gifted and suffered structural weaknesses which curtailed its operational career.

Designed by Reinhold Platz, who was not entirely convinced of the merits of a triplane layout, the Fokker machine was originally designated F I but was changed to Dr, signifying *dreidecker* (triplane) after the first three production models. The success of the Sopwith Triplane resulted in serious consideration of this layout, with no fewer than 14 German and

Above right: the most famous aircraft of World War I was Manfred von Richthofen's all-red Fokker Dr I.
Above far right: Anthony Fokker in the cockpit of a Triplane talks to General von Lossberg, while Manfred von Richthofen (second right) looks on.
Right: a standard production Dr I.
Below: the Fokker Dr I flown by the notable German ace Werner Voss.

Austrian manufacturers producing their proposals. It is often stated that the Dr I was a copy of the Sopwith machine, but Platz had not even seen the captured British aircraft before he had completed his design, although Fokker had witnessed it in action at the front.

The V 3 prototype suffered from severe vibration of its cantilever wings and the V 4 was fitted with hollow struts to minimize this. It also had redesigned ailerons and elevators and in this form went into production.

The first two models were used by *Jagdgeschwader* 1 in the late summer of 1917 and by mid-October production was in full swing. A series of fatal crashes, caused by faulty workmanship in the wings, resulted in the aircraft being grounded and it was not until late November that the troubles were overcome.

A total of 320 machines was produced and peak service was achieved in May 1918 when 171 were in front-line service. Production ceased in the same month and the Dr 1 was gradually relegated to home-defense duty after a short but spectacular career.

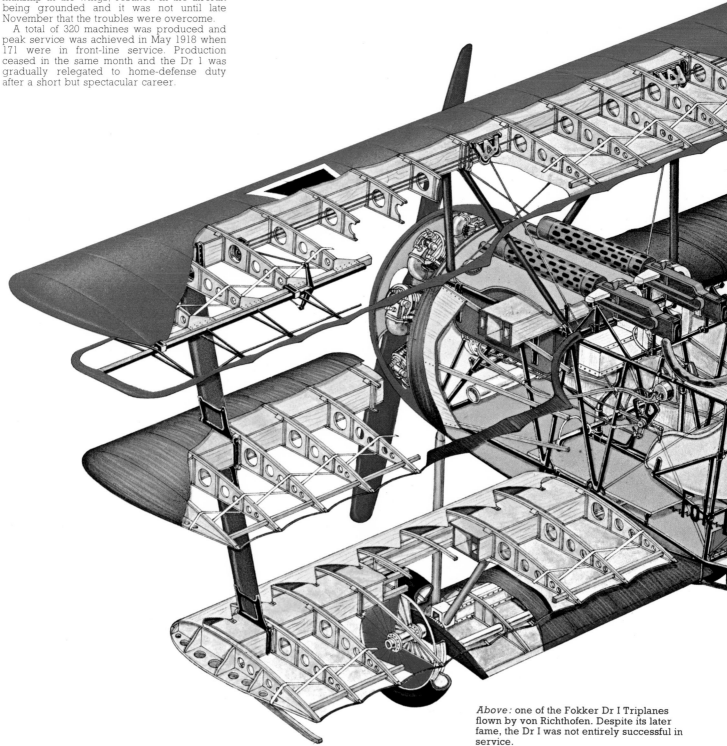

Above: one of the Fokker Dr I Triplanes flown by von Richthofen. Despite its later fame, the Dr I was not entirely successful in service.

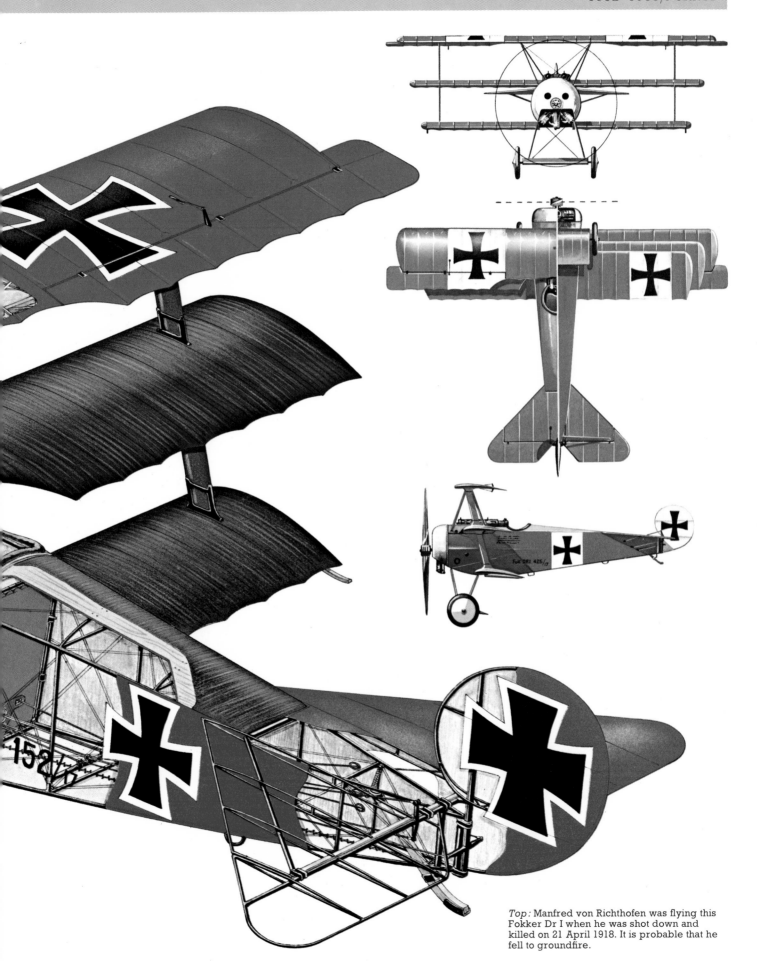

Top: Manfred von Richthofen was flying this Fokker Dr I when he was shot down and killed on 21 April 1918. It is probable that he fell to groundfire.

Fokker D VI

Year: 1917.
Manufacturer: Fokker Flugzeugwerke
G.mbH.
Type: fighter/scout.
Crew: pilot only.
Specification: Fokker D VI.
Power plant: Oberursel U II nine-cylinder
rotary engine developing 110 hp.
Dimensions: span, 25 ft 2 in; length, 20 ft 6 in;
height, 8 ft 4 in; wing area, 191 sq ft.
Weights: empty, 865 lb; loaded, 1283 lb.
Performance: maximum speed, 122.5 mph;
climb rate, 2.5 min to 3280 ft; endurance,
1.5 hr; service ceiling, 19,685 ft.
Armament: two Spandau machine guns firing
forward.

The original two prototypes were powered by
145 hp Oberursel UR III and 160 hp Siemens-
Halske Sh-3 engines. Both engines proved
troublesome so the reliable Oberursel U II was
selected for production versions, which ran
parallel to the more successful D VII, probably
as an insurance against failure of the latter.
Production was terminated after 59 aircraft had
been produced, most of which were used for
training.

Fokker D VII

Year: 1918.
Manufacturer: Fokker Flugzeugwerke
G.mbH; Albatros Werke G.mbH and O.A.W.
Type: fighter/scout.
Crew: pilot only.
Specification: Fokker D VII.
Power plant: Mercedes D III six-cylinder
water-cooled in-line engine developing
160 hp, or a similar B.M.W. D III developing
185 hp.
Dimensions: span, 29 ft 4 in; length, 23 ft;
height, 9 ft 2 in; wing area, 221.4 sq ft.
Weights: empty, 1540 lb; loaded, 1936 lb.
Performance: maximum speed, 117 mph;
climb rate, 3.8 min to 3280 ft; endurance,
1.5 hr; service ceiling, 22,900 ft.
Armament: two Spandau machine guns fixed
and synchronized to fire through propeller.

Generally regarded as the best fighting scout
to serve with the German air force during
World War I, the D VII was derived from the
V 11 for the D class (single-seat) fighting scout
competition held at Adlershof in January 1918.
Although only completed in November 1917,
Reinhold Platz's design easily won the competition and was ordered into immediate production. The V11 was modified to have a longer
fuselage and revised fin layout before being
produced as the D VII examples of which began
to reach *Jagdgeschwader* I in April 1918.
  Some 2000 were ordered but it is doubtful
if more than 1000 came off the production lines.
Some 800 were in service at the Armistice.
  One of its greatest assets was its ability to
maintain a high performance at altitude, a
characteristic which was enhanced by the use
of a B.M.W.III 185 hp engine in the D VIIF from
the summer of 1918.
  Such was the reputation earned by the D VII
that it was specifically named as one of the
aircraft to be handed to the Allies after the
surrender. Fokker managed to smuggle some
400 engines and the dismantled parts of 120
D VIIs to Holland to enable him to establish a
postwar business. Some D VIIs, converted to
two seat configuration, served with the Dutch
and Belgian air forces until 1926.

Above right: entering service in April 1918,
the Fokker D VII was reputed to be the
finest German fighter of the war.
Right: this Fokker D VII was license-built by
the Albatros Werke.

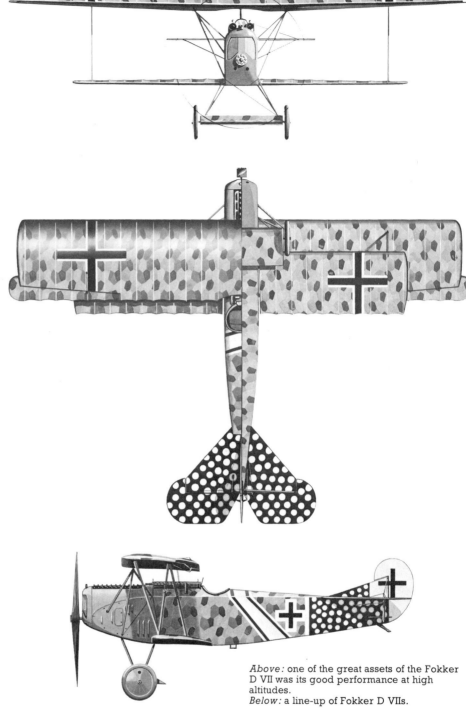

Above: one of the great assets of the Fokker D VII was its good performance at high altitudes.
Below: a line-up of Fokker D VIIs.

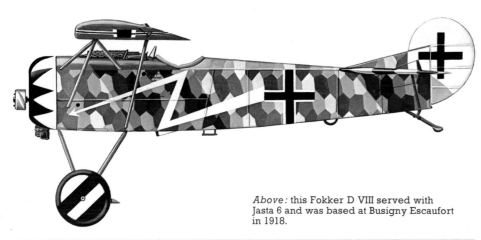

Above: this Fokker D VIII served with Jasta 6 and was based at Busigny Escaufort in 1918.

Friedrichshafen Type 33 Seaplanes

Year: 1914.
Manufacturer: Flugzeugbau Friedrichshafen G.mbH.
Type: reconnaissance/patrol/escort seaplane.
Crew: two (pilot and observer/gunner).
Specification: Friedrichshafen FF 33E.
Power plant: Benz Bz III six-cylinder water-cooled in-line engine developing 150 hp.
Dimensions: span, 55 ft; length, 34 ft 4 in; height, 12 ft 3 in; wing area, 569.2 sq ft.
Weights: empty, 2217 lb; loaded, 3636 lb.
Performance: maximum speed, 74.5 mph; climb rate, 17.5 min to 3280 ft; endurance, approximately 6 hr; service ceiling, 10,500 ft.
Armament: usually none, but some machines fitted with a Parabellum machine gun in rear cockpit.

Year: 1915.
Manufacturer: Flugzeugbau Friedrichshafen G.mbH.
Type: reconnaissance/patrol/escort seaplane.
Crew: two (pilot and observer/gunner).
Specification: Friedrichshafen FF 33L.
Power plant: Benz Bz III six-cylinder water-cooled in-line engine developing 150 hp.
Dimensions: span, 43 ft 8 in; length, 29 ft; height, 12 ft 11 in; wing area, 437.8 sq ft.
Weights: empty, 2021 lb; loaded, 3020 lb.
Performance: maximum speed, 85 mph; climb rate, 8 min to 3280 ft; endurance, approximately 5 hr; service ceiling, 14,500 ft.
Armament: one Spandau machine gun fixed to fire forward and one Parabellum machine gun in rear cockpit.

The main production Friedrichshafen Seaplanes comprised the Types FF 33, FF 39 and FF 49. Probably the most widely used German seaplanes of World War I, the Type 33 variants can be divided into two categories; the 33/33B, 33E and 33S were reconnaissance patrol aircraft and the 33F, 33H and 33L were fighters intended for armed patrols and escort duties. Over 500 of the models FF 33, 39, 49 and 59 were produced

Above and right: the Fokker D VIII parasol monoplane, which entered service in the summer of 1918, was originally designated E V.

Fokker D VIII

Year: 1918.
Manufacturer: Fokker Fluzeugwerke G.mbH.
Type: fighter/scout.
Crew: pilot only.
Specification: Fokker D VIII.
Power plant: Oberursel U II nine-cylinder rotary engine developing 110 hp.
Dimensions: span, 27 ft 4 in; length, 19 ft 3 in; height, 8 ft 6 in; wing area, 115.5 sq ft.
Weights: empty, 893 lb; loaded, 1334 lb.
Performance: maximum speed, 127.5 mph; climb rate, 2 min to 3280 ft; endurance, 1.5 hr; service ceiling, 19,680 ft.
Armament: two Spandau machine guns fixed and synchronized to fire through propeller.

The V 26 and V 28 were parasol monoplanes designed by Reinhold Platz for the second D class fighter competition at Adlershof in May/June 1918. Accepted for production, the aircraft received the *Eindecker* designation EV which was changed to D VIII in September 1918. Like the Dr 1, the D VIII suffered from wing failures due to faulty timber used by a subcontractor. By the time this problem had been overcome the war was practically over and only 85 had been delivered to front-line *Jastas* by November 1918. Like the D VII, some were salvaged by Fokker and served with the postwar Dutch Army Air Service.

Above and below: over 200 Friedrichshafen FF 49C floatplanes were built by the parent company, L.F.G. and Sablatnig.

and they operated from coastal stations as well as aboard seaplane carriers.

The FF 33 first appeared in 1914 with the then-conventional crew positions in which the gunner occupied the forward cockpit, this was followed by the B model which was fitted with a more powerful engine and had the crew positions reversed. The first major production version was the FF 33E of which 165 were manufactured. This was the first model to utilize radio equipment, most were unarmed but those fitted with a Parabellum in the rear cockpit were designated FF 33F. These were followed by the improved J version of which 100 were produced, 30 of them were later modified to the S type trainer.

The FF 33H was a fighter intended to act as an escort for the reconnaissance aircraft. It was followed by the smaller and more effective FF 33L, of which a total of 150 were eventually completed.

The FF 39 appeared in 1917 with a strengthened fuselage and a 200 hp Benz engine but only 14 were completed before the FF 49 took its place.

The FF 49 series appeared as B and C variants. The B version was an unarmed reconnaissance machine and 22 were produced. The C was equipped with a fixed Spandau and a flexible-mounted Parabellum. The final version, the FF 59C, was also Benz powered and had a redesigned fuselage and greater range than its predecessors.

Friedrichshafen G III

Year: 1917.
Manufacturer: Flugzeugbau Friedrichshafen G.mbH, Hanseatische Flugzeugwerke, and Daimler Motoren-Gesellschaft.
Type: long-range bomber.
Crew: three (pilot, gunner, bomb aimer/gunner).
Specification: Friedrichshafen G III.
Power plant: two Mercedes D IVa six-cylinder water-cooled in-line engines each developing 260 hp.
Dimensions: span, 77 ft 10 in; length, 42 ft; height, 12 ft; wing area, 1020 sq ft.
Weights: empty, 5929 lb; loaded, 8646 lb.
Performance: maximum speed, 85 mph; endurance, 5 hr; service ceiling, 14,800 ft.
Armament: two or three Parabellum machine guns manually operated in nose and rear cockpit; maximum bomb load, 3300 lb.

In service alongside the Gotha G V from mid-1917 until the end of the war, the G III carried out bombing raids throughout France and Belgium and is believed to have accompanied Gothas on raids over England. A three-bay biplane with pusher propellers, the G III was produced in greater numbers than any other aircraft in the Friedrichshafen G range. A total of 338 was produced, of which 93 were G IIIa versions with a twin biplane tail, built by Daimler, Hansa and the parent design company.

Right: the Friedsrichshafen G IIIa differed from the G III in having a biplane tail and twin fin and rudder.
Below: the Friedrichshafen G II served in limited numbers from late 1916.

Gotha Bombers

Year: 1915.
Manufacturer: Gothaer Waggonfabrik A.G.,
Luft Verkehrs G.mbH, and Siemens Schuckert
Werke G.mbH.
Type: long-range bomber.
Crew: three (pilot, gunner, bomb aimer/
gunner).
Specification: Gotha G IV.
Power plant: Two Mercedes D IVa six-
cylinder water-cooled in-line engines each
developing 260 hp.
Dimensions: span, 77 ft 10 in; length,
38 ft 11 in; height, 14 ft 1 in; wing area,
967 sq ft.
Weights: empty, 5280 lb; loaded, 7997 lb.
Performance: maximum speed, 87.5 mph;
climb rate, 28 min to 9840 ft; endurance,
approximately 6.5 hr; range, 522 miles;
service ceiling, 21,320 ft.
Armament: two Parabellum machine guns
manually operated from nose and rear
cockpits; bomb load, 1100 lb.

Gothaer Waggonfabrik entered the field of
manufacturers of large airplanes *(Grossflug-
zeuge)* in 1915 when it produced the G 1 under
license from the design of Oskar Ursinus and
Major Friedel. This machine was built in small
quantities and used for tactical support on the
Eastern and Western Fronts. It was followed
by the company's own design, the G II, which
was designed by Hans Burkhard. This conventional design carried a crew of three and was
powered by two 220 hp Benz D IV engines. It
entered service in the autumn of 1916 but
suffered from crankshaft failures and was
quickly replaced by the G III, which was fitted
with the more reliable D IVa engines. Some

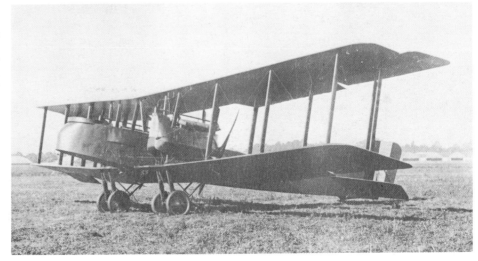

Above right: the Gotha G V bomber carried
out night raids over Britain from its
introduction in August 1917 until May 1918.
Its bomb load on such raids was some 660 lb.
Right: a Gotha G V in Allied hands.

G IIIs were fitted with a tunnel in the fuselage which enabled the gunner to operate the dorsal gun below the fuselage and cover the blind spot beneath the tail. This innovation was retained for the major production version, the G IV which was the mainstay of the German long-range strategic bombing program.

The G IV entered service in March 1917 and carried out daylight raids against England, during which its average bomb load was six 110 lb bombs. Some 230 G IVs were produced and a number were fitted with Argus As III or N.A.G. engines. Approximately 30 aircraft were transferred to Austro-Hungary where they were fitted with 230 hp Hiero engines and used on the Italian Front. The G V entered service in August 1917 and continued the night-bombing raids over England until May 1918. The G Va and G Vb were versions with a biplane tail, shorter nose, and different internal equipment. The G V and its derivitives were only produced in small quantities, with an estimated 57 at the front during August 1918.

Gotha W D 14

Year: 1916.
Manufacturer: Gothaer Waggonfabrik A.G.
Type: torpedo bomber.
Crew: three (pilot, torpedo-man, gunner).
Specification: Gotha W D 14.
Power plant: two Benz Bz IV six-cylinder water-cooled in-line engines each developing 200 hp.
Dimensions: span, 83 ft 8 in; length, 47 ft 5 in; height, 16 ft 5 in; wing area, 1465.6 sq ft.
Weights: empty, 6930 lb; loaded, 10212 lb.
Performance: maximum speed, 85 mph; climb rate, 13 min to 3280 ft; endurance, 8 hr; service ceiling, 10,500 ft.
Armament: two Parabellum machine guns manually operated from nose and rear cockpits, plus one torpedo.

The Gotha W D 14 was an attempt to produce a torpedo attack aircraft, but it turned out to be a dismal failure in this role, mainly due to its handling qualities. Sixty-nine aircraft were completed and they were tried in many roles including minelaying, reconnaissance and convoy escorts. They performed none with distinction and were eventually withdrawn from service and scrapped.

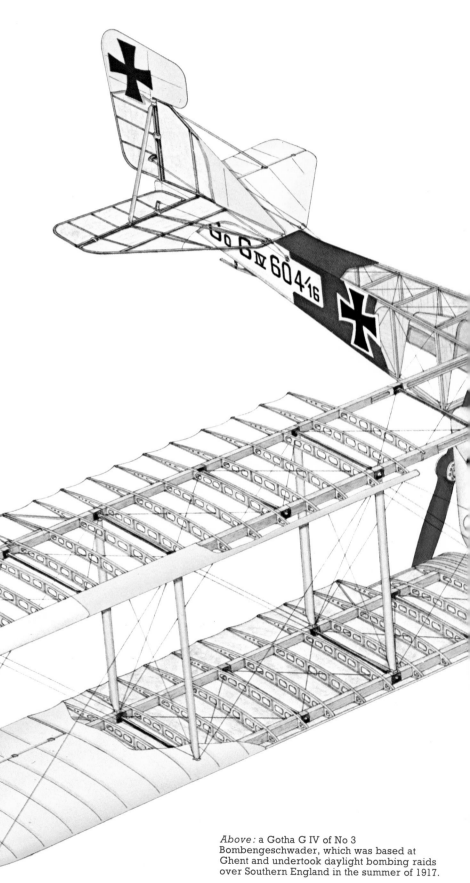

Above: a Gotha G IV of No 3 Bombengeschwader, which was based at Ghent and undertook daylight bombing raids over Southern England in the summer of 1917.

Halberstadt CL II

Year: 1917.
Manufacturer: Halberstädter Flugzeugwerke G.mbH, subcontracted to Bayerische Flugzeugwerke A.G.
Type: escort/ground attack.
Crew: two (pilot and gunner).
Specification: Halberstadt CL II.
Power plant: Mercedes D III six-cylinder water-cooled in-line engine developing 160 hp.
Dimensions: span, 35 ft 4 in; length 23 ft 11 in; height, 9 ft; wing area, 297 sq ft.
Weights: empty, 1701 lb; loaded, 2493 lb.
Performance: Maximum speed, 103.15 mph; climb rate, 5 min to 3280 ft; endurance, 3 hr; service ceiling, 16,700 ft.
Armament: one or two fixed forward-mounted Spandaus, sometimes reduced to one, and a Parabellum machine gun in rear cockpit; maximum bomb load, 110 lb.

The CL II was the first aircraft in production to meet the CL class of lightweight two-seat escort or ground-attack aircraft. It served with some distinction until 1918 and played a vital part in actions on the Somme and the Battle of Cambrai. As well as its normal bomb load it could also carry a supply of antipersonnel grenades. The CL IIa was powered by an Argus engine, but only one example was built by the BFW subcontractor.

Left: the Halberstadt CL II two-seat escort fighter was also used in the ground attack role.

Above: the Halberstadt CL IV was generally similar in performance to the CL II, but was more maneuverable.

Halberstadt CL IV

Year: 1918.
Manufacturer: Halberstädter Flugzeugwerke G.mbH, subcontracted to Luftfahrzeug Gesellschaft mbH (L.F.G. Roland).
Type: escort/ground attack.
Crew: two (pilot and gunner).
Specification: Halberstadt CL IV.
Power plant: Mercedes D III six-cylinder water-cooled in-line engine developing 160 hp.
Dimensions: span, 35 ft 3 in; length, 21 ft 6 in; height, 8 ft 9 in; wing area, 297 sq ft.
Weights: empty, 1602 lb; loaded, 2350 lb.
Performance: maximum speed, 103 mph; climb rate, 4.5 min to 3280 ft; endurance, 3.5 hr; service ceiling, 13,500 ft.
Armament: one or two fixed forward-mounted Spandaus and one Parabellum machine gun in rear cockpit; bomb load 110 lb plus antipersonnel grenades.

The CL IV was an improved version of the CL II and was similar in overall size but more maneuverable. It entered service in 1918 and gradually replaced the CL II.

Halberstadt C V

Year: 1918.
Manufacturer: Halberstädter Flugzeugwerke G.mbH; subcontracted to Automobil und Aviatik A.G.; Bayerische Flugzeugwerke and Deutsche Flugzeugwerke G.mbH.
Type: photographic reconnaissance.
Crew: two (pilot and gunner).
Specification: Halberstadt C V.
Power plant: Benz Bz IV six-cylinder water-cooled in-line engine developing 220 hp.
Dimensions: span, 44 ft 9 in; length, 22 ft 9 in; height, 11 ft; wing area, 464.4 sq ft.
Weights: empty, 2046 lb; loaded, 2730 lb.
Performance: maximum speed, 107 mph; climb rate, 3.2 min to 6560 ft; endurance, 3.5 hr; service ceiling, 17,500 ft.
Armament: one Spandau machine gun mounted on port side of forward fuselage and one Parabellum machine gun in rear cockpit.

An extremely efficient reconnaissance aircraft with a useful high-altitude performance. Entered service in midsummer 1918 and carried out useful work in trying conditions.

Below: the Halberstadt C V served in the photographic reconnaissance role from the summer of 1918 until the Armistice in November 1918.

Halberstadt D II and D III

Year: 1916.
Manufacturer: Halberstädter Flugzeugwerke G.mbH; subcontracted to Automobil und Aviatik A.G. and Hannoversche Waggonfabrik A.G.
Type: fighter/scout.
Crew: pilot only.
Specification: Halberstadt D III.
Power plant: Argus As II six-cylinder water-cooled in-line engine developing 120 hp.
Dimensions: span, 28 ft 11 in; length, 24 ft; height, 8 ft 9 in; wing area, not known.
Weights: empty, 1234 lb; loaded, 1696 lb.
Performance: maximum speed, 90 mph; climb rate, 4 min to 3280 ft; service ceiling, 19,600 ft.
Armament: one Spandau machine gun fixed to port side of fuselage firing forward.

A neat two-bay biplane which was respected by its adversaries in the early days of the war. Obsolete by 1917, it was relegated to training duties and areas of less-hostile activity.

Hannover CL II, III and IIIa

Year: 1917.
Manufacturer: Hannoverische Waggonfabrik A.G., subcontracted to Luftfahrzeug Gesellschaft mbH.
Type: escort/ground attack.
Crew: two (pilot and gunner).
Specification: Hannover CL II.
Power plant: Argus As III six-cylinder water-cooled in-line engine developing 180 hp.
Dimensions: span, 38 ft 5 in; length, 24 ft 11 in; height, 9 ft 2 in; wing area, 353 sq ft.
Weights: empty, 1577 lb; loaded, 2378 lb.
Performance: maximum speed, 103 mph; climb rate, 5.3 min to 3280 ft; endurance, 3.5 hr; service ceiling, 24,600 ft.
Armament: one Spandau machine gun fixed to fire forward and one Parabellum machine gun in rear cockpit.

Below: this Hannover CL IIIa shows the characteristic biplane tail of the series.

Above: the Argus As II powered Halberstadt D III was replaced by Albatros scouts in early 1917.

Until 1917 Hannoverische Waggonfabrik had built aircraft under license to other manufacturers, but in that year they produced the successful CL series of lightweight fighters designed to act as escorts and on ground-support duties. The design was unique in that it employed a short-span biplane tail which gave the gunner a wider arc of fire. The main differences between the types was in engines and wing-tip configuration. The aircraft were sturdy and because of their relatively small size were often mistaken for single-seat scouts; this quite often proved costly owing to the rear cockpit mounted Parabellum. They served until the end of the war by which time a total of 1056 had been manufactured, of which 537 were CL IIIs.

Above: the tough, all-metal Junkers J I was a popular ground attack aircraft with its crews.

Junkers J 1

Year: 1917.
Manufacturer: Junkers Flugzeugwerke A.G.
Type: ground attack/infantry cooperation.
Crew: two (pilot and gunner).
Specification: Junkers J 1.
Power plant: Benz Bz IV six-cylinder water-cooled in-line engine developing 200 hp.
Dimensions: span, 52 ft 6 in; length, 29 ft 10 in; height, 11 ft 2 in; wing area, 533.52 sq ft.
Weights: empty, 3885 lb; loaded, 4787 lb.
Performance: maximum speed, 97 mph; climb rate, 32 min to 6560 ft; endurance, 2 hr; service ceiling, 13,100 ft.
Armament: two Spandau machine guns fixed to fire forward and one Parabellum machine gun in rear cockpit.

Of steel tube with Duralumin skinning, the military designated J 1 was in fact the J 4 as far as the factory designation was concerned. Designed by Hugo Junkers, who patented his first aircraft design in 1910, the J 1 was a large airplane with no outboard supporting wing struts. It entered service in 1917 and was popular with crews because its metal skin offered a high degree of protection. Most of its work was carried out at low altitude and it was used to drop supplies to the infantry. A total of 227 aircraft was built.

Above: the all-metal Junkers CL I.

Junkers CL I

Year: 1918.
Manufacturer: Junkers Flugzeugwerke A.G.
Type: ground attack.
Crew: two (pilot and gunner).
Specification: Junkers CL I.
Power plant: Mercedes D IIIa six-cylinder water-cooled in-line engine developing 180 hp.
Dimensions: span, 39 ft 6 in; length, 25 ft 11 in; height, 7 ft 9 in; wing area, 253 sq ft.
Weights: empty, 1562 lb; loaded, 2310 lb.
Performance: maximum speed, 100 mph; climb rate, 3.9 min to 3280 ft; endurance, 2 hr; service ceiling, 19,685 ft.
Armament: two fixed forward-firing Spandau machine guns and one Parabellum machine gun in rear cockpit.

Derived from the D 1 which was built for the D class fighter contests, the CL 1 was put into production in 1918 to replace the Halberstadt CL series. A low-wing monoplane of all-metal construction, it proved to be strong and maneuverable and could carry bombs as well as its machine-gun armament. A total of 47 was produced by the time of the Armistice. A prototype seaplane version was developed but did not enter production.

L.F.G. Roland C II

Year: 1915.
Manufacturer: Luftfahrzeug Gesellschaft mbH (L.F.G.); subcontracted to Linke-Hoffmann Werke A.G.
Type: reconnaissance and escort.
Crew: two (pilot and gunner).
Specification: L.F.G. Roland C II.
Power plant: Mercedes D III six-cylinder water-cooled in-line engine developing 160 hp.
Dimensions: span, 33 ft 10 in; length, 25 ft 3.5 in; height, 9 ft 6 in; wing area, 281 sq ft.
Weights: empty, 1680 lb; loaded, 2824 lb.
Performance: maximum speed, 103 mph; climb rate, 6 min to 3280 ft; endurance, up to 5 hr; service ceiling, approximately 15,000 ft.
Armament: one Parabellum machine gun in rear cockpit. Later some aircraft fitted with a Spandau firing forward.

Entering service in 1916, the C II proved to be a reliable reconnaissance machine with tricky handling qualities. It was nicknamed *Walfisch* because of its rotund whale-shaped fuselage. Several hundred were produced and the later D series fighters, which had much slimmer fuselages and twin-machine-gun armament, owed a lot to their design. The most successful of the D series was the D VI, which was produced only in limited quantities as a back up in case of failure of the Fokker D VII, to which in some respects it was superior.

L.V.G. C Series

Year: 1915.
Manufacturer: Luft-Verkehrs Gesellschaft mbH; subcontracted to Ago Flugzeugwerke G.mbH, Otto-Werke G.mbH, and D.F.W.
Type: reconnaissance and artillery observation.
Crew: two (pilot and observer).
Specification: L.V.G. C V.
Power plant: Benz Bz IV six-cylinder water-cooled in-line engine developing 200 hp.
Dimensions: span, 44 ft 9 in; length, 26 ft 6 in; height, 10 ft 6 in; wing area, 464.16 sq ft.
Weights: empty, 2228 lb; loaded, 5372 lb.
Performance: maximum speed, 103 mph; climb rate, 35 min to 13,120 ft; endurance, 3.5 hr; service ceiling, 21,300 ft.
Armament: one Spandau machine gun fixed to fire forward, one Parabellum machine gun in rear cockpit.

Below: the L.V.G. C VI offered improved visibility for the crew.

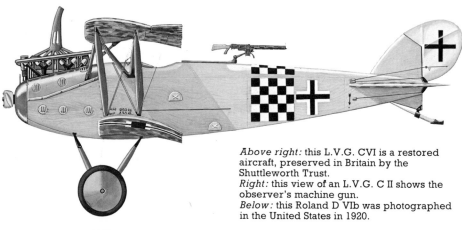

The first L.V.G. armed reconnaissance aircraft was the C I which, like the three models to follow, was designed by Franz Schnieder and was basically a B I airframe fitted with a 150 hp engine and defensive armament. The high attrition rate of the unarmed B types brought about the need to develop what was known as the C class, and Schneider was quickly able to modify his earlier airframe to meet these requirements. The C I entered service in 1915 and was the first operational German aircraft in which the observer was provided with a Schnieder ring-mounted Parabellum.

It was quickly followed by the C II which was more or less identical to the B II but was fitted with a Mercedes D III engine and armed with the observer operated Parabellum, which was later supplemented by a fuselage mounted forward-firing Spandau.

The C III and C IV models were not produced in any quantity. The C III was slightly smaller than the C II and the observer was located in the front seat. The C IV was a larger version of the C II powered by a 220 hp Mercedes D IV engine.

The C V brought about a major step in design and performance and was produced in some quantity. It bore a very close resemblance to the D.F.W. C V, probably because the same designer was responsible for both. The C V could carry a 254 pound bomb load and saw widespread service on the Western Front where it proved itself to be a good all-round airplane.

The C VI made its debut in 1918 and about 1000 were built. It had an increased performance over the C V as well as improved aerodynamics. The final version was the 240 hp Benz engined C VIII which incorporated structural improvements and revised control surfaces, but it was too late to see service and it is believed that only the prototype was completed.

Above right: this L.V.G. CVI is a restored aircraft, preserved in Britain by the Shuttleworth Trust.
Right: this view of an L.V.G. C II shows the observer's machine gun.
Below: this Roland D VIb was photographed in the United States in 1920.

Pfalz E I to E IV

Year: 1914.
Manufacturer: Pfalz Flugzeugwerke G.mbH.
Type: fighter/scout.
Crew: pilot only.
Specification: E II.
Power plant: Oberursel U 1 nine-cylinder rotary engine developing 100 hp.
Dimensions: span, 33 ft 6 in; length, 21 ft 2 in; height, 8 ft 5 in; wing area, 172 sq ft.
Weights: empty, 902 lb; loaded, 1364 lb.
Performance: maximum speed, 94 mph; climb rate, 9.75 min to 6560 ft; endurance, 2 hr.
Armament: one Spandau machine gun firing forward.

A series of monoplane fighters which saw limited service during 1915/16 after which they were relegated to training as more maneuverable and reliable biplanes became available.

Pfalz D III and D IIIa

Year: 1917.
Manufacturer: Pfalz Flugzeugwerke G.mbH.
Type: fighter/scout.
Crew: pilot only.
Specification: Pfalz D III.
Power plant: Mercedes D III six-cylinder water-cooled in-line engine developing 160 hp.
Dimensions: span, 30 ft 10 in; length, 22 ft 10 in; height, 8 ft 9 in; wing area, 237.75 sq ft.
Weights: empty, 1532 lb; loaded, 2056 lb.
Performance: maximum speed, 103 mph; climb rate, 7 min to 5000 ft; endurance, 2.5 hr; service ceiling, 17,000 ft.
Armament: two Spandau machine guns fixed to fire forward.

Having completed production of the E series fighters, Pfalz embarked on a program of license-built Rolands until 1917 when it produced its own D series. The D III and IIIa were both well-liked although they were marginally inferior in performance to their contemporary Fokker and Albatros rivals. Using a monocoque fuselage the aircraft were extremely strong. Some 600 were produced and over 400 were still in service in 1918. The D IIIa was powered by a 180 hp Mercedes D IIIa engine and could be distinguished from the D III by its rounded wing and tail-plane tips.

Above: a Pfalz D IIIa in the markings of Vizefeldwebel Max Holtzem, who flew with the Bavarian Jasta 16b. In April 1918 433 D IIIas were at the Front.

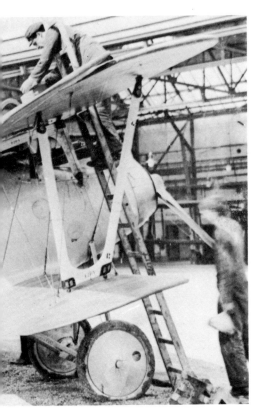

Above: the Pfalz D IIIa differed from the D III in having a more powerful engine and rounded rather than square wingtips and tailplane tips.
Above right: a captured Pfalz D IIIa.

Pfalz D XII

Year: 1918.
Manufacturer: Pfalz Flugzeugwerke G.mbH.
Type: fighter/scout.
Crew: pilot only.
Specification: Pfalz D XII.
Power plant: Mercedes D IIIa six-cylinder water-cooled in-line engine developing 160 hp.
Dimensions: span, 29 ft 6 in; length, 20 ft 10 in; height, 8 ft 10 in; wing area, 236.3 sq ft.
Weights: empty, 1571 lb; loaded, 1973 lb.
Performance: maximum speed, 106 mph; climb rate, 3.4 min to 3280 ft; endurance, 2.5 hr; service ceiling, 18,500 ft.
Armament: two Spandau machine guns fixed to fire forward.

The D XII was a logical development of the D III but never received the recognition it deserved as it was subjected to unfair comparison with the Fokker D VII. It entered service in 1918 and soon proved to be popular with pilots, who quickly found that in some respects it was better than its vaunted rival. It equipped 10 *Jastas* as well as home-defense units and 180 were in service at the time of the Armistice. If it had not been over-shadowed by the D VII it may well have proved to have been one of the best D type aircraft used by the Germans.

Left: the Pfalz D III entered service in August 1917 and by the end of the year 276 were with front line units.
Above right: the last of the Pfalz single seaters was the D XV, which was officially tested in November 1918.
Right: although it was overshadowed by the more famous Fokker D VII, the Pfalz D XII was an excellent fighter aircraft.

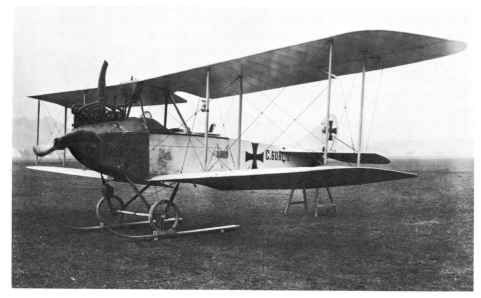

Above: this Rumpler C I is fitted with a temporary ski undercarriage.

Rumpler C Series

Year: 1915.
Manufacturer: Rumpler Flugzeugwerke G.mbH; subcontracted to Germania-Flugzeugwerke, Märkische Flugzeugwerke, Hannoverische Waggonfabrik, Bayerische Rumpler-Werke and Albert Rinne Flugzeugwerke.
Type: reconnaissance and general duties.
Crew: two (pilot and observer).
Specification: Rumpler C I.
Power plant: Mercedes D III six-cylinder water-cooled in-line engine developing 160 hp.
Dimensions: span, 39 ft 10 in; length 25 ft 9 in; height, 10 ft 1 in; wing area, 385 sq ft.
Weights: empty, 1744 lb; loaded, 2866 lb.
Performance: maximum speed, 95 mph; endurance, 4 hr; service ceiling, 16,600 ft.
Armament: one Spandau machine gun fixed to fire forward and one Parabellum machine gun in rear cockpit; bomb load 220 lbs.

The C I was a development of the unarmed B I which served from 1915–1918. It was a docile and extremely efficient aircraft which carried out invaluable photographic reconnaissance and visual reconnaissance on all fronts.

Rumpler C IV, C VII and Rubild

Year: 1917.
Manufacturer: Rumpler Flugzeugwerke G.mbH.
Type: long-range visual and photographic reconnaissance.
Crew: two (pilot and observer).
Specification: Rumpler C VII.
Power plant: Maybach Mb IV six-cylinder water-cooled in-line engine developing 240 hp.
Dimensions: span, 41 ft 2 in; length, 26 ft 11 in; height, 11 ft 1 in; wing area, 363 sq ft.
Weights: empty, 2310 lb; loaded, 3267 lb.
Performance: maximum speed, 110 mph; climb rate, 2.3 min to 3280 ft; endurance, 3.5 hr; service ceiling, 23,944 ft.
Armament: one Spandau machine gun fixed to fire forward, one Parabellum machine gun in rear cockpit. Spandau removed from C VII (Rubild).

The Rumpler C I was replaced by the successful C IV which was a more powerful version of the 220 hp C III development aircraft. It had an outstanding high-altitude performance and was popular with crews. The C VII followed it into production and its high-compression Maybach engine gave it more power reserves at altitude; its crews were equipped with heated suits and oxygen so that they could retain their efficiency at these high (*sic*) operating levels.

The Rubild, which is believed to have been a C VII, carried more photographic equipment at the expense of its forward-firing Spandau.

Siemens-Schuckert D III and D IV

Year: 1917.
Manufacturer: Siemens-Schuckert Werke G.mbH.
Type: fighter/scout.
Crew: pilot only.
Specification: Siemens-Schuckert D IV.
Power plant: Siemens-Halske Sh III and IIIa 11-cylinder rotary engine developing 160 hp.
Dimensions: span, 27 ft 5 in; length, 18 ft 9 in; height, 8 ft 11 in; wing area, 163.25 sq ft.
Weights: empty, 1190 lb; loaded, 1620 lb.
Performance: maximum speed, 118.75 mph; climb rate, 1.9 min to 3280 ft; endurance, 2 hr; service ceiling, 26,240 ft.
Armament: two Spandau machine guns fixed to fire forward.

Developed from the D II, IIa and IIb prototypes designed by Harald Wolff, the D III was potentially one of the most efficient D types to emerge from the German aircraft industry. Eighty D IIIs were built and served with eight *Jastas*, where their superb rate of climb, maneuverability and handling made them very popular as well as successful. Minor overheating problems were encountered but were overcome during the summer of 1918. The D IV had an even better climb rate but only half of the ordered 280 had been delivered by the Armistice. Although tricky to land, the D IV was considered by many to be the best single-seat fighter still serving in 1918, being faster and more maneuverable than the Fokker D VII especially at altitudes above 13,000 ft.

Right: the Siemens-Schuckert D IV of late 1918 was fast and maneuverable, with an excellent rate of climb, but few reached Front line units.

Above: the giant Zeppelin Staaken R VI was produced by the parent company and by Aviatik, O.A.W. and Schütte-Lanz.

Zeppelin Staaken R VI

Year: 1917.
Manufacturer: Zeppelin Werke Staaken G.mbH; subcontracted to Automobil und Aviatik A.G., Ostdeutsche Albatros Werke G.mbH and Luftfahrzeugbau Schütte-Lanz.
Type: long-range heavy bomber.
Crew: seven (pilot, observer and five gunners, one of whom was also the bomb aimer).
Specification: Staaken R VI.
Power plant: four Maybach Mb IV 245 hp or Mercedes D IVa 260 hp six-cylinder water-cooled in-line engines.
Dimensions: span, 138 ft 6 in; length, 72 ft 6 in; height, 20 ft 8 in; wing area, 3959 sq ft.
Weights: empty, 17,426 lb; loaded, 26,066 lb.
Performance: maximum speed, 85 mph; climb rate, 43 min to 9840 ft; duration, up to 10 hr depending on load; service ceiling, 14,170 ft.
Armament: four Parabellum machine guns manually operated from nose. dorsal and ventral positions, some aircraft fitted with additional Parabellums; bomb load, 4409 lb.

The R VI was the major production version of the Zeppelin R series of long-range bombers. Eighteen R VIs were produced and they equipped two units operating from the Ghent area. During the period December 1917–May 1918 they carried out many raids over London, dropping 1000 kg bombs, the largest to be used in World War I, and lost none of their number to Allied action. Only two machines were lost in combat but eight were written off in accidents. Various other versions were produced including a seaplane variant of the R VI.

PROTOTYPES

Below: three Zeppelin-Staaken R XVs were constructed in 1918.
Right: the Siemens-Schuckert D Dr I crashed during its maiden flight in 1917 and was not rebuilt. Power was provided by two engines mounted fore-and-aft in a central nacelle.

Left: the experimental L.V.G. D III first flew in 1917. Its wing bracing was unusual in that the landing wires were replaced by struts, but standard flying wires were retained.
Right: the Sablatnig SF 4 was built in both biplane and triplane versions, the latter being illustrated. Neither version was put into production.
Below: an L.F.G. Roland D II and an Albatros C V are parked on the airfield of Flieger Abteilung 250.

Below: the Imperial Naval Yards built various two-seat seaplanes in small quantities. The K.W. (Danzig) 1105, powered by a 150 hp Benz III engine, was constructed at the Danzig Yard.
Bottom: the N.F.W. B I trainer was built by National Flugzeug-Werke in 1915.
Far right: an L.F.G. Roland D II scout.

Below: the remarkable Junkers J9 (D I) was a single-seat, all-metal monoplane. Ordered into production in 1918, only a few examples had reached the Front by the end of hostilities.
Bottom: the Junkers J9 was fitted with a crash pylon aft of the cockpit to protect the pilot in the event of the aircraft overturning.

Below: the bizarre Fokker V8 was powered by a 120 hp Mercedes D II and used many Fokker V6 components.
Right: the Fokker V3 cantilever triplane embodied many features of the Dr I, but it was unsuccessful.
Far right: the Gotha Ursinus GUH G I.

Above: the Daimler L6, which was powered by a 185 hp Daimler IIIb, participated in the D-type fighter competitions in June 1918.
Top: one of the early unarmed two-seat reconnaissance aircraft in German service was the Aviatik B.I.

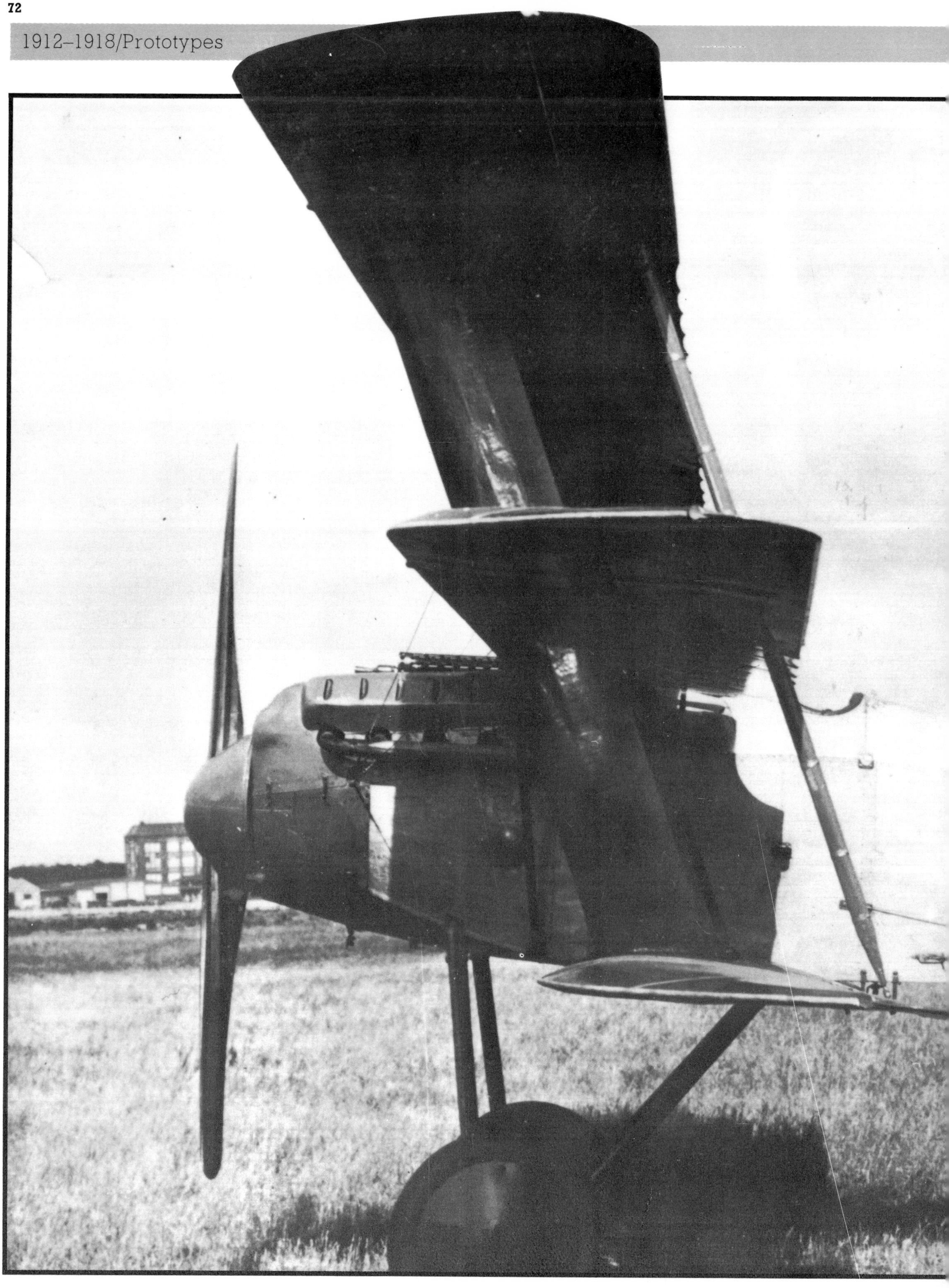

Below: the Albatros Dr II triplane was powered by a Benz IVB 195 hp eight-cylinder vee-engine.
Right: the Ago C IV was a fast and efficient reconnaissance aircraft, but its time-consuming and expensive construction techniques limited the number in service.

Alb.DR Ⅱ.

Left: unarmed reconnaissance aircraft such as this Albatros B II were used on front-line duties before the introduction of the armed C-types.
Below: a small quantity of Albatros B III aircraft were built in 1915, the aircraft illustrated being an example captured by the Royal Flying Corps.

Part Two
1919-

Above: known as the 'Flying Pencil,' the Dornier Do 17 operated alongside the He 111 in the early raids against Britain. This Do 17Z-2 served with the Geschwader Stab of KG 3.

1945

Arado Ar 65

Year: 1931.
Manufacturer: Arado Flugzeugwerke G.mbH.
Type: single-seat fighter.
Crew: pilot only.
Specification: Ar 65E.
Power plant: one BMW VI 7.3 12-cylinder liquid-cooled engine developing 750 hp.
Dimensions: span, 36 ft 9 in; length, 27 ft 7 in; height, 11 ft 3 in; wing area, 322.917 sq ft.
Weights: empty, 3329 lb; loaded, 4255 lb.
Performance: maximum speed, 186 mph at 5415 ft; cruising speed, 153 mph at 4595 ft; initial climb rate, 2086 ft per min; service ceiling, 24,935 ft.
Armament: two 7.9 mm MG 17 machine guns with 500 rounds per gun.

Generally considered to be the first warplane of the Luftwaffe, the Ar 65 first flew in 1931 and entered service in 1933. Design work was carried out in contravention of the Treaty of Versailles and the aircraft remained in production until early 1936, by which time most Ar 65s had been relegated to the training role.

Arado Ar 66

Year: 1932.
Manufacturer: Arado Flugzeugwerke G.mbH.
Type: trainer.
Crew: two.
Specification: Ar 66C (major production).
Power plant: Argus As 10C inverted eight-cylinder liquid-cooled engine developing 240 hp.
Dimensions: span, 32 ft 10 in; length, 27 ft 3 in; height, 9 ft 8 in; wing area, 318.94 sq ft.
Weights: empty, 1995 lb; loaded, 2932 lb.
Performance: maximum speed, at sea level 130 mph; cruising speed, 109 mph; climb rate, 4 min 6 sec to 3280 ft; service ceiling, 14,765 ft.
Armament: none. Some versions modified to carry 4.5–9 lb antipersonnel bombs.

The Ar 66 entered service with the Luftwaffe in 1933 and continued to equip training schools until well into World War II. Exact production figures are not available but it is likely that some 10,000 of all versions were produced. The aircraft were used on the Eastern Front and in Finland by *Störkampfstaffeln* (Harassing Squadrons) for night-interdiction work. Sixteen *Staffeln* used the Ar 66 and one of these was operated by Soviet ex-POWs.

Arado Ar 68

Year: 1933.
Manufacturer: Arado Flugzeugwerke G.mbH.
Type: single-seat fighter.
Crew: pilot only.
Specification: Ar 68E-1 and Ar 68F-1.
Power plant: E-1 Junkers Jumo 210 Ea 12-cylinder liquid-cooled engine developing 680 hp. F-1 BMW VI 7.3Z developing 750 hp.
Dimensions: span, 36 ft 1 in; length, E-1 31 ft 2 in, F-1 31 ft; height, 10 ft 10 in; wing area, 293.855 sq ft.
Weights: empty, E-1 3527 lb, F-1 3351 lb; loaded E-1 4453 lb, F-1 4299 lb.
Performance: speed, E-1 190 mph at sea level, 208 mph at 8695 ft, F-1 205 mph at sea level 200 mph at 8695 ft; climb rate, E-1 2480 ft per min, F-1 2205 ft per min.
Armament: two fuselage-mounted 7.9 mm MG 17 machine guns and (optional) six 22 lb SC 10 fragmentation bombs.

The last biplane fighter to enter Luftwaffe service, the Ar 68 was designed to replace the He 51 which in turn had replaced the earlier Ar 65. Performance of the BMW-powered

prototype did not reach expectations so the second prototype was fitted with the Junkers Jumo engine. Although performance was superior to the He 51 the Luftwaffe General Staff were not convinced that this was so, but a comparison demonstration between the two aircraft in which Udet flew the Ar 68, proved the aircraft to be superior and it was put into production in 1936.

The E version equipped most *Jagdgruppen* by the time the Bf 109 entered service in 1937. It was used on trials during the Spanish Civil War but by this time it had been overtaken by the monoplane fighter.

By the start of World War II most Ar 68s had been relegated to the training role, equipping advanced flying training schools. Some aircraft were pressed into service as night fighters but only operated for a very short period. A development of the aircraft, fitted with an 815 hp BMW 132J nine-cylinder radial engine driving a three-bladed propeller, arrestor hook and catapult spools, was known as the Ar 197. This aircraft was intended for use aboard the planned aircraft carriers *Graf Zeppelin* and *Peter Strasser*, but it was superseded by a modified version of the Bf 109E known as the Bf 109T.

Arado Ar 76

Year: 1935.
Manufacturer: Arado Flugzeugwerke G.mbH.
Type: light fighter/trainer.
Crew: pilot only.
Specification: Ar 76A.
Power plant: one Argus As 10 C Series 1, eight-cylinder inverted-V air-cooled engine developing 240 hp.
Dimensions: span, 31 ft 2 in; length, 23 ft 8 in; height, 8 ft 5 in; wing area, 143.59 sq ft.
Weights: empty, 1653 lb; loaded, 2359 lb.
Performance: maximum speed, 166 mph; cruising speed, 137 mph; climb rate, 1417 ft per min; service ceiling, 21,000 ft.
Armament: two 7.9 mm MG 17 machine guns; bomb load, three 22 lb bombs. Training version had one 7.9 mm MG 17.

Designed to a specification which called for a lightweight home-defense fighter which could also be used as an advanced trainer, the Ar 76 was placed second in evaluation trials to the Fw 56 and only a small batch was produced. These were issued to *Jagdfliegerschulen* in 1936.

Arado Ar 80

Year: 1934.
Manufacturer: Arado Flugzeugwerke G.mbH.
Type: single-seat fighter.
Crew: pilot only.
Specification: Ar 80 V2.
Power plant: Junkers Jumo 210C 12-cylinder liquid-cooled engine developing 600 hp.
Dimensions: span, 35 ft 9 in; length, 33 ft 10 in; height, 8 ft 8 in; wing area, 226 sq ft.
Weights: empty, (unarmed) 3620 lb; loaded, 4684 lb.
Performance: maximum speed, 217 mph at sea level, 258 mph at 8250 ft; climb rate, 1870 ft per min; service ceiling, 32,800 ft.
Armament: two 7.9 mm MG 17 machine guns.

The Ar 80 V2 was an esthetically pleasing aircraft. One prototype was fitted with a Rolls-Royce Kestrel engine. However weight and drag exceeded expectations and no production was undertaken. In 1937 the Ar 80 V3, the Jumo 210C-powered third prototype, was pressed into service as a flying test bed for Fowler flaps. A second seat was installed for a flight-test observer and the converted aircraft flew again in 1938.

Arado Ar 81

Year: 1935.
Manufacturer: Arado Flugzeugwerke G.mbH.
Type: dive bomber.
Crew: two (pilot and gunner).
Specification: Ar 81 V3.
Power plant: Junkers Jumo 210Ca 12-cylinder liquid-cooled engine developing 640 hp.
Dimensions: span, 36 ft 1 in; length, 37 ft 9 in; height, 11 ft 10 in; wing area, 383.20 sq ft.
Weights: empty, 4244 lb; loaded, 6768 lb.
Performance: maximum speed, 186 mph at sea level, 214 mph at 13,120 ft; climb rate, 11 min to 13,120 ft; service ceiling, 25,256 ft.
Armament: one 7.9 mm MG 17 machine gun firing forward and one 7.9 mm MG 15 on flexible mounting in rear cockpit; bomb load, one 550 lb bomb on external cradle.

The Ar 81 V3 was designed as a result of Ernst Udet's support for the dive bomber after he had witnessed dive-bombing techniques demonstrated by Curtiss Helldivers. Although superior in performance to the Junkers Ju 87, the fact that it was a biplane made its production seem a retrograde step, so it was dropped in favor of the monoplane. Only three examples were built.

Arado Ar 95

Year: 1936.
Manufacturer: Arado Flugzeugwerke G.mbH.
Type: torpedo bomber/reconnaissance floatplane.
Crew: two (pilot and observer/gunner).
Specification: Ar 95A-1.
Power plant: one BMW 132Dc nine-cylinder air-cooled radial engine developing 850 hp.
Dimensions: span, 41 ft; length, 36 ft 5 in; height, 17 ft 1 in; wing area, 488.50 sq ft.
Weights: empty, 5588 lb; loaded, 7843 lb.
Performance: maximum speed, 171 mph at sea level, 187 mph at 9840 ft; climb rate, 2.3 min to 3280 ft; service ceiling, 23,950 ft.
Armament: one 7.9 mm MG 17 machine gun firing forward, one 7.9 mm MG 15 on flexible mounting; bomb load; one torpedo beneath fuselage or one 827 lb bomb and six 110 lb bombs on wing racks.

Initial trials indicated that the aircraft would not be suitable for the design use so a respecification resulted in a much modified wheeled version, the Ar 195 for the proposed aircraft carrier program. Export orders for the Ar 95A-1 were diverted to the Luftwaffe and only three prototype Ar 195s were completed.

Above: the Avia C-2 was the version of the Ar 96B built in Czechoslovakia, where it remained in production until 1948, 394 being produced.

Six preproduction Arado Ar 95A-0 floatplanes went to the Condor Legion in 1938 and in 1939 three of these were passed to the Spanish, who flew them until 1948. One Luftwaffe *Staffel*, 3/ SAGr 125, flew the Ar 95A-1 and when Germany invaded the Soviet Union it operated on the flanks of the advance in the Baltic. When SAGr 125 moved to Romania later in 1941 the Ar 95s passed to SAGr 127.

Arado Ar 96

Year: 1938.
Manufacturer: Arado Flugzeugwerke G.mbH.
Type: advanced trainer.
Crew: two (pilot and pupil).
Specification: Ar 96B-2.
Power plant: Argus As 410A-1 12-cylinder inverted-V air-cooled engine developing 465 hp.
Dimensions: span, 36 ft 1 in; length, 29 ft 11 in; height, 8 ft 6 in; wing area, 184.06 sq ft.
Weights: empty, 2854 lb; loaded, 3747 lb.
Performance: speed, 205 mph at sea level, cruising speed 183 mph; climb rate, 6.8 min to 9843 ft; service ceiling, 23,295 ft.
Armament: one 7.9 mm MG 17 firing forward on front cowling. Some versions modified to carry bombs for training ground-attack and dive-bomber pilots. At least one variant fitted with a 7.9 mm MG 15 in rear cockpit for air gunner training.

The Ar 96 was the most important advanced trainer to serve with the Luftwaffe. The A version entered service in 1939 but the bulk production type was the B, which began to join the training schools in 1940. Over 11,546 were built during the war but the aircraft stayed in production in Czechoslovakia until 1948. An advanced version, known as the Ar 396, was made by the French SIPA works where it remained in production as the S 11 and S 12 after the Liberation.

Left: the Arado Ar 95B was derived from the Ar 95 floatplane and it was intended for carrier operations. As performance was disappointing, the Ar 95B was not produced.

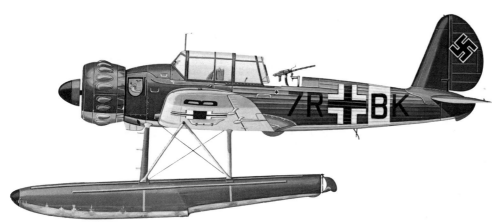

Arado Ar 232

Year: 1941.
Manufacturer: Arado Flugzeugwerke G.mbH.
Type: general purpose transport.
Crew: four (pilot, observer, radio operator, engineer/gunner).
Specification: Ar 232 B-0.
Power plant: four BMW-Bramo 323R-2 Fafnir nine-cylinder air-cooled radial engines each developing 1000 hp.
Dimensions: span, 109 ft 11 in; length, 77 ft 2 in; height, 18 ft 8 in; wing area, 1535 sq ft.
Weights: empty, 28,175 lb; loaded, 44,090 lb.
Performance: maximum speed, 191 mph at 13,120 ft; cruising speed, 180 mph at 6560 ft; climb rate, 15.8 min to 13,120 ft; service ceiling, 22,640 ft.
Armament: one 13 mm MG 131 on flexible mount in nose, one 20 mm MG 151 cannon on forward dorsal turret, and one or two 13 mm MG 131 machine guns in rear of fuselage. Could also accommodate eight hand-held 7.9 mm MG 34s firing through side windows.

The Ar 232 was a medium-range transport initially designed with two engines but converted to four when availability of BMW 801 became problematic. A unique multiwheeled undercarriage earned it the nickname *Tausendfüssler* (millipede) in Luftwaffe service. Only 22 aircraft were completed. They were operated by I and II/TG 5 and *Transport Staffel* 5 of I/KG 200.

Arado Ar 196A-1 to A-5

Year: 1938.
Manufacturer: Arado Flugzeugwerke G.mbH.
Type: shipboard reconnaissance/coastal-patrol floatplane.
Crew: two (pilot and observer/gunner).
Specification: Ar 196A-3.
Power plant: one BMWK nine-cylinder air-cooled radial engine developing 960 hp.
Dimensions: span, 40 ft 10 in; length, 36 ft; height, 14 ft 7 in; wing area, 304.62 sq ft.
Weights: empty, 5148 lb; loaded, 7282 lb.
Performance: speed, 194 mph at 3280 ft, cruising speed 166 mph; climb rate, 1358 ft per min; service ceiling, 22,965 ft.
Armament: two 20 mm MG FF cannons, one 7.9 mm MG 17 machine gun firing forward, and one 7.9 mm MG 15 machine gun on flexible mounting in rear cockpit; bomb load, two 110 lb SC 50 bombs on external wing racks.

Designed to equip German warships, the Ar 196 became one of the most widely used floatplanes outside the Pacific Theater in World War II. Making its service debut in the Autumn of 1939, the aircraft became standard equipment on

Above: an Arado Ar 196A floatplane of 2./SAGr 125, serving in the Aegean.

Germany's capital ships, the complement varying from six on battleships such as the *Tirpitz* and *Bismarck*, to two on light cruisers. Apart from shipboard use, the Ar 196 also equipped several coastal-patrol units where its use gradually developed from reconnaissance to anti-shipping strikes. One early notable success was the capture of the submarine HMS *Seal* by two Ar 196A-4s of 1/*Küstenfliegergruppe* 706. The floatplane was also used to harass RAF Coastal Command aircraft operating in the Bay of Biscay.

The A-3 version was produced in the greatest quantity and proved to be a formidable opponent in the right hands. It served with distinction in all theaters but it was mainly used in the Mediterranean, Norway and the Balkans. A total of 546 aircraft of all versions were produced and it remained in service until the close of hostilities in May 1945.

Below left: SAGr 126 began to operate in the Greek islands in spring 1943.
Below right: this pair of Ar 196A-3 floatplanes belong to 2./SAGr 125.

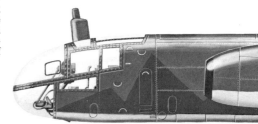

Arado Ar 234A, B, & C

Year: 1943.
Manufacturer: Arado Flugzeugwerke G.mbH.
Type: single-seat reconnaissance bomber.
Crew: pilot only.
Specification: Ar 234B-2.
Power plant: two Junkers Jumo 004B Orkan axial-flow turbojets, each rated at 1980 lb s.t.
Dimensions: span, 46 ft 4 in; length, 41 ft 6 in; height, 14 ft 1 in; wing area, 284.17 sq ft.
Weights: empty, 11,464 lb; loaded, 18,541 lb; maximum load with rocket boosters, 21,715 lb.
Performance: maximum speed, 461 mph at 19,685 ft, 435 mph at 32,800 ft; climb rate, 12.8 min to 19,685 ft.
Armament: two 20 mm MG 151 cannon fixed to fire aft; bomb load, a maximum weight of 3300 lb of various combinations of bombs.

Postwar advances in aircraft design owe a great deal to the efforts made in aeronautical research by the Germans, especially in the field of turbojet-powered aircraft. In 1940 Dipl Ing Walter Blume and Ing Rebeski of Arado started work on the design of a medium-range reconnaissance aircraft which was to be powered by the BMW and Junkers turbojets which were then beginning test-bench trials. The result was the Ar 234, the first jet bomber to reach operational status with any air force. Although the airframe was of orthodox construction, a novel approach was adopted for the undercarriage. A trolly was used for takeoff which was then jettisoned, the aircraft landing on retractable skids. Although this worked well after initial teething troubles had been sorted out, it proved impractical as the aircraft was difficult to maneuver after landing. In the event of a landing away from its home base its subsequent recovery would require the transportation of takeoff trollies, or the availability of such trollies at a variety of airfields. Subsequently the B version was fitted with a narrow-track tricycle undercarriage which resulted in increased weight and required careful ground maneuvering by the pilot. Performance however, was not adversely affected, and when the B-2 version began to be operated by KG 76, it proved hard to intercept and was really only vulnerable during takeoff and landing. The weight and carrying capacity was roughly equivalent to a Hawker Hunter, and with the advantage of height, speed and a computer bombsight it could have achieved considerable success if it had been available earlier and in greater quantity. A four-engined version, designated Ar 234C, was also built but did not reach operational status. Although a total of 274 aircraft were built (of which 210 were the B version), something less than 100 actually saw operational service. An interesting proposed design was the Ar 234 V16 which was fitted with a crescent wing similar to that later adopted for the Victor bomber.

Arado Ar 240

Year: 1940.
Manufacturer: Arado Flugzeugwerke G.mbH.
Type: long-range reconnaissance/heavy fighter bomber.
Crew: two (pilot, observer/gunner or radar operator).
Specification: Ar 240A-0.
Power plant: two Daimler-Benz DB 601E 12-cylinder liquid-cooled engines each developing 1475 hp.
Dimensions: span, 43 ft 9 in; length, 42 ft; height 13 ft; wing area, 336.91 sq ft.
Weights: empty, 13,669 lb; loaded, 20,834 lb.
Performance: maximum speed, 384 mph at 19,685 ft, cruising speed, 345 mph at 19,685 ft; climb rate, 11 min to 19,685 ft; service ceiling, 34,450 ft.
Armament: two 7.9 mm MG 17 machine guns firing forward, two 7.9 mm MG 81 machine guns in dorsal and ventral barbettes. The C-03 version had four 20 mm MG 151 cannons and two 13 mm MG 131 machine guns plus an external bomb load of 3968 lb.

The Ar 240 was fitted with a revolutionary defense system using remotely operated barbettes. Only 15 aircraft were built and they saw limited service. An improved version known as the Ar 440 was developed from the Ar 240 but only four were built as the Do 335 offered a better performance envelope.

Below: the Ar 234 could be used both as a dive bomber and as a level bomber. The periscopic sight used in the former role can be seen above the cockpit of this aircraft and a bombing computer was also fitted.

Below: an Arado 234B-2 jet bomber of 8 Staffel of Kampfgeschwader 76, which commenced operations early in 1945.

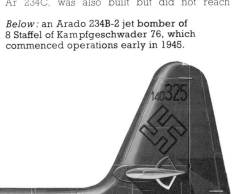

Bachem Ba 349 (Natter)

Year: 1944.
Manufacturer: Bachem-Werke G.mbH.
Type: single-seat interceptor.
Crew: pilot only.
Specification: Ba 349 B-1.
Power plant: one Walter HWK 509C-1 rocket motor developing maximum thrust of 4410 lb plus two or four solid fuel boosters.
Dimensions: span, 13 ft 2 in; length, 19 ft 9 in; height, 7 ft 5 in; wing area, 50.59 sq ft.
Weights: empty, 1940 lb; loaded, (with booster rockets) 4290 lb, (with fuel but without booster rockets) 3900 lb.
Performance: maximum speed, 620 mph at 16,400 ft; cruising speed, 495 mph; climb rate, 37,400 ft per min; service ceiling, 45,920 ft.
Armament: 24 73 mm Hs 217 Föhn or 33 55 mm R4M rockets. Proposal was also made to fit two 30 mm MK 108 cannons.

The Ba 349 B-I was developed in a desperate attempt to combat the increasing intrusions by the USAAF daylight raids. The aircraft was ramp launched and after interception the pilot used an ejector seat to save himself and the rocket motor was recovered by parachute. Several test flights had been made and 36 aircraft produced before the manufacturing facility was overrun by the Allies in April 1945.

Blohm und Voss Ha 137

Year: 1935.
Manufacturer: Hamburger Flugzeugbau G.mbH.
Type: dive bomber/close support.
Crew: pilot only.
Specification: Blohm und Voss Ha 137 V4.
Power plant: one Junkers Jumo 210Aa 12-cylinder liquid-cooled engine developing 610 hp.
Dimensions: span, 36 ft 7 in; length, 31 ft 1 in; height, 9 ft 2 in; wing area, 252.95 sq ft.
Weights: empty, 4000 lb; loaded, 5324 lb.
Performance: maximum speed, 186 mph at sea level, cruising speed, 180 mph at 6560 ft; climb rate, 4 min to 6560 ft (unloaded); service ceiling, 22,965 ft.
Armament: two 7.9 mm MG 17 machine guns in fuselage and one 7.9 mm MG 17 or 20 mm MG FF cannons mounted in each undercarriage leg fairing; bomb load, four 110 lb SC 50 bombs on wing racks.

A sturdy, well-designed aircraft which was not proceeded with after the four prototypes were built, as Udet attached little importance to the close-support role.

Blohm und Voss Ha 138, BV 138A, B, & C

Year: 1937.
Manufacturer: Hamburger Flugzeugbau G.mbH and Blohm und Voss Abt. Flugzeugbau.
Type: long-range maritime-reconnaissance flying boat.
Crew: five (two pilots, observer, radio operator, engineer). Two crews could be carried for long-endurance patrols.
Specification: Blohm und Voss Bv 138 C-1.
Power plant: three Junkers Jumo 205D six-cylinder vertically-opposed diesel engines each developing 880 hp.
Dimensions: span, 88 ft 4 in; length, 65 ft 2 in; height, 19 ft 4 in; wing area, 1205.56 sq ft.
Weights: empty, 25,948 lb; loaded, 38,912 lb (maximum).
Performance: maximum speed, at sea level 171 mph; cruising speed, 146 mph at 3280 ft; climb rate, 24 min to 10,390 ft; service ceiling, 31,967 ft.
Armament: two 20 mm MG 151 cannons in bow and hull turrets, one 13 mm MG 131 in open position aft of engine and one 7.9 mm MG 15 in starboard hatch (optional); bomb load, three 110 lb bombs on wing racks, or six 110 lb bombs or four 331 lb depth charges.

Hamburger Flugzeugbau GmbH, the aircraft subsidiary of the famous shipbuilders Blohm und Voss, produced two land-based aircraft, the Ha 135 and Ha 137, before predictably turning their attention to waterborne aircraft. This came about in the winter of 1933–34 when the technical department of the *Luftfahrtkommissariat* (C-Amt) issued a tentative specification for an ocean-going reconnaissance flying boat. Under the guidance of Dr Ing Richard Vogt the design team produced three alternatives, *Projekte* 8, 12 and 13. Eventually a compromise between *Projekts* 8 and 12 was reached and

after a long gestation period the first prototype, Ha 138 V1 carrying the civil registration D-ARAK, made its maiden flight on 15 July 1937. Various problems of an aerodynamic and hydrodynamic nature were encountered, and it was not until 1939 that the redesigned aircraft, now carrying the designation BV 138A-01, left the water for the first time. Despite serviceability problems and an obvious need for structural strengthening of the hull, trials were satisfactory overall and a first production order for 25 aircraft was placed.

The first and second BV 138A-1s were pressed into service during the Norwegian campaign as transports. From the fourth A-1 structural strengthening was carried out, resulting in the B-0. The next 14 machines were produced as B-1s, which had improved defensive armament.

The definitive version was the C-1 and 227 of the total BV 138 production of 279 were C-1s. Some B-0 models were converted to the role of minesweepers and were designated Bv 138 MS.

The aircraft served in most theaters and its hull shape earned it the nickname *der Fliegende Holzschuh* (the flying clog). One of the last operations of the war was carried out by a BV 138 of 3(F)SAGr 130. It flew to Berlin on 1 May 1945 to collect two couriers who were entrusted with Hitler's will but the couriers could produce no identification and so the pilot refused to take them and evacuated 10 wounded soldiers instead.

Below: this Blohm und Voss BV 138C-1 of SAGr 125 operated over the Black Sea during 1943.
Bottom: a BV 138 C-1 of SAGr 125 pictured on patrol over Arctic waters. This flying boat's distinctive hull shape earned it the nickname of 'Flying Clog.' Despite early problems with the flying boat's hull and floats, it became a most seaworthy craft.

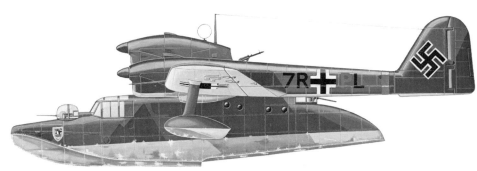

Above: one of Lufthansa's Blohm und Voss Ha 139s aboard the *Schwabenland.*

Blohm und Voss Ha 139

Year: 1936.
Manufacturer: Hamburger Flugzeugbau G.mbH.
Type: long-range reconnaissance floatplane.
Crew: four (pilot, observer, engineer, radio operator).
Specification: Blohm und Voss Ha 139 B/U.
Power plant: four Junkers Jumo 205C six-cylinder vertically-opposed diesel engines with 12 pistons in double-ended cylinders each developing 600 hp.
Dimensions: span, 96 ft 10 in; length, 65 ft 10 in; height, 15 ft 9 in; wing area, 1399.31 sq ft.
Weights: empty, approximately 29,000 lb; loaded, 41,888 lb.
Performance: maximum speed, 179 mph at 9840 ft, cruising speed, 124 mph; service ceiling, 16,400 ft.
Armament: four 7.9 mm MG15 machine guns mounted in nose and fuselage.

Designed for Deutsche Lufthansa, the three aircraft completed were pressed into wartime service but were eventually scrapped owing to a lack of spares.

Blohm und Voss BV 141 A and B

Year: 1938.
Manufacturer: Blohm und Voss Abt. Flugzeugbau.
Type: tactical reconnaissance and army cooperation.
Crew: three (pilot, observer, radio operator/gunner).
Specification: BV 141 A-04.
Power plant: one BMW 132N nine-cylinder air-cooled radial engine developing 960 hp.
Dimensions: span, 50 ft 8 in; length, 39 ft 10 in; height, 13 ft 6 in; wing area, 461.233 sq ft.
Weights: empty, 6982 lb; loaded, 8598 lb.
Performance: maximum speed, 211 mph at sea level, cruising speed, 193 mph; service ceiling, 29,530 ft.
Armament: two 7.9 mm MG 17s firing forward, two 7.9 mm MG 15s on flexible mountings firing aft; bomb load, four 110 lb bombs on underwing racks.

The BV 141 was designed by Dr Ing Richard Vogt but failed to achieve production status. Thirteen examples were built and saw very limited service. The asymmetric layout was not popular although it was favored by Blohm und Voss in other design proposals.

Blohm und Voss BV 142

Year: 1938.
Manufacturer: Blohm und Voss Abt. Flugzeugbau.
Type: maritime and strategic reconnaissance.
Crew: six.
Specification: BV 142 V2/U1.
Power plant: four BMW 132H nine-cylinder air-cooled radial engines each developing 880 hp.
Dimensions: span, 96 ft 11 in; length, 67 ft 2 in; height, 14 ft 7 in; wing area, 1399.30 sq ft.
Weights: empty, 24,427 lb; loaded, 36,508 lb.
Performance: maximum speed, 232 mph at sea level; cruising speed, 202 mph at 6560 ft; service ceiling, 29,530 ft.
Armament: five 7.9 mm MG 15 machine guns in nose, ventral, dorsal turret, and beam positions; bomb load, four 220 lb or eight 110 lb bombs carried internally.

The BV 142 was a land version of the Ha 139 employing many common components. Only four were built, initially as Atlantic mailplanes but they were pressed (unsuccessfully) into military use in 1940 – 42, mainly as transports.

Below: the fourth BV 222A-0 airframe was modified to accept Jumo diesel engines and redesignated BV 222 V7.

Blohm und Voss BV 222 Wiking

Year: 1940.
Manufacturer: Blohm und Voss Abt Flugzeugbau.
Type: long-range maritime-patrol and reconnaissance flying boat.
Crew: 10.
Specification: BV 222C-09.
Power plant: six Junkers Jumo 207C six-cylinder vertically opposed 12-piston diesel engines each developing 1000 hp.
Dimensions: span, 150 ft 11 in; length, 121 ft 5 in; height, 35 ft 9 in; wing area, 2744.8 sq ft.
Weights: empty, 67,572 lb; loaded (maximum), 108,026 lb.
Performance: maximum speed, 205 mph at sea level; cruising speed, 189 mph; climb rate, 473 ft per min; service ceiling, 23,950 ft.
Armament: one 13 mm MG 131 machine gun in bow, and four firing from beam positions, three 20 mm MG 151 cannons in dorsal turret and two wing turrets.

The BV 222 Wiking, was the largest flying boat to see operational service in World War II. It was bigger than both the Short Sunderland and Kawanishi H8K but fewer were produced. Like many German military aircraft, it was

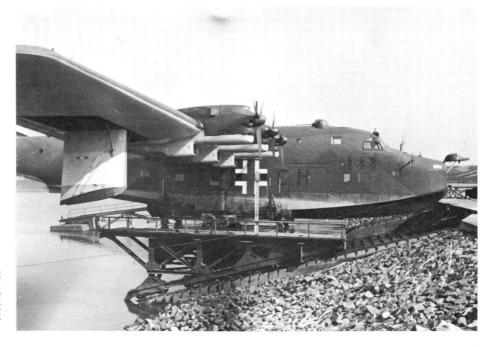

designed originally for civilian use; in this case to carry 24 passengers on the Atlantic route. Wartime conditions prevailed when the BMW-Bramo Fafnir-engined prototype made its first flight in September 1940, so flight tests were designed to assess the aircraft's military use. Early transport flights on behalf of the Luftwaffe were carried out in Norway and the Mediterranean by the civil flight-test crew.

The second and third aircraft were fitted with defensive armament, which was fitted retrospectively to the first.

A maritime transport *Staffel* was formed to operate the aircraft, mainly in the Middle East, but in 1943 modifications to armament and the fitting of radar saw a change in role to maritime reconnaissance. The BV 222 V9 made its maiden flight on 1 April 1943 fitted with Jumo diesel engines and revised defensive armament.

The aircraft had more success in the transport role than it did as a reconnaissance aircraft, but as Allied air superiority increased it proved vulnerable to marauding fighters. Nonetheless it could give a good account of itself and on one occasion a BV 222 surprised a patrolling RAF Lancaster bomber and dispatched it into the sea. The deteriorating war conditions never allowed the flying boat to reach its full potential and the envisioned large-scale production never materialized; a total of only 12 aircraft were completed and used by the Luftwaffe.

Blohm und Voss BV 238

Year: 1944.
Manufacturer: Blohm und Voss Abt. Flugzeugbau.
Type: transport/maritime-patrol and bomber flying boat.
Crew: 10.
Specification: BV 238 V-1.
Power plant: six Daimler-Benz DB 603A 12-cylinder liquid-cooled engines each developing 1750 hp.
Dimensions: span, 197 ft 5 in; length, 142 ft 9 in; height, 44 ft; wing area, 3930 sq ft.
Weights: empty, 111,985 lb; loaded (maximum), 176,400 lb.
Performance: maximum speed, 264 mph at 19.685 ft; range, 3788 miles; service ceiling and climb rate not recorded.
Armament: none.

Although having to concede to the Tupolev ANT 20 the distinction of being the world's largest aircraft to fly at the time of its maiden flight in April 1944, the BV 238 was certainly the heaviest. Envisioned as a replacement for the BV 138, a quarter-scale prototype known as the FGP 227 was initially produced to assess the design envelope as occurred with the British Short Stirling. Trials were still in progress when the only completed aircraft (the V1) was destroyed by Mustang fighters on Lake Schaal in April 1944.

Blohm und Voss BV 40

Year: 1944.
Manufacturer: Blohm und Voss Abt Flugzeugbau.
Type: single-seat interceptor (glider).
Crew: pilot only.
Specification: BV 40A.
Power plant: none.
Dimensions: span, 25 ft 11 in; length, 18 ft 9 in; height, 5 ft 4 in; wing area, 93.65 sq ft.
Weights: empty, 1844 lb; loaded, 2094 lb.
Performance: maximum speed, (in dive) 560 mph; maximum towed speed, 344 mph; climb rate, one aircraft and Bf 109 tug, 12 min to 23,000 ft.
Armament: two 30 mm MK 108 cannons.

The critical shortage of fuel and basic materials saw many improvised design proposals materialize from a variety of aircraft designers. One of these came from the versatile team led by Dr Ing Richard Vogt and was for a glider fighter which was to be towed to altitude by a standard fighter, then released to make a head-on diving attack at the bomber formations.

The advantage of minimum use of raw materials, few skilled man-hours for assembly and pilots trained only to a basic standard, had certain attractions. Flight trials commenced in 1944 but development was overtaken by the so-called lightweight rocket-powered fighters and the planned fighter program was abandoned. Use of the aircraft as a 'stand-off' bomb and towed fuel tank were investigated but also eventually discarded.

Below: the BV 238 V1 pictured while under test on Lake Schaal in April 1944. It was shortly afterwards destroyed by strafing P-51 Mustangs.

Bücker Bü 131 Jungmann

Year: 1934.
Manufacturer: Bücker Flugzeugbau G.mbH.
Type: trainer.
Crew: two (pupil and pilot).
Specification: Bü 131B.
Power plant: one Hirth HM 504A-2 four-cylinder in-line engine developing 105 hp.
Dimensions: span, 24 ft 3 in; length, 21 ft 9 in; height, 7 ft 5 in; wing area, 145.3 sq ft.
Weights: empty, 860 lb; loaded, 1500 lb.
Performance: maximum speed, 114 mph at sea level; cruising speed, 106 mph; climb rate, 6.3 min to 3280 ft; service ceiling, 9840 ft.
Armament: none.

Formed at Johannisthal in 1932 by the former World War I German Navy pilot Carl Bücker, the company bearing his name met with immediate success with its first model. It was conceived by Anders Andersson, a Swedish designer with a flair for incorporating superb handling qualities into his aircraft. The Bü 131 was first issued to Luftwaffe training schools for *ab initio* training in 1935 and served throughout the war. When it was supplanted by the Bü 181 some machines found their way to night ground-attack units and were used on the Eastern Front in this role. The Bü 131 was adopted by the Imperial Japanese Army Air Force as a standard trainer designated as the Kokusai Ki-86. It was also built under license in Czechoslovakia where it was known as the C-104. Production continued postwar.

Bücker Bü 133 Jungmeister

Year: 1935.
Manufacturer: Bücker Flugzeugbau G.mbH.
Type: advanced trainer.
Crew: pilot only.
Specification: Bü 133 C.
Power plant: one Siemens Sh 14A-4 seven-cylinder air-cooled radial engine developing 160 hp.
Dimensions: span, 21 ft 8 in; length, 19 ft 9 in; height, 7 ft 3 in; wing area, 129.12 sq ft.
Weights: empty, 937 lb; loaded, 1290 lb.
Performance: maximum speed, 137 mph at sea level; cruising speed, 124 mph; climb rate, 2.8 min to 3280 ft; service ceiling, 14,760 ft.
Armament: none.

Above: many examples of the Bücker Bü 133 Jungmeister are today flown by private pilots. The aircraft's superb aerobatic qualities made it an ideal military advanced trainer.

Utilizing many components of the Bü 131, the Jungmeister was a very aerobatic advanced trainer which had immediate potential for training fighter pilots at advanced flying schools. Built under license in Switzerland and Spain, the aircraft soon earned itself a wonderful reputation and many examples are still flying today.

Bücker Bü 181 Bestmann

Year: 1939.
Manufacturer: Bücker Flugzeugbau G.mbH.
Type: multipurpose trainer.
Crew: two.
Specification: Bü 181 D.
Power plant: one Hirth HM 504A four-cylinder in-line engine developing 105 hp.
Dimensions: span, 34 ft 9 in; length, 25 ft 9 in; height, 6 ft 9 in; wing area, 145.3 sq ft.
Weights: empty, 1047 lb; loaded, 1687 lb.
Performance: maximum speed, 130 mph at sea level; cruising speed, 126 mph; climb rate, 5.18 min to 3280 ft; service ceiling, 16,404 ft.
Armament: none.

Following the unsuccessful Bü 134 monoplane and the limited production Bü 180 sports monoplane, came the Bü 181 side-by-side, dual control, cabin monoplane. Selected as the Luftwaffe's standard basic trainer in 1940, the Bü 181 gradually replaced the biplane Bü 131. It was also used in communication roles, as a glider tug and a tactical weapons-transport aircraft. Several thousand aircraft were built, including 708 by Fokker in Holland. Production continued in Czechoslovakia after the war, and the soundness of the design is evidenced by the license granted by the Czechs to the Heliopolis Aircraft Works in Egypt during the 1950s.

Right: a Bucker Bü 133 in Luftwaffe service shows its aerobatic prowess. The Jungmeister equipped many wartime fighter pilot schools and other training units and also served with the air forces of Spain and Switzerland.

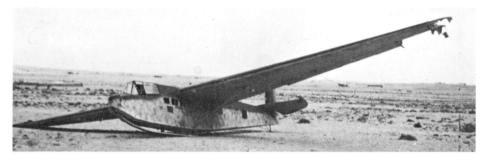

Above: a DFS 230 troop carrying glider lies abandoned on a desert airfield.

DFS 230

Year: 1937.
Manufacturer: Deutsches Forschungsinstitut für Segelflug Gothaer Waggonfabrik; Hartwig; Erla and others.
Type: 10-seat assault glider.
Crew: two.
Specification: DFS 230B-1.
Power plant: none.
Dimensions: span, 72 ft 2 in; length, 36 ft 11 in; height, 9 ft; wing area, 444.12 sq ft.
Weights: empty, 1896 lb; loaded, 4630 lb.
Performance: maximum gliding speed, 180 mph; towed speed, 130 mph; fully loaded glide angle, 1.18.
Armament: one 7.9 mm MG 15 machine gun on flexible mount in forward fuselage, two 7.9 mm MG 34 machine guns attached to forward fuselage and fixed to fire forward.

An impressive demonstration by the famous German woman pilot, Hanna Reitsch, in 1938 helped to convince Luftwaffe officers that the assault glider could play an important part in military operations. This was vindicated by the DFS 230 during World War II when it took part in many famous operations including the capture of the Belgian fort of Eben-Emael on the Albert Canal in May 1940, the invasion of Crete and the rescue of Benito Mussolini from his mountain prison in the Hotel Rifugio. Over 1500 examples were built, the greatest quantities being of the A and B versions. A more streamlined aircraft, which was to be known as the F and capable of carrying 15 troops, was not produced.

Dornier Do 11

Year: 1932.
Manufacturer: Dornier Metallbauten Switzerland.
Type: heavy bomber.
Crew: four (pilot, observer, engineer/gunner, radio operator/gunner).
Specification: Do 11D.
Power plant: two Siemens Sh 22B-2 nine-cylinder air-cooled radial engines each developing 650 hp.
Dimensions: span, 86 ft 3 in; length, 61 ft 8 in; height, 18 ft; wing area, 1160.3 sq ft.
Weights: empty, 13,173 lb; loaded, 18;080 lb.
Performance: maximum speed, 161 mph at sea level; cruising speed, 140 mph at 3280 ft; climb rate, 7 min to 3280 ft; service ceiling, 13,450 ft.
Armament: three 7.9 mm MG 15 machine guns on flexible mountings in nose, dorsal and ventral positions; bomb load, 2205 lb

The Treaty of Versailles' ban on the development of military aircraft, was flouted in many ways, one of which was the design and development of aircraft by German-owned subsidiary companies operating in other countries. One of these was the Dornier works at Altenrhein, Switzerland, which produced the Do 11, ostensibly as a freighter but in reality a heavy bomber. The aircraft was equipped with a retractable undercarriage which gave so many problems that it was eventually locked down. Operated by the German State Railways in the guise of a freighter, it was in fact used for long-range navigation exercises by clandestine Luftwaffe crews. With the Ju 52 it formed the backbone of the Luftwaffe bomber squadrons in 1934 but was obsolete by 1939.

Dornier Do 15 Wal

Year: 1922.
Manufacturer: Construzioni Meccaniche Aeronautiche (CMASA) (Dornier's Italian Subsidiary).
Type: maritime-reconnaissance flying boat.
Crew: four (pilot, observer, engineer/gunner, radio operator/gunner).
Specification: Do 15 (Militar-Wal 33).
Power plant: two BMW VI 7.3 12-cylinder liquid-cooled engines each developing 750 hp.
Dimensions: span, 76 ft 2 in; length, 59 ft 9 in; height, 18 ft 1 in; wing area, 1033 sq ft.
Weights: empty, 11,872 lb; loaded (maximum), 17,637 lb.
Performance: maximum speed, 137 mph at sea level; cruising speed, 118 mph at 3280 ft; climb rate, 35 min to 9840 ft; service ceiling, 9840 ft.
Armament: three 7.9 mm MG 15 machine guns, in bow and two dorsal positions; bomb load, four 110 lb bombs on external racks.

Below: the Dornier Do 11D was one of the bomber aircraft operated by Germany in defiance of the Versailles Treaty.

Above: the Dornier Do 15 Wal flying boat was extensively used by both civil and military operators during the interwar years. Some 30 Wals were built for the Luftwaffe.

The prototype Wal made its debut in 1922 and incorporated many features used in the flying boats designed by Dipl Ing C Dornier in World War I. Various versions were produced over the years and equipped Dutch and Spanish units. The Wal 33 was the ultimate design and first flew in 1933. It was used by Deutsche Lufthansa and, with the addition of armament, became serviceable with pseudo-civil/military organizations in 1934. By the end of 1938 it had been retired from military use and was replaced by the Do 18, although some examples soldiered on in training establishments and others were used for armament experiments with the 13mm MG 131 machine gun.

Dornier Do 17E, F, K, P

Year: 1934.
Manufacturer: Dornier-Werke G.mbH.
Type: medium bomber.
Crew: three (pilot, observer, radio operator/gunner).
Specification: Do 17E-1.
Power plant: two BMW V1 7.3 12-cylinder liquid-cooled engines each developing 750 hp.
Dimensions: span, 59 ft 1 in; length, 53 ft 4 in; height, 14 ft 2 in; wing area, 592.02 sq ft.
Weights: empty, 9920 lb; loaded, 15,520 lb.
Performance: maximum speed, 220 mph at sea level; cruising speed, 163 mph at 13,120 ft; range, 932 miles; service ceiling, 16,730 ft.
Armament: two 7.9 mm MG 15, one firing downward from ventral position, one firing aft from rear of flight deck; bomb load, 1650 lb.

Dornier Do 17M and Do 17Z

Year: 1939.
Manufacturer: Dornier-Werke G.mbH.
Type: medium bomber.
Crew: four (pilot, observer, radio operator/gunner, engineer/gunner).
Specification: Do 17Z-2.
Power plant: two BMW-Bramo 323P Fafnir nine-cylinder air-cooled radial engines each developing 1000 hp.
Dimensions: span, 59 ft; length, 51 ft 10 in; height, 15 ft; wing area, 592.02 sq ft.
Weights: empty, 11,484 lb; loaded, (maximum) 19,481 lb.
Performance: maximum speed, 186 mph at sea level; cruising speed, 186 mph at 13,120 ft; range, 720 miles; service ceiling, 26,900 ft.
Armament: six 7.9 mm MG 15 machine guns displaced, two firing from side windows, one above and one below fuselage, and two forward from front windows; bomb load, 2205 lb.

Dornier 215

Year: 1939.
Manufacturer: Dornier-Werke G.mbH.
Type: medium reconnaissance bomber.
Crew: four (pilot, observer, radio operator/gunner, engineer/gunner).
Power plant: two Daimler-Benz DB 601Aa 12-cylinder liquid-cooled engines each developing 1100 hp.
Dimensions: span, 59 ft; length, 51 ft 10 in; height, 15 ft; wing area, 592.02 sq ft.
Weights: empty, 12,730 lb; loaded (maximum), 19,400 lb.
Performance: maximum speed, 239 mph at sea level; cruising speed, 255 mph at 13,120 ft; range, 1520 miles; service ceiling 29,530 ft.
Armament: six 7.9 mm MG 15 machine guns displaced, two aft firing, one above and one below fuselage, and two firing forward on flexible mounts; bomb load, 2205 lb.

Below: a Dornier Do 17P-1.

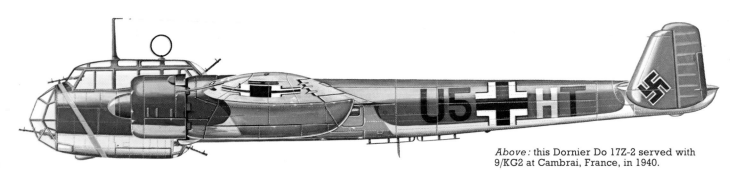

Above: this Dornier Do 17Z-2 served with 9/KG2 at Cambrai, France, in 1940.

Dubbed 'The Flying Pencil,' the Dornier 17 series of medium bombers was probably the most well-known bomber to those on the receiving end of their lethal loads in the early days of World War II. The aircraft originated as a result of a specification from Deutsche Lufthansa for a six-seat high-speed mailplane, which Dornier met with three prototypes. Each had a single fin and rudder and an exceptionally small cross-sectional fuselage. After tests Lufthansa rejected the aircraft since they considered the passenger accommodations inadequate. However, Flugkapitän Robert Untucht saw in the aircraft the possibility of development to a medium-bomber configuration. The *Technische Amt* of the RLM saw merit in the suggestion and in the summer of 1935 the Do 17 V4 appeared. This aircraft had the revised twin-fin layout of the definitive version, and the original cabin windows were deleted. The V4 was followed by the V5 and V6, the latter being powered by Hispano Suiza engines.

The initial production model was the E-1 which was produced in parallel with the F-1 reconnaissance version. By July 1937, when the aircraft was demonstrated at the Military Aircraft Competition in Zurich, where it outpaced contemporary fighters which were also on show, the first two models were already being issued to Luftwaffe bomber and reconnaissance squadrons. In 1938 the Bramo 323-powered Do 17M and the DB 600-engined reconnaissance and pathfinder versions, the S and U, reached production status, but in 1939 a return was made to the radial engine for the Do 17Z.

In the spring of 1937 one *Staffel* of Do 17F-1s was operating in Spain with the Condor Legion, and these were joined by Do 17Es and Ps which were handed to the Spanish Nationalists when the Civil War ended.

The outbreak of the war in Europe saw 9 *Kampfgruppen* equipped with a total of 370 Do 17s, the majority being the Z-1 model. Although not involved in the Norwegian campaign, the aircraft was in the thick of the fighting in France and the Battle of Britain. In Britain its

Above left: a Dornier Do 17Z-2 operating over England in 1940.
Left: a Do 215B-4 illustrates the deeper forward fuselage introduced on the Do 17S, when compared with the Do 17 (below).

weak defensive armament was highlighted but it was shown that it could absorb much punishment.

During 1940 some aircraft were used for intruder missions over British airfields, where their long loiter time gave them an advantage over other aircraft which may have appeared more suited for this role. The aircraft also operated in the Middle East and on the Eastern Front before being relegated to second-line duties in 1943. The Do 215 was basically an export version of the Do 17Z which was developed because of Yugoslavian interest. A preproduction Do 17Z was reequipped with a pair of Gnome-Rhône radials but it did not perform better than the Do 17K, which was already in production. However, an increase in performance did result from the fitting of DB 601 in-line engines and this aircraft, the Do 215 V3, was demonstrated to several potential foreign customers. A Swedish order resulted but an embargo was placed on delivery and eventually the aircraft reached the Luftwaffe as the Do 215A and B. The success of the Do 17Z-10 in the intruder role brought about the conversion known as the Do 215B-4 for this duty, and such aircraft joined 4/NJG 1 in late 1940. The Do 215B-5 was equipped with two nose-mounted 20 mm MG FF cannons and four 7.9 mm MG 17 machine guns as well as the infrared sensor for the Spanner-Anlage with a Q-Rohr screen in the cockpit. Despite the introduction of FuG 202 Lichtenstein radar, the days of the Do 215 as a night fighter were numbered, and by 1942 most aircraft had been replaced by the Ju 88 and Bf 110 and were relegated to test flying of new equipment.

Above: the Dornier Do 18 undertook reconnaissance and rescue work, a Do 18D-1 of 3/Ku Gr 406 is shown.

Dornier Do 18

Year: 1935.
Manufacturer: Dornier Werke G.mbH.
Type: patrol and reconnaissance flying boat.
Crew: four (pilot, observer, engineer/gunner, radio operator/gunner).
Specification: Do 18G-1.
Power plant: two Junkers Jumo 205D six-cylinder 12-piston diesel engines each developing 880 hp.
Dimensions: span, 77 ft 9 in; length, 63 ft 7 in; height, 17 ft 6 in; wing area, 1054.86 sq ft.
Weights: empty, 13,180 lb; loaded, 23,800 lb.
Performance: maximum speed, 166 mph at 6560 ft; cruising speed, 142 mph; climb rate, 7.8 min to 3280 ft; service ceiling, 13,800 ft.
Armament: one 13 mm MG 131 machine gun in open nose position, one 20 mm MG 151 in dorsal turret; bomb load, two 110 lb bombs on wing racks.

Like many German World War II aircraft, the Do 18 was originally designed as a civilian long-range mailplane for Deutsche Lufthansa, to replace the Do 15 Wal. The tandem-mounted engines in which one propeller pushed and the other pulled, gave the aircraft a unique appearance and overcame any asymmetric handling problems. In March 1938 a Do 18F D-ANHR established a long-distance record of 5214 miles in 43 hrs, for seaplanes. In Luftwaffe service the flying boat carried out a number of roles including search-and-rescue, reconnaissance and antishipping strikes. A total of 152 were produced. It had the distinction of being the first Luftwaffe type to fall to British aircraft in World War II.

Dornier Do 19

Year: 1936.
Manufacturer: Dornier Werke G.mbH.
Type: long-range strategic bomber.
Crew: proposed nine (two pilots, radio operator, bomb aimer, five gunners).
Specification: Do 19 V1.
Power plant: four Bramo (Siemens) 322H-2 nine-cylinder air-cooled radial engines each developing 715 hp.
Dimensions: span, 114 ft 10 in; length, 83 ft 6 in; height, 18 ft 11 in; wing area, 1724.38 sq ft.
Weights: empty, 26,158 lb; loaded, (maximum) 40,785 lb.
Performance: maximum speed, 196 mph at sea level; cruising speed, 155 mph at 6560 ft; climb rate, 3.4 min to 3280 ft; service ceiling, 18,370 ft.
Armament: two 7.9 mm MG 15 machine guns in nose and tail, two 20 mm MG FF cannons in power-operated dorsal and ventral turrets; bomb load, not known.

The absence of a true strategic bomber was to cost the Luftwaffe dearly during World War II. In the so-called 'Ural Bomber' the basic require-

ments for such an aircraft were available, but after the death of General Wever in 1936 the aircraft lost its true champion and development was abandoned; with it, it is often argued, went Germany's chance to wage a true strategic bomber offensive. The only completed aircraft was used as a transport in the Polish campaign.

Dornier Do 22

Year: 1935.
Manufacturer: AG für Dornier Flugzeug Switzerland.
Type: light reconnaissance torpedo bomber.
Crew: three (pilot, observer, gunner).
Specification: Do 22.
Power plant: one Hispano Suiza 12Ybrs 12-cylinder liquid-cooled engine rated at 775 hp.
Dimensions: span, 53 ft 2 in; length, 43 ft 2 in; height, 15 ft 11 in; wing area, 484.20 sq ft.
Weights: empty, 5610 lb; loaded, 8800 lb.
Performance: maximum speed, 217 mph at 13,120 ft; cruising speed, 186 mph; climb rate, 2.1 min to 3280 ft; service ceiling, 26,247 ft.
Armament: one 7.62 mm or 7.9 mm machine gun firing forward and one or two similar on Scarff ring in rear cockpit; bomb load, one 1760 lb torpedo or four 110 lb bombs on external racks.

Left: a Dornier Do 22 floatplane of the Royal Yugoslav Air Force.
Below left: the first prototype of the Do 19 heavy bomber under test.
Right: this Dornier Do 24T-1 is fitted with a 20 mm cannon in the dorsal turret.
Below: the Dornier Do 23 was developed from the unsuccessful Do 11, entering service in the summer of 1935.

The Do 22 was not ordered by the Luftwaffe. The total production of 31 machines were sold abroad, mainly to Greece, Finland and Yugoslavia. Four aircraft supplied to Yugoslavia were operated by the Allies in the Mediterranean when Yugoslavia was overrun. A land plane version known as the Do 22L was flown but not put into production.

Dornier Do 23

Year: 1935.
Manufacturer: Dornier-Werke G.mbH.
Type: heavy day and night bomber.
Crew: four (pilot, observer, engineer/gunner, radio operator/gunner).
Specification: Do 23G.
Power plant: two BMW VIU 12-cylinder liquid-cooled engines each developing 750 hp.
Dimensions: span, 84 ft; length, 61 ft 8 in; height, 17 ft 9 in; wing area, 1147.43 sq ft.
Weights: empty, 12,346 lb; loaded, (maximum) 20,282 lb.
Performance: maximum speed, 161 mph; cruising speed, 130 mph; climb rate, 4 min to 3280 ft; service ceiling, 13,780 ft.
Armament: three 7.9 mm MG 15 machine guns in ventral, nose and dorsal positions; bomb load, 2205 lb.

The definitive variant of the disastrous Do 11, the Do 23 equipped some *Kampfgruppen* for a very short period, but were phased out in 1936. Total production was 210 and the aircraft's only claim to fame was its starring role in many propaganda films depicting the reborn Luftwaffe. It was also used in early aerial-mine-sweeping experiments.

Dornier Do 24

Year: 1937.
Manufacturer: Dornier-Werke G.mbH; production by various subcontractors including Weser, Aviolanda. Potez-Cams and postwar by CASA in Spain.
Type: transport and air-sea rescue flying boat.
Crew: six (two pilots, observer, engineer, radio operator/gunner, gunner).
Specification: Do 24T-1.
Power plant: three BMW-Bramo 323R-2 Fafnir nine-cylinder air-cooled radial engines each developing 1000 hp.
Dimensions: span, 88 ft 7 in; length, 72 ft 4 in; height, 18 ft 10 in; wing area, 1162.50 sq ft.
Weights: empty, 20,723 lb; loaded, (maximum) 35,715 lb.
Performance: maximum speed, 206 mph at 8530 ft; cruising speed, 180 mph at sea level; climb rate, 6 min to 6560 ft; service ceiling, 24,605 ft.
Armament: two 7.9 mm MG 15 machine guns in bow and stern turrets, one 20 mm Hispano Suiza cannon in dorsal turret.

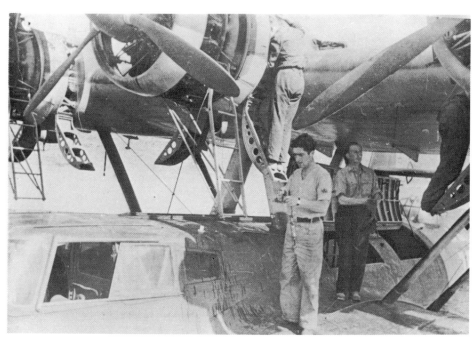

Above: mechanics work on the engines of a Dornier Do 24.

The Do 24 was one of the few German aircraft designed from the outset to meet the needs of a foreign government, in this case that of the Netherlands. The third prototype was the first to fly powered by Wright Cyclone engines and together with 11 others was delivered as the Do 24K before the war started. The original two aircraft were powered by Jumo 205 diesel engines and they were used in Norway as transports. A total of 294 of all versions were built, most of which served in the search and rescue role. This sturdy flying boat performed its designated role well, and postwar license-produced versions were still in service in the early 1970s.

Dornier Do 26

Year: 1938.
Manufacturer: Dornier-Werke G.mbH.
Type: long-range reconnaissance and transport flying boat.
Crew: four (pilot, observer, radio operator/gunner, engineer/gunner).
Specification: Do 26D-0.
Power plant: four Junkers Jumo 205D six-cylinder, 12-piston diesel engines each rated at 880 hp.
Dimensions: span, 98 ft 5 in; length, 80 ft 9 in; height, 22 ft 6 in; wing area, 1291.67 sq ft.
Weights: empty, 24,912 lb; loaded (maximum), 49,600 lb.
Performance: maximum speed, 184 mph at sea level; cruising speed, 160 mph; climb rate, 8.2 min to 3280 ft; service ceiling, 14,760 ft.
Armament: one 20 mm MG 151 cannon in bow turret, three 7.9 mm MG 15 machine guns in lateral midship blisters and aft of rear planing step.

An elegant gull-winged flying boat contrasting with previous designs from Dornier. Five aircraft were built and served with 1 *Staffel* of *Küstenfliegergruppe* 406 in Norway. Two were destroyed by RAF Hurricanes on 28 May 1940 and the other three operated on communications tasks until servicing problems were encountered, which necessitated the withdrawal from service of the survivors.

Below: the Dornier Do 26 was designed as a commercial flying boat for Lufthansa, however military versions took part in the invasion of Norway, being withdrawn from front line use shortly afterwards.

Above: the bulbous nose and closely-cowled engines of the Dornier Do 217 are clearly evident on this bomber. The Do 217K-1 carries the emblem of Luftflotte 2 on its nose.

Dornier Do 217E, K, M, & N

Year: 1938.
Manufacturer: Dornier-Werke G.mbH.
Type: heavy night bomber.
Crew: four (pilot, observer, radio operator/gunner, engineer/gunner).
Specification: Do 217M-1.
Power plant: two Daimler-Benz DB 603A 12-cylinder, liquid-cooled engines each developing 1850 hp.
Dimensions: span, 62 ft 4 in; length, 55 ft 9 in; height, 16 ft 4 in; wing area, 613.54 sq ft.
Weights: empty, 19,985 lb; loaded, 36,817 lb.
Performance: maximum speed, 348 mph at 18,700 ft; cruising speed, 248 mph; climb rate, 3.3 min to 3280 ft; service ceiling, 24,170 ft loaded, 31,200 ft unloaded.
Armament: four 7.9 mm MG 81 machine guns, two each in nose and lateral positions, two 13 mm MG 131 in ventral position, and electrically operated dorsal turret; bomb load, 5550 lb.

The first prototype Do 217 crashed in September 1938 almost exactly a month after its maiden flight, but despite this inauspicious start to its career the aircraft progressed to become a useful addition to the Luftwaffe's inventory.

Based on the Do 17 the Do 217, although externally similar, this was in fact an entirely new design based on a requirement for a bomber capable of carrying a much more substantial load.

First production version was the E which was

equipped with BMW 801A radial engines and began to join Luftwaffe squadrons in the reconnaissance role in late 1940 and as a bomber in March 1941. The E-5 was designed to carry the Hs 293 stand-off bomb on underwing ETC 2000/XII carriers and the missile's Telefunken guidance control system in the bomb-aimer's position.

The F and G designations were not used and the H was an experimental high-altitude machine with DB 601 engines. The J-1 and J-2 were interim designs for a night-fighter version, which had faired-over bomb bays, increased nose armament and FuG 202 Lichtenstein BC radar. Entering service with KG 2 in 1942, the Do 217K had a completely redesigned bulbous nose which increased crew comfort and carried heavier defensive armament. The K-1 had a tail fairing housing a braking parachute and was involved in experiments in which it carried four L5 torpedoes. The K-2 was designed to carry Fritz X FX 1400 stand-off bombs and had its wing span increased to 81 ft 5 in, and operated these missiles with III/KG 100 for the first time in August 1943. The K-3 was similar to the K-2, but it had later guidance equipment to control its missiles.

The M-1, which was basically a K-1, was fitted with DB 603A in-line engines to safeguard against a shortage of BMW radial engines. In the night-fighter role, modified M-1s were redesignated Do 217N. The Do 217P was an high-altitude version of the E fitted with DB 603B engines which were supercharged by a DB 605T engine installed in the fuselage driving a two-stage supercharger. The final version was the Do 217R, five examples of which were built. This was a launcher for Hs 293a missiles used by III/KG 100. A total of 1750 of 11 variants of the Do 217 was built.

Dornier Do 317 A This aircraft was envisaged as a high-altitude heavy bomber based on the Do 217. After many stop-start situations it was eventually abandoned and the six completed prototypes were completed as Do 217R. (See previous description.)

Dornier Do 335

Year: 1943.
Manufacturer: Dornier-Werke G.mbH.
Type: fighter.
Crew: one.
Specification: Do 335A-1.
Power plant: two Daimler-Benz DB 603E-1 12-cylinder, inverted-vee, liquid-cooled engines each developing 1900 hp.
Dimensions: span, 45 ft 3 in; length, 45 ft 5 in; height, 16 ft 5 in; wing area, 414.41 sq ft.
Weights: empty, 16,005 lb; loaded, 21,160 lb.
Performance: maximum speed, 474 mph at 21,325 ft; cruising speed, 426 mph at 23,610 ft; climb rate, 55 sec to 3280 ft; service ceiling, 37,400 ft.
Armament: one 30 mm MK 103 cannon, two 15 mm MG 151 cannons plus a varied bomb load in proposed fighter/bomber configuration.

Indecision by the RLM delayed production and entry into service of this powerful fighter which was potentially the fastest piston-engined fighter of the era. The unique twin-engined layout, in which one engine was installed in the nose and the other in the tail, was patented by Dr Ing Dornier in 1937 and proved in the Hütter designed Gö 9 test bed. Dornier was instructed to concentrate on bomber aircraft and was consequently granted a development contract for a twin-engined intruder capable of carrying a 1100 lb bomb load. By the time that this decision was reversed and the go-ahead given for the fighter version, irrecoverable delays had occurred.

Flight tests revealed the vast potential of the aircraft, by which time a heavy-fighter (Zerstörer) version as well as a two seat night fighter had been envisioned. Twenty-eight aircraft had been completed by the time the Dornier factory was overrun and a further 70 were in various stages of construction.

Below: the Dornier Do 335 Pfeil mounted two DB 603E engines in an unusual push-pull arrangement.

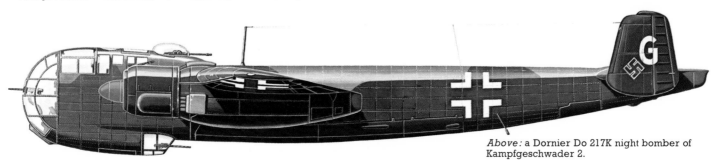

Above: a Dornier Do 217K night bomber of Kampfgeschwader 2.

Fieseler Fi 98

Year: 1935.
Manufacturer: Gerhard Fieseler Werke
G.mbH.
Type: dive bomber.
Crew: one.
Specification: Fi 98a.
Power plant: one BMW 132A-3 nine-cylinder,
air-cooled radial engine developing 650 hp.
Dimensions: span, 37 ft 9 in; length, 24 ft 3 in;
height, 9 ft 10 in; wing area, 274.48 sq ft.
Weights: empty, 3197 lb; loaded, 4762 lb.
Performance: maximum speed, 183 mph at
6560 ft; cruising speed, 168 mph; climb rate,
1 min 7 sec to 3280 ft; service ceiling, 29,530 ft.
Armament: two 7.9 mm MG 17 machine guns
firing forward; bomb load, four 110 lb bombs.

Designed to meet the requirement of the
embryo Luftwaffe for a dive bomber, this neat
two-bay biplane received little support and
only two prototypes were produced as a back-
up against failure of the favored Henschel Hs
123.

Fieseler Fi 103 'Reichenberg'

Year: 1944.
Manufacturer: Gerhard Fieseler Werke
G.mbH.
Type: expendable attack aircraft.
Crew: one.
Specification: Fi 103 'Reichenberg' VI.
Power plant: one Argus As 014 pulse-jet
rated at 660 lb thrust.
Dimensions: span, 18 ft 9 in; length, 26 ft 3 in.
Weights: loaded, 4960 lb.
Performance: maximum speed, 497 mph at
8000 ft.
Armament: one 1874 lb warhead.

This manned version of the Fi 103 *Vergeltung-
swaffe Eins* (V1) Flying Bomb was championed
by Hanna Reitsch and Otto Skorzeny. The
proposal was for the aircraft to be air launched
against its target and the pilot to bale out after
aiming the machine. A total of 175 was produced,
but it did not achieve operational status. The
unmanned version was produced in quantities
exceeding 30,000 and launched against targets
in England from June 1944–March 1945.

Below: the Fieseler Fi 103 (V1 flying bomb)
was produced in a manned version, but this
saw no service.

Above: a Fieseler Fi 156 Storch ambulance
aircraft lies abandoned on Gambut airfield,
Libya, 1942.

Fieseler Fi 156 A, C, D & E

Year: 1936.
Manufacturer: Gerhard Fieseler Werke
G.mbH. Most service aircraft produced by
Morane Saulnier in France and Mraz in
Czechoslovakia.
Type: air observation post, army co-
operation, communications, rescue, and
casualty evacuation.
Crew: three.
Specification: Fi 156C-2.
Power plant: one Argus As 10C-3 eight-
cylinder, air-cooled engine developing
240 hp.
Dimensions: span, 46 ft 9 in; length, 32 ft 6 in;
height, 10 ft; wing area, 279.86 sq ft.
Weights: empty, 2050 lb; loaded, 2920 lb.
Performance: maximum speed, 109 mph at
sea level; cruising speed, 81 mph; climb rate,
905 ft per min; service ceiling, 15,090 ft.
Armament: one 7.9 mm MG 15 on flexible
mount in rear of cabin.

In response to an RLM requirement issued in
1935 for an army cooperation, liaison and
casualty-evacuation aircraft, Fieseler designed

a high-wing monoplane to compete with the
Messerschmitt Bf 163 and the Siebel Si 201. One
example of the Bf 163 and two of the very unusual
Si 201 were produced. However the contract
went to Fieseler whose cabin monoplane could
accommodate a crew of three and had high-lift
devices which gave it a remarkable short
take-off landing (STOL) capability. The prototype carried the civil registration D-IKVN and
first flew in the spring of 1936 and was fitted
with light-alloy, full-span, fixed leading-edge
slots.

The aircraft began to reach Luftwaffe units
in the winter of 1937 in the A-1 version and this
was followed by the C-1 which was modified in
light of service experience. The D was produced in parallel with the C and had improved
access to the cabin for stretcher cases.

The Storch (Stork) was used on every front
by the Luftwaffe and carried out invaluable
work in all its designed roles. A total of 2549
aircraft was produced during the war and
production continued postwar by Morane Saulnier as the M.S. 500 and 502 Criquet, as well as
in Czechoslovakia as the K-65 Cap.

Fieseler Fi 167

Year: 1938.
Manufacturer: Gerhard Fieseler Werke
G.mbH.
Type: shipboard torpedo/reconnaissance
aircraft.
Crew: two (pilot, observer/gunner).
Specification: Fi 167A-0.
Power plant: one Daimler-Benz DB 601B
12-cylinder, liquid-cooled engine developing
1100 hp.
Dimensions: span, 44 ft 4 in; length, 37 ft 5 in;
height, 15 ft 9 in; wing area, 489.76 sq ft.
Weights: empty, 6173 lb; loaded (maximum),
10,690 lb.
Performance: maximum speed, 199 mph at
sea level; cruising speed, 155 mph; climb
rate, 2.7 min to 3280 ft; service ceiling,
24,600 ft.
Armament: one 7.9 mm MG 17 machine gun
firing forward and one 7.9 mm MG 15 on
flexible mount in rear cockpit; bomb load,
2205 lb, or one 1686 lb torpedo.

Designed specifically for the aircraft carrier
program the Fi 167 had a remarkable STOL
performance which even exceeded that of the
Storch. When the carrier program was abandoned, completed examples were used for
coastal trials with *Erprobungsstaffel* 167. When
work on the carriers was resumed, the Fi 167
was considered obsolete and its role passed to
a navalized version of the Ju 87. Completed aircraft were sold to Rumania.

Flettner Fl 282 Kolibri

Year: 1941.
Manufacturer: Anton Flettner G.mbH.
Type: observation helicopter.
Crew: two (pilot, observer).
Specification: Fl 282B.
Power plant: one BMW-Bramo Sh 14A seven-cylinder, air-cooled radial engine developing 160 hp.
Dimensions: rotor diameter, 39 ft 2 in; length, 21 ft 6 in; height, 7 ft 2 in; disc area, 1281 sq ft.
Weights: empty, 1675 lb; loaded, 2205 lb.
Performance: maximum speed, 93 mph at sea level; cruising speed, 71 mph; climb rate, 300 ft per min; service ceiling, 10,800 ft.
Armament: none.

The most highly developed of all German helicopters, the Kolibri was the first such aircraft to reach mass production status, although in the event only 24 were manufactured. A production order for 1000 was placed in 1944, but was terminated as a result of Allied bombing. The helicopter was tried by the German Navy in the Baltic, operating from a platform on the cruiser *Köln*. Some were used for convoy protection work in the Mediterranean, but little is known of their operational work.

Focke Achgelis Fa 223 Drache, Fa 266 Hornisse

Year: 1940.
Manufacturer: Focke Achgelis Flugzeugbau G.mbH.
Type: transport/rescue helicopter.
Crew: two (pilot, observer).
Specification: Fa 223E.
Power plant: one BMW 301R nine-cylinder, air-cooled radial developing 1000 hp.
Dimensions: rotor span, 80 ft 5 in; length, 40 ft 2 in; height, 14 ft 4 in; disc area, 2435 sq ft.
Weights: empty, 7000 lb; loaded (maximum), 9500 lb.
Performance: maximum speed, 109 mph (limited to avoid rotor vibration to 75 mph); cruising speed, 75 mph; climb rate, 800 ft per min; service ceiling, 16,000 ft.
Armament: none.

This advanced design twin-rotor helicopter was planned for antisubmarine patrol, reconnaissance, transport and rescue. Thirty examples were built and all tried in the various design roles. However production was interrupted by Allied air raids and only a few aircraft were used operationally.

Above: an example of the Focke Achgelis Fa 330 gyrokite under test by the British at the end of World War II.

Focke Achgelis Fa 330 Bachstelze

Year: 1942.
Manufacturer: Focke Achgelis Flugzeugbau G.mbH.
Type: gyro-kite.
Crew: one.
Specification: Fa 330.
Power plant: none.
Dimensions: rotor diameter, 24 ft; length, 14 ft 6 in; disc area, 450 sq ft.
Weights: empty, 181 lb; loaded, 363 lb.
Performance: maximum towing speed, 25 mph; service ceiling, approximately 400 ft.
Armament: none.

The Fa 330 was an ingenious method to increase the vision of a surfaced U-Boat by towing a gyrokite behind a submarine. It was used in the South Atlantic, Gulf of Aden and Indian Ocean but problems encountered with rapid recovery in the event of surprise attack led to its eventual withdrawal from service.

Focke-Wulf Fw 44 Stieglitz

Year: 1932.
Manufacturer: Focke-Wulf Flugzeugbau G.mbH.
Type: trainer.
Crew: two (pilot and pupil).
Specification: Fw 44C.
Power plant: one Siemens Sh 14a seven-cylinder, air-cooled radial engine developing 150 hp.
Dimensions: span, 29 ft 6 in; length, 23 ft 11 in; height, 8 ft 10 in; wing area, 215.20 sq ft.
Weights: empty, 1158 lb; loaded, 1919 lb.
Performance: maximum speed, 115 mph at sea level; cruising speed, 107 mph; climb rate, 5.5 min to 3280 ft; service ceiling, 12,792 ft.
Armament: none.

A sports aircraft design of 1932, the Fw 44 was widely exported and used by the Luftwaffe at training schools throughout World War II.

Below: Focke-Wulf Fw 44 Stieglitz trainers are lined up before World War II. The type was also built under license in Sweden.

Left: the major production version of the Focke Wulf Stieglitz was the Fw 44C, which was powered by a 150 hp Siemens Sh 14A radial engine.

Focke-Wulf Fw 56 Stösser

Year: 1933.
Manufacturer: Focke-Wulf Flugzeugbau G.mbH.
Type: fighter/advanced trainer.
Crew: one.
Specification: Fw 56A-1.
Power plant: one Argus As 10C Series III eight-cylinder, inverted-Vee, air-cooled engine developing 240 hp.
Dimensions: span, 34 ft 7 in; length, 25 ft 1 in; height, 8 ft 4 in; wing area, 150.69 sq ft.
Weights: empty, 1477 lb; loaded, 2171 lb.
Performance: maximum speed, 166 mph at sea level; cruising speed, 152 mph at sea level; climb rate, 1650 ft per min; service ceiling, 20,340 ft.
Armament: two 7.9 mm MG 17 machine guns and three 22 lb bombs.

Designed to meet a specification for a Home-defense fighter, the parasol-winged Fw 56 proved to be an agile aerobatic aircraft with a good rate of climb. Between 1935 – 40 extensive production was undertaken and models were exported to Hungary and Austria. Approximately 1000 machines were produced and although these were out of front-line service by 1939, they equipped fighter-pilot training schools in World War II. Some aircraft were used for experiments in towing gliders, as well as being the upper component in a Fw 56/DFS 230 pickaback scheme.

Focke-Wulf Fw 58 Weihe

Year: 1935.
Manufacturer: Focke-Wulf Flugzeugbau G.mbH.
Type: multirole crew trainer/transport.
Crew: two (pilot, observer) plus six trainees or passengers.
Specification: Fw 58C.
Power plant: two Argus As 10C eight-cylinder, inverted-Vee, air-cooled engines each developing 240 hp.
Dimensions: span, 68 ft 11 in; length, 45 ft 11 in; height, 12 ft 9 in; wing area, 505.9 sq ft.
Weights: empty, 5291 lb; loaded, 7936 lb.
Performance: maximum speed, 162 mph at sea level; cruising speed, 150 mph; climb rate, 3.48 min to 3280 ft; service ceiling, 18,372 ft.
Armament: none.

Designed as a light transport, the Fw 58 was used as a utility aircraft by the Luftwaffe in the same way as the RAF used Avro Ansons. The Fw 58B could carry a small bomb load and some were fitted with floats, when they became Fw 58BW. The major production version was the Fw 58C which served as a crew trainer, communications aircraft and ambulance. In the latter role it was dubbed by Luftwaffe personnel *Leukoplast-Bomber* (sticking plaster or band-aid bomber). It was also used for crop spraying and to protect German troops by spraying suspected infected areas on the Eastern Front with germicide.

Left: the Focke Wulf Fw 56 Stösser advanced fighter trainer made its first flight in late 1933.
Right: the major production model of the Focke-Wulf Weihe was the Fw 58C, here illustrated in pre-war civil markings. This twin-engined light transport and crew trainer matched the RAF's Anson in versatility.

Focke-Wulf Fw 187 Falke

Year: 1937.
Manufacturer: Focke-Wulf Flugzeugbau G.mbH.
Type: heavy fighter.
Crew: two (pilot, observer).
Specification: Fw 187A-0.
Power plant: two Junkers Jumo 210Ga 12-cylinder, liquid-cooled engines each developing 730 hp.
Dimensions: span, 50 ft 2 in; length, 36 ft 6 in; height, 12 ft 8 in; wing area, 327.22 sq ft.
Weights: empty, 8157 lb; loaded, 11,023 lb.
Performance: maximum speed, 322 mph at sea level; cruising speed, 287 mph; climb rate, 3445 ft per min; service ceiling, 32,810 ft.
Armament: two 20 mm MG FF cannons and four 7.9 mm MG 17 machine guns.

Above: the Focke-Wulf Fw 187 twin-engined Zerstörer was not adopted by the Luftwaffe.

Possessing excellent handling characteristics, coupled with a tight turning rate and a maximum speed higher than that of the Bf 109, the prototype Fw 187 appeared to have an assured future, yet the RLM showed scant interest. Six models were built and one of these, the V6, which was powered by DB 600 engines, achieved a top speed of 390 mph. Production was not proceeded with and although the three prototypes were followed by a preproduction order for three A versions, these were withdrawn from service when the RLM discovered that JG 77 had been using them in Norway. The completed aircraft were used to defend the Focke-Wulf factory at Bremen.

Focke-Wulf Fw 189 Uhu

Year: 1938.
Manufacturer: Focke-Wulf Flugzeugbau
G.mbH, SNCASCO and Breguet in France and
Aero in Czechoslovakia.
Type: tactical reconnaissance and army
cooperation.
Crew: three (pilot, observer, gunner).
Specification: Fw 189A-2.
Power plant: two Argus As 410A-1, 12-
cylinder, inverted-Vee, air-cooled engines
each developing 465 hp.
Dimensions: span, 60 ft 4 in; length, 39 ft 5 in;
height, 10 ft 2 in; wing area, 409.03 sq ft.
Weights: empty, 6239 lb; loaded (maximum),
9193 lb.
Performance: maximum speed, 217 mph at
7875 ft; cruising speed, 190 mph; climb rate,
1017 ft per min; service ceiling, 22,967 ft.
Armament: two 7.9 mm MG 17 machine guns
in the wing roots, two 7.9 mm MG 81 machine
guns in a dorsal position and two 7.9 mm
MG 81 in tail; bomb load, four 110 lb bombs on
external racks.

The twin-boom layout of this unconventional
reconnaissance aircraft caused something of a
stir when it became known to the Allies in 1941.
It had already been in Luftwaffe service since
the spring of 1940.
   Designed to a specification issued by the
RLM calling for an advanced successor to the
Hs 126, the Fw 189 went through various design
changes, most of which improved its aerodynamic handling, before it emerged in the preproduction A-0 form.
   Attempts to convert it to the attack role were
not entirely successful and it was far more
effective when carrying out its designed function. Ten trainer versions, designated B-1,
were produced but major production was confined to the A series. Several modifications and
design projects including fitting the aircraft
with Schräge Musik and FuG 212 radar were
carried out.
   The 'Flying Eye' as it was popularly known,
served mainly in the Soviet Union and the
Eastern Front, but one *Staffel* operated in the
Middle East. Total production reached 864 and
together with the Hs 126 it performed the
majority of the tactical-reconnaissance roles
required by the Luftwaffe.

Above right: the unusual Focke-Wulf
Fw 189 Uhu carried out much useful
reconnaissance work on the Eastern
Front. This Fw 189A-2 is fitted with
underwing bomb racks.
Right: bombs are loaded onto the racks of a
Fw 189A-2 of a Panzer support unit in the
Soviet Union.
Below: this Focke-Wulf Fw 189A-1 served
with 5(H)/12 on the Eastern Front during
1941. The Fw 189 was progressively
issued to the Aufklarungsstaffeln (H) in
1941–42.

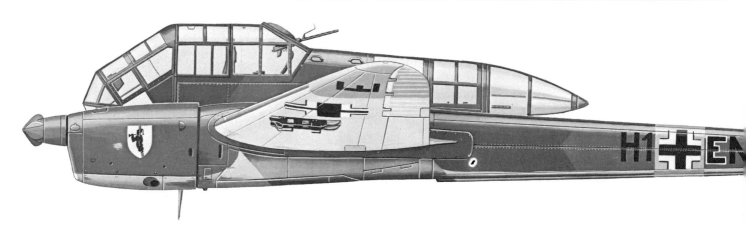

Focke-Wulf Fw 190 A series

Year: 1939.
Manufacturer: Focke-Wulf Flugzeugbau G.mbH and subcontractors.
Type: fighter.
Crew: one.
Specification: Fw 190A-3.
Power plant: one BMW 801D-2 14-cylinder, air-cooled radial developing 1700 hp.
Dimensions: span, 34 ft 5 in; length, 28 ft 10 in; height, 12 ft 11 in; wing area, 196.98 sq ft.
Weights: empty, 6393 lb; loaded, 8770 lb.
Performance: maximum speed, 312 mph at sea level; cruising speed, 278 mph; climb rate, 2830 ft per min; service ceiling, 34,775 ft.
Armament: two 7.9 mm MG 17 in upper front fuselage, two 20 mm MG 151 in wing roots, two 20 mm MG FF in outer wing bays.

Focke-Wulf Fw 190D series

Year: 1943.
Manufacturer: Focke-Wulf Flugzeugbau G.mbH and subcontractors.
Type: close-support fighter.
Crew: one.
Specification: Fw 190F-3.
Power plant: one BMW 801D-2 14-cylinder, air-cooled radial engine developing 1700 hp.
Dimensions: span, 34 ft 5 in; length, 29 ft 5 in; height, 12 ft 11 in; wing area, 196.98 sq ft.
Weights: empty, 7328 lb; loaded (maximum), 10,850 lb.
Performance: maximum speed, 342 mph at sea level; cruising speed, 280 mph; climb rate (without stores), 2110 ft per min; service ceiling, 34,775 ft.
Armament: two 7.9 mm MG 17 machine guns in fuselage decking, two 20 mm MG 151 cannons in wing roots; bomb load, 551 lb on wing and fuselage racks.

Focke-Wulf Fw 190F series

Year: 1942.
Manufacturer: Focke-Wulf Flugzeugbau G.mbH and subcontractors.
Type: fighter, fighter/bomber.
Crew: one.
Specification: Fw 190D-9.
Power plant: one Junkers Jumo 213A-1 12-cylinder, liquid-cooled engine rated at 1776 hp, or 2240 hp with MW 50 water/methanol injection.
Dimensions: span, 34 ft 5 in; length, 33 ft 5 in; height, 11 ft; wing area, 196.98 sq ft.
Weights: empty, 7694 lb; loaded (maximum), 10,670 lb.
Performance: maximum speed, 357 mph at sea level, 426 mph at 21,650 ft; climb rate, 2.1 min to 6560 ft; service ceiling, 39,372 ft.
Armament: two 13 mm MG 131 cannons in top decking, two 20 mm MG 151 cannons in wing roots; bomb load, one 1102 lb bomb on center-line fuselage rack.

In late 1937 project work on a single-seat fighter to supplement the Bf 109 was started by Focke-Wulf Flugzeugbau under the guidance of Dipl Ing Kurt Tank and Ober-Ing R. Blaser. The end result was to cause the RAF a severe jolt when the Fw 190 first encountered the Spitfire Mk V in September 1941.

Design initially centered around the DB 601 liquid-cooled engine and the BMW 139 two-row radial. It came as something of a surprise when the RLM, who were known to be opposed to radial-engined fighters, opted for the latter type of power unit, and selected the BMW

Left: this Focke-Wulf Fw 190A-4/U4 served with a fighter reconnaissance unit based in southern France in 1944.
Below: a Focke-Wulf Fw 190A-4 of Jagdgeschwader 2 in France.

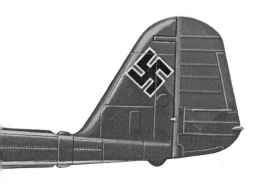

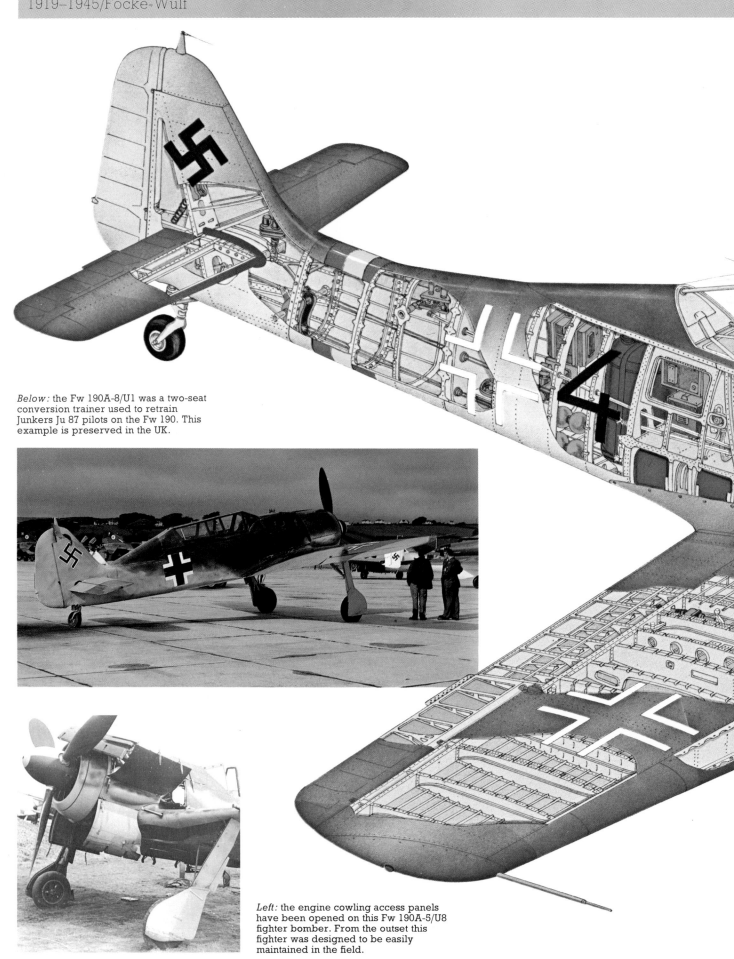

Below: the Fw 190A-8/U1 was a two-seat conversion trainer used to retrain Junkers Ju 87 pilots on the Fw 190. This example is preserved in the UK.

Left: the engine cowling access panels have been opened on this Fw 190A-5/U8 fighter bomber. From the outset this fighter was designed to be easily maintained in the field.

Below: a cutaway view of the Focke-Wulf Fw 190D-9, illustrating the unusual installation of the Junkers Jumo 213 inline engine with an annular radiator, which gave it the appearance of a radial engine. This aircraft carries the markings of III/JG 54, which was assigned to the defence of the Reich.

Left: this Fw 190D-9 is preserved by the United States Air Force Museum at Wright-Patterson Air Force Base, Ohio. It carries the emblem of Jagdgeschwader 3 'Udet.'

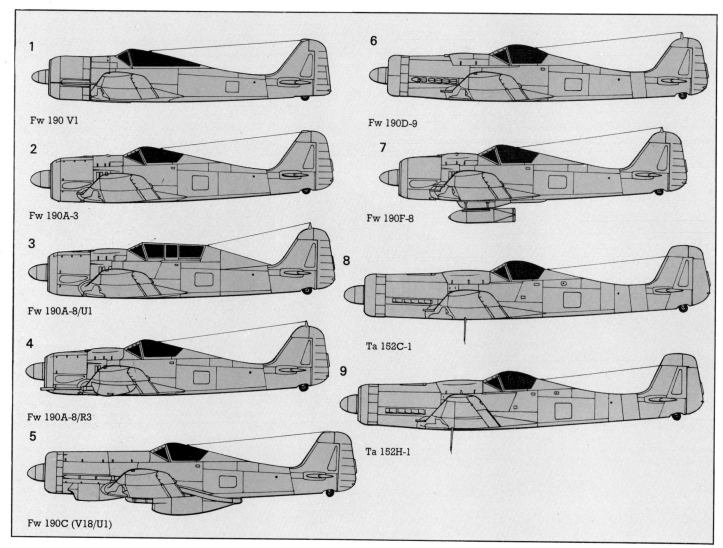

1 Fw 190 V1

2 Fw 190A-3

3 Fw 190A-8/U1

4 Fw 190A-8/R3

5 Fw 190C (V18/U1)

6 Fw 190D-9

7 Fw 190F-8

8 Ta 152C-1

9 Ta 152H-1

engined version for further detailed work. This began in earnest in 1938 and on 1 June 1939 the prototype, carrying the civil registration D-OPZE, made its maiden flight from Bremen.

Following a successful development program using a variety of prototypes, the first A-1s were introduced into the Luftwaffe in March 1941 by a team from JG 26. In August of that year the Sixth *Staffel* of JG 26 took delivery of their first aircraft at Le Bourget and the following month they met the Spitfire in combat for the first time. The nimble Focke-Wulf design immediately proved superior to this opponent in every respect apart from the turning circle, but on balance this was a small price to pay since the overall superiority of the radial engine fighter enabled it to dictate combat terms. It was not until after an A-3 model had mistakenly landed at RAF Pembry, that the true performance envelope of the German fighter could be assessed; this resulted in the introduction of the Spitfire Mk IX, which proved to be a more worthy adversary.

The A Series was developed in a series of subtypes (listed below), each having changes in armament, equipment and engine modifications including methanol/water injection, nitrous oxide injection, or a combination of both. Some versions were fitted with autopilots and bad weather/night flying equipment, also radar for use in the night interception role.

The F Series was developed from the A and concentrated on the ground support role, armed with bombs, rockets and cannons. The G, which in fact preceded the F in production, had modified landing gear and a strengthened structure which enabled it to carry a bomb load out of all proportion to its size, which incidently was one of the smallest for a fighter of World War II. The C was a design project with a turbo-supercharger aimed at improving the aircraft's high altitude performance and, like the B, was not proceeded with.

The D was virtually a complete redesign with increased span and a longer fuselage. It became generally known as the *Langnasen-Dora*, a reference to the increased length of its nose which housed a Jumo 213 engine.

The D was potentially the best of the breed with a turn of speed that left conventionally-powered contemporary fighters standing, and its superb quality soon won over those Luftwaffe fighter pilots who were suspicious of its

Type	Engine	Armament	Remarks
Fw 190A-1	BMW 801C-1	4 X MG 17, 2 X MG FF	
Fw 190A-2	BMW 801C-2	2 X MG 17, 2 X MG 151, 2 X MG FF	
Fw 190A-3	BMW 801D-2	as A-2	
Fw 190A-4	As A-3	as A-2	Fitted with FuG 16Z-Y
Fw 190A-5	As A-3	as A-2	Fitted with BSK 16 gun camera in longer fuselage
Fw 190A-6	As A-3	2 X MG 17, 4 X MG 151	Modified wing
Fw 190A-7	As A-3	2 X MG 131, 4 X MG 151	Fitted with Revi 16b
Fw 190A-8	As A-3	2 X MG 131, 4 X MG 151	Fitted with FuG 16Z repositioned fuselage rack
Fw 190D-9	Jumo 213A	2 X MG 131, 2 X MG 151	Provision for Wfr 21 underwing rockets
Fw 190F-1	BMW 801D-2	2 X MG 17, 2 X MG 151	Fighter-bomber version of A-4 with wing racks
Fw 190F-2	As F-1	as F-1	New blown canopy
Fw 190F-3	As F-1	as F-1	
Fw 190F-8	As F-1	2 X MG 131, 2 X MG 151	Based on A-6
Fw 190F-9	BMW 801TS	As F-8	Based on A-8
Fw 190G-2	BMW 801D-2	2 X MG 17, 2 X MG 151	Based on A-4 with long-range wing tanks
Fw 190G-3	As G-2	As G-2	With PKS 11 autopilot
Fw 190G-8	As G-2	2 X MG 131, 2 X MG 151	Based on A-8

Above: a Focke-Wulf Fw 190G-3 of
II Gruppe, Schlachtgeschwader 10
flying over Romania in 1944.

'bomber' engine. Used for top cover over airfields from which the German jet fighters operated, the D proved a formidable adversary and would no doubt have enjoyed considerable success if its late introduction into front-line service had not coincided with the operational limitations created by fuel shortages.

There can be no doubt that the Fw 190 was one of the most successful single-seat fighters of World War II and the soundness of its design is evidenced by the use made of similar techniques after the war in developing such aircraft as the Hawker Sea Fury, and others. A total of 20,001 of all versions of the Fw 190 was produced.

The following table lists the main production variants, but it should be remembered that they could be fitted with additional armament and equipment using *Rüstatz* and/or *Umrüst-Bausatz* conversions.

Focke-Wulf Ta 152

Year: 1944.
Manufacturer: Focke-Wulf Flugzeugbau G.mbH.
Type: fighter, fighter/bomber.
Crew: one.
Specification: Ta 152B-5/R 11.
Power plant: one Junkers Jumo 213E-1 12-cylinder, liquid-cooled engine rated at 1750 hp.
Dimensions: span, 36 ft 1 in; length, 35 ft 1 in; height, 11 ft; wing area, 209.89 sq ft.
Weights: empty, 8642 lb; loaded (maximum), 11,900 lb.
Performance: maximum speed, 342 mph at sea level; cruising speed, 315 mph; service ceiling, 34,000 ft.
Armament: one 30 mm MK 103 cannon firing through spinner and two 30 mm MK 103 cannons in wing roots; bomb load, 1100 lb on fuselage center-line rack.

The short-span and long-span (Ta 152H) versions of the Fw 190 carried the designer's name in abbreviated form (Ta) as their type designation. There is considerable conjecture as to how many aircraft were produced, but the total is generally thought to be some 215 with about 67 achieving service status. The aircraft were used to protect jet fighter bases and were

operated by JG 301. One version with a very high-aspect ratio wing was designated Ta 153. This model was built but then abandoned so as not to cause congestion on production lines during a critical stage of the war.

Focke-Wulf Ta 152H

Year: 1944.
Manufacturer: Focke-Wulf Flugzeugbau G.mbH.
Type: high-altitude fighter.
Crew: one.
Specification: Ta 152H-1.
Power plant: one Junkers Jumo 213E-1 12-cylinder, liquid-cooled engine developing 1750 hp or 2050 hp with MW 50 Methanol/water injection.
Dimensions: span, 47 ft 4 in; length, 35 ft 2 in; height, 11 ft; wing area, 250.80 sq ft.
Weights: empty, 8642 lb; loaded (maximum), 11,502 lb.
Performance: maximum speed, 332 mph at sea level; cruising speed, 311 mph at 22,965 ft; climb rate, 3445 ft per min; service ceiling, 48,550 ft.
Armament: one 30 mm MK 108 cannon firing through spinner, two 20 mm MG 151 cannons in wing roots.

Focke-Wulf Ta 154

Year: 1943.
Manufacturer: Focke-Wulf Flugzeugbau G.mbH.
Type: two seat night/all weather fighter.
Crew: two (pilot and radar operator).
Specification: Ta 154A-1.
Power plant: two Junkers Jumo 213E 12-cylinder, inverted-Vee liquid-cooled engines, each developing 1750 hp.
Dimensions: span, 53 ft 6 in; length, 41 ft 3 in; height, 11 ft 10 in; wing area, 348.75 sq ft.
Weights: empty, 14,122 lb; loaded (maximum), 19,687 lb.
Performance: maximum speed, 404 mph at 23,250 ft, 332 mph at sea level; climb rate, 10 min to 19,680 ft; service ceiling, 35,760 ft.
Armament: two 20 mm MG 151 cannons and two 30 mm MK 108 cannons.

The need for defensive fighters was never seriously considered by the RLM until it was far too late to produce and develop successful aircraft. Kurt Tank's Ta 154, which was hailed as the German Mosquito, came close to becoming

Below: the Focke-Wulf Ta 152H-1 high-altitude fighter saw little combat.

Above: the Ta 154 night fighter was Germany's equivalent to the DH Mosquito, but it saw no service.

a very successful combat type. However, problems such as finding the producer of a suitable glue after the original manufacturer was bombed brought a premature end to the fighter. Constructed mainly of wood, the Ta 154 was designed specifically to combat the RAF night bomber and there can be little doubt that if production had proceeded it would have presented a real threat.

Focke-Wulf Fw 191

Year: 1942.
Manufacturer: Focke-Wulf Flugzeugbau G.mbH.
Type: medium bomber.
Crew: four (pilot, observer, engineer, radio operator).
Specification: Fw 191B.
Power plant: two Daimler-Benz DB 610A 24-cylinder, liquid-cooled engines each developing 2870 hp.
Dimensions: span, 85 ft 3 in; length, 64 ft 5 in; height, 18 ft 4 in; wing area, 758.86 sq ft.
Weights: empty, 35,940 lb; loaded, 52,600 lb.
Performance: maximum speed, 352 mph at 12,965 ft; climb rate, 1500 ft per min; service ceiling, 28,800 ft.
Armament: one 20 mm MG 151 cannon or two 13 mm MG 131 machine guns in nose barbette, two 20 mm MG 151 in ventral and dorsal barbettes and one 20 mm MG 151 or two 13 mm MG 131 machine guns in tail; bomb load, 4400 lbs, or two 3300 lb LT 1500 torpedoes, or torpedo/bomb combination.

Plagued by underpowered engines in early test flights, plus a complex and troublesome electrical system, the Fw 191 was finally abandoned in 1943 after the building of three prototypes.

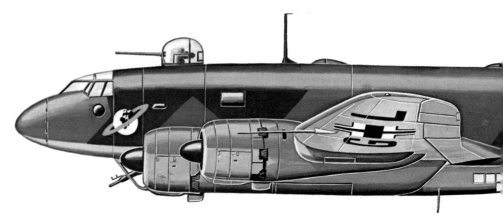

Above: the crew of a Focke-Wulf Fw 200 Condor prepares for a sortie.
Below: the FW 191 bomber was pressurized for high altitude operation.

Focke-Wulf Fw 200 Condor

Year: 1937.
Manufacturer: Focke-Wulf Flugzeugbau G.mbH with Hamburger Flugzeugbau.
Type: maritime reconnaissance bomber.
Crew: seven (pilot, copilot, observer, radio-operator, engineer, two gunners or radar operator/gunner).
Specification: Fw200C-3/U4.
Power plant: four BMW-Bramo 323 R-2 Fafnir nine-cylinder, air-cooled radial engines each developing 1200 hp with methanol-water injection.
Dimensions: span, 107 ft 9 in; length, 76 ft 11 in; height, 20 ft 8 in; wing area, 1290 sq ft.
Weights: empty, 28,550 lb; loaded (maximum), 50,045 lb.
Performance: maximum speed, 224 mph at 15,750 ft; cruising speed, 172 mph at sea level; service ceiling, 19,685 ft; endurance at economic cruising speed, 14 hr.
Armament: two 7.9 mm MG 15 machine guns, three 13 mm MG 131 machine guns and one 20 mm MG 151 cannon in dorsal turrets, beam hatches and ventral gondola; bomb load, 4626 lb.

Although not an outstanding warplane, the Fw 200 established a formidable record bearing in mind the relatively few (263) operated by the Luftwaffe. Like so many military aircraft of World War II, the Condor was originally designed to a civil requirement and captured many prewar records in the hands of DLH. Oberst-

Gotha Go 145

Year: 1934.
Manufacturer: Gothaer Waggonfabrik A.G.; subcontracted to Ago, Focke-Wulf, BFW (Messerschmitt) and under license to CASA in Spain.
Type: primary trainer.
Crew: two (pilot and pupil).
Specification: Go 145C.
Power plant: one Argus As 10C eight-cylinder, inverted-Vee, air-cooled engine developing 240 hp.
Dimensions: span, 29 ft 6 in; length, 28 ft 6 in; height, 9 ft 6 in; wing area, 234.10 sq ft.
Weights: empty, 1940 lb; loaded, 3043 lb.
Performance: maximum speed, 132 mph at sea level; cruising speed, 112 mph; climb rate, 5.5 min to 3280 ft; service ceiling, 12,140 ft.
Armament: usually none; but some aircraft fitted with 7.9 mm MG 15 in rear cockpit for gunnery training.

A conventional wood and fabric-covered single-bay biplane, the Go 145 served in the training role throughout the war and with the Spanish air force long after hostilities ceased. Nearly 10,000 were produced and in 1942 they were used in the Soviet campaign on night harassing missions, a duty that continued until 1944, but their main use was as trainers.

Gotha Go 242 and Go 244

Year: 1941.
Manufacturer: Gothaer Waggonfabrik A.G. and subcontractors.
Type: transport glider.
Crew: two (pilot and copilot), plus 21 fully equipped troops.
Specification: Go 242A-1.
Power plant: none.
Dimensions: span, 80 ft 4 in; length, 51 ft 10 in; height, 14 ft; wing area, 693.19 sq ft.
Weights: empty, 7055 lb; loaded (maximum), 16,094 lb.
Performance: maximum speed, 180 mph (gliding); cruising speed under tow, 130 mph; rate of climb under tow, 15 min to 6560 ft.
Armament: four 7.9 mm MG 15 machine guns and up to four 7.9 mm MG 34 machine guns.

The twin-boom layout and center fuselage pod chosen by Dipl Ing Albert Kalkert for the Go 242 assault glider was a foretaste of the configuration of many postwar heavy transport aircraft.

Above: this Fw 200C-3/U1 served with 3 Staffel of Kampfgeschwader 40. KG 40 was the main user of the type.
Top: a Condor runs up its engines.

leutnant Oscar Petersen was mainly instrumental in getting the aircraft into Luftwaffe service as an improvised reconnaissance aircraft and as such it earned notoriety on both sides. Regarded by the Allies as a danger to convoys, it was known as the 'Scourge of the Atlantic.' The Fw 200 carried out antishipping strikes as well as reconnaissance work and was also used to shadow shipping while acting as an airborne command post for U-boats. The weak structure of the aircraft resulted in many of them breaking their backs on landing or taking-off with heavy loads and this tendency, together with the thin undersurface structure which gave little or no protection to fuel and electrical systems, did little to endear them to their crews.

The first military production variant was the Fw 200C-1, which was fitted with 850 hp BMW 132 engines, one 20 mm MG FF cannon and three MG 15 machines. This version equipped 1/KG 40 which operated from Bordeaux-Merignac during the Battle of Britain. The C-2 was basically the same aircraft, but it had redesigned outboard nacelles allowing the carriage of either 550 lb bombs or 66 Imperial gallon drop tanks with reduced drag. The C-3 was an improved design which began to reach units in 1941 and included a stronger rear spar and fuselage. This was powered by BMW-Bramo 323R-2 radials and had increased defensive armament. The C-4 followed and was equipped with FuG Rostock search radar which was later replaced by FuG Hohentwiel, which had a blind-bombing capability. An attempt was made to increase the aircraft's offensive qualities by producing the C-6, which could carry two

Henschel Hs 293 missiles. The definitive version, which could also carry missiles was designated C-8.

Although it virtually disappeared from operational use in 1944, the Fw 200 served until the end of the war, reverting to its original role of a transport aircraft in the last year of its life. Total production was 276 and in its heyday as an antishipping aircraft, it claimed the destruction of over 90,000 tons of shipping from August–September 1940.

Below: the Gotha Go 145 trainer was used as a light attack aircraft by some 15 *staffeln* on the Eastern Front.

Above: the Gotha Go 242 was the Luftwaffe's standard transport glider from 1942.

Over 1500 Go 242s were built making it the most widely used offensive aircraft produced by Gotha in World War II. The aircraft entered service in 1942 and was most often towed by standard He 111 tugs and the five-engined He 111Z. It could be fitted with rocket-assisted take-off packs and could carry heavy loads including vehicles such as the Kübelwagen. The Go 244 was a powered version of the glider using Gnome/Rhône, Soviet Shvetsov or BMW engines. It was used in limited numbers in the Middle East and Western Desert, but proved to be vulnerable and was soon withdrawn. A total of 133 Go 244s was produced.

Gotha-Kalkert Ka 430

Year: 1944.
Manufacturer: Gothaer Waggonfabrik AG.
Type: assault glider.
Crew: two (pilot and copilot), plus accommodation for 12 troops, or vehicles.
Specification: Ka 430A-0.
Power plant: none.
Dimensions: span, 64 ft; Length, 43 ft 4 in; height, 13 ft 8 in; wing area, 429.48 sq ft.
Weights: empty, 3990 lb; loaded (maximum), 10,140 lb.
Performance: maximum gliding speed, 199 mph; maximum towing speed, 186 mph.
Armament: one 13 mm MG 131 in manually operated turret.

Designed by Albert Kalkert after he had left Gotha, the KA 430 was a logical development of the Go 242. Trials proved successful and a production order was placed, but only 12 aircraft were completed when the overall war situation brought about the end of the project in 1944.

Heinkel He 8

Year: 1927.
Manufacturer: Ernst Heinkel A.G.
Type: reconnaissance floatplane.
Crew: two (pilot, observer).
Specification: He 8.
Power plant: one Armstrong-Siddeley Jaguar engine developing 450 hp.
Dimensions: span, 55 ft 1 in; length, 38 ft 1 in; height, 14 ft 5 in; wing area, 507 sq ft.
Weights: empty, 3693 lb; loaded, 5126 lb.
Performance: maximum speed, 134 mph at sea level; cruising speed, 106 mph; climb rate, 3 min to 3280 ft; service ceiling, 19,685 ft.
Armament: none.

An early Heinkel monoplane floatplane, the He 8 was sold to the Danish Government in 1928 and produced under license for the Danish Navy. Approximately 25 were built and they served until April 1940.

Heinkel He 42

Year: 1931.
Manufacturer: Ernst Heinkel A.G.
Type: maritime reconnaissance floatplane.
Crew: two (pilot, observer/gunner).
Specification: He 42C-2.
Power plant: one Junkers Jumo L-5Ga engine developing 380 hp.
Dimensions: span, 45 ft 11 in; length, 34 ft 10 in; height, 14 ft 1 in; wing area, 603 sq ft.
Weights: empty, 2980 lb; loaded (maximum), 5336 lb.
Performance: maximum speed, 124 mph at sea level; cruising speed, 115 mph; climb rate, 13.24 min to 6560 ft; service ceiling, 14,700 ft.
Armament: one 7.9 mm MG 15 on flexible mount in rear cockpit.

A total of 85 Heinkel He 42s was produced and the type saw extensive service with the prewar Luftwaffe. The first version was a dual-control trainer and the C-2 was an armed reconnaissance version. The aircraft served in minor operational roles with the Luftwaffe until 1944.

Heinkel He 45

Year: 1932.
Manufacturer: Ernst Heinkel A.G.
Subcontracted to Gotha, BFW, and Focke-Wulf.
Type: light reconnaissance bomber.
Crew: two (pilot, observer/gunner).
Specification: He 45C.
Power plant: one BMW VI 7.3 12-cylinder, liquid-cooled engine developing 750 hp.
Dimensions: span, 37 ft 9 in; length, 34 ft 9 in; height, 11 ft 10 in; wing area, 372.32 sq ft.
Weights: empty, 4641 lb; loaded, 6052 lb.
Performance: maximum speed, 180 mph at sea level; cruising speed, 137 mph; climb rate, 2.4 min to 3280 ft; service ceiling, 18,045 ft.
Armament: one 7.9 mm MG 17 fixed to fire forward and one 7.9 mm MG 15 machine gun on flexible mount in rear cockpit.

The He 45 featured prominently in Erhard Milch's production plan for military aircraft issued in 1934, the Heinkel He 45 was used in some quantity by the Luftwaffe. Initially it served as a trainer, then later in the bombing and reconnaissance roles. A total of 512 of all versions was produced, but by the outbreak of World War II only 21 remained in front-line service. These proved to be so outdated that they were soon relegated to training. Some aircraft were delivered to Bulgaria and a quantity of He 45b versions were exported to the Chinese Nationalists.

Right: a number of Heinkel He 45s were returned to service as night attack aircraft in 1942–43.

Left: by the end of 1935 both *Gruppe* of Jagdgeschwader 132 'Richthofen' had equipped with the He 51 fighter. In 1936 He 51s saw action in Spain.

Heinkel He 46

Year: 1931.
Manufacturer: Ernst Heinkel A.G. Subcontracted to Siebel, Gotha, Fieseler and MIAG.
Type: short-range reconnaissance and army cooperation.
Crew: two (pilot, observer/gunner).
Specification: He 46C.
Power plant: one Bramo 322B SAM nine-cylinder, air-cooled radial engine developing 650 hp.
Dimensions: span, 45 ft 11 in; length, 31 ft 2 in; height, 11 ft 2 in; wing area, 354.13 sq ft.
Weights: empty, 3890 lb; loaded (maximum), 5070 lb.
Performance: maximum speed, 155 mph at sea level; cruising speed, 130 mph; climb rate, 2.6 min to 3280 ft; service ceiling, 19,685 ft.
Armament: one 7.9 mm MG 17 on flexible mount in rear cockpit; bomb load, 440 lb.

First flown as a sesquiplane designated He 46a, the aircraft was modified to a parasol wing layout with the He 46b. Featuring prominently in the build up of the clandestine Luftwaffe, the aircraft saw service in the Spanish Civil War but had been mainly replaced by the Hs 126 at the time of the campaigns in France and the Low Countries in 1940. It soldiered on in the Eastern Front until 1943. Total production was 481 machines and the aircraft was used by Hungary and Bulgaria.

Heinkel He 50

Year: 1931.
Manufacturer: Ernst Heinkel A.G. and BFW.
Type: dive bomber and reconnaissance bomber.
Crew: one in dive-bomber configuration, two (pilot and observer) in reconnaissance role.
Specification: He 50A.
Power plant: one Bramo 322B SAM nine-cylinder, air-cooled radial engine developing 650 hp.
Dimensions: span, 37 ft 9 in; length, 31 ft 6 in; height, 14 ft 5 in; wing area, 374.58 sq ft.
Weights: empty, 3871 lb; loaded, 5776 lb.
Performance: maximum speed, 143 mph at sea level; cruising speed, 115 mph; climb rate, 3 min to 3280 ft; service ceiling, 21,000 ft.
Armament: as divebomber, one 7.9 mm MG 17 machine gun firing forward; bomb load, 1102 lb. As reconnaissance bomber, one 7.9 mm MG 15 machine gun on flexible mount in rear cockpit; bomb load, 550 lb.

A sturdy two-bay biplane of wood and metal construction, the He 50 was designed to meet a Japanese specification for a two-seat dive bomber. Demonstrated to the Defense Ministry in 1932, the aircraft proved well capable of carrying out its task and a preproduction order was placed. Although early prototypes were underpowered the problem was overcome by weight saving and reengining with the fourth prototype. Total production was 90 and the aircraft saw service on the Eastern Front flown by Estonian volunteers in 1943.

Heinkel He 51

Year: 1933.
Manufacturer: Ernst Heinkel A.G. Subcontracted to Ago, Erla, Arado and Fieseler.
Type: fighter.
Crew: one.
Specification: He 51B-1.
Power plant: one BMW VI 7.3Z 12-cylinder, liquid-cooled engine developing 750 hp.
Dimensions: span, 36 ft 1 in; length, 27 ft 7 in; height, 10 ft 6 in; wing area, 292.78 sq ft.
Weights: empty, 3247 lb; loaded, 4189 lb.
Performance: maximum speed, 205 mph at sea level; cruising speed, 174 mph; climb rate, 1.4 min to 3280 ft; service ceiling, 25,260 ft.
Armament: two 7.9 mm MG 17 machine guns, fixed to fire forward.

The scant interest taken by Germany's former enemies in the violations of the Treaty of Versailles prompted German aircraft manufacturers to concentrate more and more on thinly disguised military aircraft posing as civil and sports machines. Among these was the range of fighters designed by the Günter brothers which culminated in the He 51. When the reborn Luftwaffe was revealed to the world in March 1935, JG 132 was equipped and combat ready with this neat biplane fighter. By January 1936 75 of the A-1 versions had been produced and later in the year the improved B-0 and B-1 models began to appear. In November 1936, 36 A-1 versions went to Spain with the Condor Legion and were sufficiently successful for the Spanish to place an order for 30.

Some aircraft were fitted with floats and in this configuration were eventually designated He 51B-2. The introduction of monoplane fighters led to the gradual decline of the He 51 in its prime role. The C-1 operated in Spain as a ground-attack aircraft, but its performance was disappointing and the type suffered a high attrition rate. Relegation to the training role followed and by 1938 most aircraft were with fighter training schools. A total of 725 He 51s was produced.

Heinkel He 70

Year: 1932.
Manufacturer: Ernst Heinkel A.G.and Manfred Weiss Flugzeug und Motorenfabrik.
Type: light reconnaissance bomber.
Crew: three (pilot, observer, radio operator/ gunner).
Specification: He 70F-2.
Power plant: one BMW VI 7.3Z 12-cylinder, liquid-cooled engine developing 750 hp.
Dimensions: span, 48 ft 7 in; length, 39 ft 4 in; height, 10 ft 2 in; wing area, 392.88 sq ft.
Weights: empty, 5203 lb; loaded, 7630 lb.
Performance: maximum speed, 203 mph at sea level; cruising speed, 208 mph.
Armament: one 7.9 mm MG 15 machine gun on flexible mount in rear cockpit; bomb load, 660 lb.

Inspired by the Lockheed Orion, the He 70 was perhaps the most esthetically-pleasing aircraft to come from the drawing board of the Günter brothers, and its clean flowing lines had great influence on many aircraft subsequently designed for the Luftwaffe. Although a success as a high speed transport in the hands of DLH, its service record was somewhat more dismal. It was used as a strategic reconnaissance aircraft for a brief period, but it eventually found its niche as a transport and communications machine. A total of 306 was built and some continued to serve in Spain until the early 1950s. An export version, the He 170, was delivered to Hungary and the more powerful He 270 never passed the prototype stage.

Below: conceived as a high-speed civil transport, the He 70 was not a success as a military aircraft.

Heinkel He 59

Year: 1931.
Manufacturer: Ernst Heinkel A.G. Subcontracted to Walter Bachmann AG and Arado Flugzeugwerke.
Type: torpedo bomber/ reconnaissance floatplane.
Crew: four (pilot, observer, radio operator/ gunner, gunner).
Specification: He 59B-2.
Power plant: two BMW VI 6.0 ZU 12-cylinder, liquid-cooled engines each rated at 660 hp.
Dimensions: span, 77 ft 9 in; length, 57 ft 1 in; height, 23 ft 3 in; wing area, 1649 sq ft.
Weights: empty, 11,023 lb; loaded, 20,062 lb.
Performance: maximum speed, 137 mph at sea level; cruising speed, 115 mph, climb rate, 4.7 min to 3280 ft; service ceiling, 11,480 ft.
Armament: two 7.9 mm MG 15 machine guns in open nose and dorsal positions and one 7.9 mm MG 15 in closed ventral position; bomb load, 2205 lb, or one torpedo weighing either 1543 lb or 2205 lb, slung externally.

Landplane and seaplane prototypes of the He 59 were produced, but the wheeled model never achieved production status. The aircraft achieved some notoriety in the opening days of the campaign against England, when, thinly disguised as a rescue aircraft carrying the Red Cross symbol, it carried out reconnaissance and mine-laying duties. A more noteworthy achievement was the use of the aircraft to land troops on the River Maas to capture the Rotter- dam bridges. Produced in a variety of versions, the floatplane carried out sterling work in training, air-sea rescue (including over the Black Sea from 1941 to 1943), reconnaissance and minelaying.

Heinkel He 60

Year: 1933.
Manufacturer: Ernst Heinkel A.G. Subcontracted to Arado and Weser.
Type: short-range reconnaissance floatplane.
Crew: two (pilot, observer/gunner).
Specification: He 60C.
Power plant: one BMW VI 6.0 ZU 12-cylinder, liquid-cooled engine developing 660 hp.
Dimensions: span, 42 ft 5 in; length, 37 ft 9 in; height, 16 ft 2 in; wing area, 581.25 sq ft.
Weights: empty, 5313 lb; loaded (maximum), 7840 lb.
Performance: maximum speed, 140 mph at 3280 ft; cruising speed, 118 mph; climb rate, 3.8 min to 3280 ft; service ceiling, 16,400 ft.
Armament: one 7.9 mm MG 15 machine gun on flexible mount in rear cockpit.

Above: this Heinkel He 59B-2 operated in the Middle East. By 1943 the type was relegated to second-line duties.

Designed to operate from warships, the He 60 eventually saw most of its active service from coastal bases carrying out reconnaissance duties. Of sturdy construction, the aircraft could absorb a great deal of punishment both from enemy action and heavy seas. The He 60C equipped all major German warships until replaced by the Arado Ar 196 and it was issued to all four of the coastal reconnaissance units. It remained in service until 1943, by which time a total of 250 had been produced.

Above: a line-up of Heinkel He 72A Kadett training aircraft pictured in the mid-1930s. The He 72A was the initial production version, powered by a 150 hp Argus As 8R.

Heinkel He 72 Kadett

Year: 1933.
Manufacturer: Ernst Heinkel A.G.
Type: primary trainer.
Crew: two (pilot and pupil).
Specification: He 72B-1.
Power plant: one Siemens SH 14A seven-cylinder, air-cooled radial engine developing 160 hp.
Dimensions: span, 29 ft 6 in; length, 24 ft 7 in; height, 8 ft 10 in; wing area, 222.80 sq ft.
Weights: empty, 1190 lb; loaded, 1907 lb.
Performance: maximum speed, 115 mph at sea level; cruising speed, 106 mph; climb rate, 6 min to 3280 ft; service ceiling, 11,483 ft.
Armament: none.

Alongside the Fw 44, Ar 66 and Go 145, the Kadett was one of the most important primary trainers used by the Luftwaffe. It was built in some quantity and used by several National Socialist Flying Corps units in the mid 1930s. The He 72B-3 Edelkadett was an improved version with spatted wheels and 30 aircraft were built for civil use. Another development was the more refined He 172, which had a fully cowled engine, but only one example was manufactured. The aircraft was also used for communications and reconnaissance work, as well as serving as a flying test bed for the liquid-fuelled Walter rocket engine.

Left: this Heinkel He 60C served with the Luftwaffe in northern Russia during 1942, where this floatplane soldiered on until the winter of 1943. The He 60 was originally a shipboard reconnaissance floatplane, but it was relegated to shore duties in 1939.

Heinkel He 74

Year: 1934.
Manufacturer: Ernst Heinkel A.G.
Type: fighter/advanced trainer.
Crew: one.
Specification: He 74B.
Power plant: one Argus As 10C Series 1 eight-cylinder, inverted-Vee, air-cooled engine developing 240 hp.
Dimensions: span, 26 ft 9 in; length, 21 ft 2 in; height, 7 ft 2 in; wing area, 160.60 sq ft.
Weights: empty, 1697 lb; loaded, 2242 lb.
Performance: maximum speed, 174 mph at sea level; cruising speed 146 mph; climb rate, 2.6 min to 3280 ft; service ceiling, 15,750 ft.
Armament: one 7.9 mm MG 17 machine gun.

Virtually a scaled-down version of the He 51, the He 74 was Heinkel's entry in a competition for a *Heimatschutzjäger* (home defense fighter). The specification called for a monoplane and so the Günter brothers' biplane probably had little chance from the outset. The winner proved to be the Fw 56 and, despite the Heinkel's outstanding performance, only three prototypes were constructed.

Below: the Heinkel He 72BW was a floatplane version of the Kadett primary trainer, but no production was undertaken and only one prototype was built. The landplane trainer was widely used by civil and military flying schools in the 1930s and it operated on military communications and liaison duties early in World War II.

Heinkel He 100

Year: 1938.
Manufacturer: Ernst Heinkel A.G.
Type: fighter.
Crew: one.
Specification: He 100D-1.
Power plant: one Daimler-Benz DB 601Aa 12-cylinder, inverted-Vee, liquid-cooled engine developing 1175 hp.
Dimensions: span, 30 ft 10 in; length, 36 ft 11 in; height, 11 ft 10 in; wing area, 155.0 sq ft.
Weights: empty, 3990 lb, loaded, 5511 lb.
Performance: maximum speed, 415 mph at 16,400 ft; cruising speed, 342 mph; climb rate, 3280 ft per min; service ceiling, 34,440 ft.
Armament: one nose-mounted 20 mm MG FF cannon and two wing-mounted 7.9 mm MG 17 machine guns.

After losing the production contract for the Luftwaffe's new monoplane fighter to the Messerschmitt Bf 109, Heinkel proposed an improved version of the He 112. This was originally to be designated He 113, but it was changed to He 100. The aircraft had many advanced features and in March 1939 a special version, the He 100 V8, obtained the absolute air-speed record for Germany.

Twelve aircraft were produced but although they were photographed in spurious unit markings and used for propaganda purposes, they never equipped a Luftwaffe unit. The completed machines were used to form a factory-defense unit at Heinkel's Rostock-Marienehe works, but never fired their guns in anger.

Above: a He 111H-8 in winter camouflage.
Left: this Heinkel He 111H-3 served with Kampfgeschwader 1 in 1940.

Heinkel He 111 Series

Year: 1935.
Manufacturer: Ernst Heinkel A.G. Subcontracted to SNCASO, Fabrica de Avione SET Rumania and CASA, Spain.
Type: medium bomber.
Crew: four (pilot, observer, radio operator/gunner, engineer/gunner).
Specification: He 111B-2.
Power plant: two Daimler-Benz DB 600CG 12-cylinder, liquid-cooled, inverted-Vee engines each developing 950 hp.
Dimensions: span, 74 ft 2 in; length, 57 ft 5 in; height, 14 ft 5 in; wing area, 942.92 sq ft.
Weights: empty, 12,875 lb; loaded (maximum), 22,046 lb.
Performance: Maximum speed, 186 mph at sea level; cruising speed, 174 mph; climb rate, 30 min to 14,765 ft; service ceiling, 22,966 ft.
Armament: three 7.9 mm MG 15 machine guns on flexible mount in nose cone, open dorsal turret and retractable 'dustbin'; bomb load, 3307 lb.

Below: this Heinkel He 111P-2 served with Kampfgeschwader 55's 5 Staffel at Chartres, France, in 1940.

Specification: He 111P-4.
Year: 1938.
Crew: five (pilot, observer, radio operator/gunner, engineer/gunner, gunner).
Power plant: two Daimler-Benz DB 601A-1 12-cylinder, liquid-cooled engines each developing 1100 hp.
Dimensions: span, 74 ft 2 in; length, 53 ft 9 in; height, 13 ft 2 in; wing area, 942.92 sq ft.
Weights: empty, 14,936 lb; loaded (maximum), 29,762 lb.
Performance: maximum speed, 225 mph at sea level; cruising speed, 194 mph; climb rate, 7 min to 3280 ft; service ceiling, 26,250 ft.
Armament: six 7.9 mm MG 15 machine guns, in nose cone on flexible mounting, in nose fixed, in two beam windows and in open dorsal turret and ventral gondola; some aircraft also fitted with one 7.9 mm MG 17 machine gun in tail cone; bomb load, 2204 lb internally and 2204 lb externally on racks.
Specification: He 111 H-16.
Year: 1943.
Crew: five (pilot, observer, radio-operator/gunner, engineer/gunner, gunner).
Power plant: two Junkers Jumo 211F-2 12-cylinder, liquid-cooled engines each developing 1350 hp.
Dimensions: span, 74 ft 2 in; length, 53 ft 9 in; height, 13 ft 1 in; wing area, 931.07 sq ft.
Weights: empty, 19,136 lb; loaded (maximum), 30,865 lb.
Performance: maximum speed, 227 mph at sea level; cruising speed, 197 mph; climb rate, 8.5 min to 6560 ft; service ceiling, 27,890 ft.
Armament: one 20 mm MG FF cannon in nose, one 13 mm MG 131 machine gun in dorsal position, two 7.9 mm MG 81 machine guns in rear ventral gondola, two 7.9 mm MG 15 or MG 81 machine guns in beam positions; the nose cannon could also be replaced by a 7.9 mm MG 15 machine gun and the beam positions with twin 7.9 mm MG 81 machine guns; bomb load, 7165 lb, made up of various bombs carried internally and on external racks.

The graceful lines of the He III derive from the earlier He 70, many advanced design features of which were incorporated in the larger twin-engined bomber. Design work began in 1934 and from the start the aircraft was planned to perform in the bombing role for the then-secret Luftwaffe.

The first prototype, registered D-ALIX, was delivered to Lufthansa as a high-speed transport aircraft and was later used for clandestine reconnaissance work. In late 1935 Heinkel received instructions to proceed with the A Series in the bomber configuration and examples were delivered to Rechlin in 1936, where they proved to be very disappointing.

All 10 of the preproduction A-0s were stripped of their military equipment and shipped to China, which had shown interest in the aircraft. The more powerful B Series followed and was quickly approved for service with the Luft-

waffe. In the winter of 1936 He 111Bs joined KG 154 at Hannover-Langenhagen. The Spanish Civil War presented an ideal opportunity to evaluate the new bomber under combat conditions, so two *Staffeln* of KG 88 were equipped with 30 He 111B-1s which reached Spain in February 1937.

The C and G versions were produced as transports in parallel to the bombers and these began operating with DLH in 1937. A bottleneck in production of DB 600 engines, which in any case were mostly earmarked for the Bf 109, brought a premature end to the He 111D, which never achieved service status. Work was concentrated on the E which was powered by Jumo 211 engines. The He 111F had a redesigned wing, but production was delayed to avoid holdups of the current models then coming off the lines. In the end the F was not produced for the Luftwaffe, but a quantity went to Turkey where they served until 1946. The supply situation with DB 600 engines eased somewhat by the summer of 1938 and an F-4 version was fitted with these engines and designated He 111J. This aircraft had no internal bomb bays being designed to carry torpedoes on external racks, but this decision was changed and the 90 completed aircraft were modified to have bomb bays and were delivered alongside F-4s, to which, apart from the engines, they were identical in all respects.

The P had a completely redesigned nose, which did away with the stepped windshield of the earlier versions and introduced the fully glazed nose with offset nose bubble, which characterized the whole range of wartime He 111s. The P was not produced in any great quantities and in 1939 it began to be replaced by the H, which was probably the most successful of the range. Fitted with Jumo 211 engines the H series went through many minor and major design changes, most of which concentrated on the fitting of armor, more-effective defensive armament and greater carrying capacity.

The need for an effective torpedo bomber was fulfilled by the H-6 which was intended to be the last of the line, but the failure of the Ju 288 and He 177 resulted in the He 111 being put back into production and subjected to further development long after it became obsolescent. The H-21 was modified to carry the Fieseler Fi 103 flying bomb under its port or starboard wing and was redesignated H-22. This version began operating in late 1944 with KG 3, air launching the missiles against targets in England. The final version was the H-23 which was to carry 14 parachutists on special saboteur missions.

A proposed high-altitude version to be known as the He 111R was abandoned, but more success was met by one of the most unusual aircraft to see Luftwaffe service, the He 111Z. This aircraft was basically two H-6s joined together by a new wing section carrying a fifth Jumo 211 engine. Twelve *Zwilling* (twin) He 111Zs were produced and used as glider tugs.

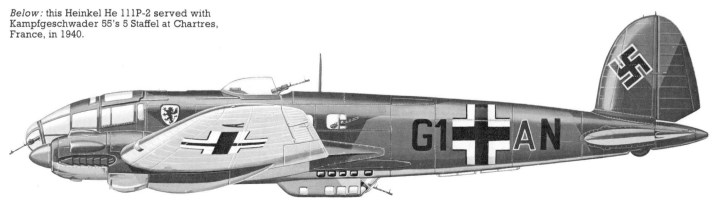

Above: a Heinkel He 111H-3 of 5/KG 27 operating over the Eastern Front in April 1942. This sub-type could be used for anti-shipping work.

The He 111 stayed in production for nine years, during which over 7300 were built. A testimony to its sound basic concept is the fact that it remained in production in Spain until 1956.

The He 111 carried out its various tasks well, although it was forced to continue in front-line service long after it should have been removed, by which time it was being opposed by much-superior designs which it had no chance of meeting on equal terms.

Heinkel He 112

Year: 1935.
Manufacturer: Ernst Heinkel A.G.
Type: fighter.
Crew: one.
Specification: He 112 B-0.
Power plant: one Junkers Jumo 210Ea 12-cylinder, liquid-cooled engine developing 680 hp.
Dimensions: span, 29 ft 10 in; length, 30 ft 6 in; height, 12 ft 7 in; wing area, 182.99 sq ft.
Weights: empty, 3571 lb; loaded, 4960 lb.
Performance: maximum speed, 267 mph at sea level; cruising speed, 301 mph at 13,120 ft; climb rate, 2.6 min to 6560 ft; service ceiling, 27,890 ft.
Armament: two 7.9 mm MG 17 machine guns in fuselage and two wing-mounted 20 mm MG FF cannons, plus six 22 lb bombs on wing racks.

Built to the same specification as the Bf 109, the He 112 was considered by many to have a greater potential than the Messerschmitt fighter to which it lost the production contract after trials at Travemünde in October 1935. The redesigned B version proved to be faster than the Bf 109 and an order for 30 was received from Japan. Twelve of these were dispatched in 1938, but a second batch was diverted to the Luftwaffe because of the Sudeten crisis. After the signing of the Munich Agreement, the aircraft were returned to Heinkel for export. Approximately 68 of all versions were produced but only those serving with the Rumanian Air Force saw operational service in World War II.

Heinkel He 114

Year: 1936.
Manufacturer: Ernst Heinkel A.G.
Type: reconnaissance floatplane.
Crew: two (pilot, observer/gunner).
Specification: He 114A-2.
Power plant: one BMW 132K nine-cylinder, air-cooled radial engine developing 960 hp.
Dimensions: span, 44 ft 7 in; length, 38 ft 2 in; height, 17 ft 2 in; wing area, 455 sq ft.
Weights: empty, 5070 lb; loaded (maximum), 8090 lb.
Performance: maximum speed, 205 mph at sea level; cruising speed, 168 mph; climb rate, 4.3 min to 3280 ft; service ceiling, 16,075 ft.
Armament: one 7.9 mm MG 15 machine gun on flexible mount in rear cockpit; two 110 lb bombs on external racks.

Designed to replace the He 60, the sesquiplane He 114 encountered a lot of early handling troubles both on the water and in the air. It was outdated by the time the war started but saw limited service with the Luftwaffe, mainly in Greece and Crete. It was also operated by Rumania and Sweden. Production ceased in 1939 when 98 aircraft had been manufactured.

Heinkel He 115

Year: 1936.
Manufacturer: Ernst Heinkel A.G.
Type: multirole float seaplane.
Crew: three (pilot, observer, radio operator/gunner).
Specification: He 115C-1.
Power plant: two BMW 132K nine-cylinder, air-cooled radial engines each developing 960 hp.
Dimensions: span, 73 ft 1 in; length, 56 ft 9 in; height, 21 ft 8 in; wing area, 933.23 sq ft.
Weights: empty, 15,146 lb; loaded, 23,545 lb.
Performance: maximum speed, 180 mph at sea level; cruising speed, 168 mph.
Armament: two 7.9 mm MG 15 on flexible mounts in nose and dorsal positions, one 15 mm MG 151 cannon fixed forward, two 7.9 mm MG 17 machine guns fixed to fire aft in engine nacelles; bomb load, 2756 lb, or one 1102 lb torpedo, or mines.

A sturdy twin-float monoplane, the He 115 handled very well and was able to perform a variety of roles, including mine laying, casualty evacuation, reconnaissance and torpedo bomb-

ing. A total of 142 were produced, and three of these which had been bought by Norway, were used by the RAF in the Mediterranean after their escape to England in 1940. In 1943 the He 115 was put back into production and this, coming at a time when priority was being given to defensive fighters, speaks volumes for the esteem in which the aircraft was held.

Bottom left: the Heinkel He 112B-1 was evaluated by the Royal Hungarian Air Force, three being purchased.
Right: a Heinkel He 115B-1 serving with *Küstenfliegergruppe* 406, which was based in Norway.
Below: this Heinkel He 114C-1 of the Romanian Air Force's Escadrila 102 operated over the Black Sea.
Bottom: this He 115B-1 carries the emblem of Kü Fl Gr 206, but the fuselage code indicates Kü Fl Gr 106.

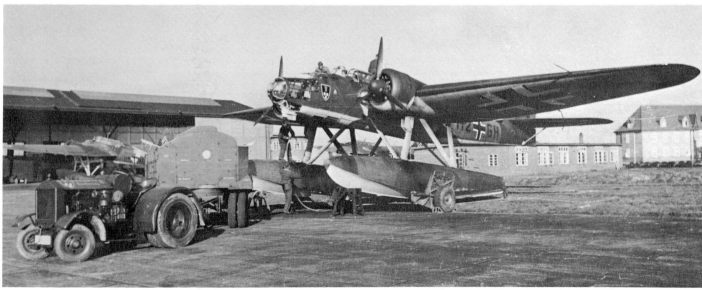

Heinkel He 116

Year: 1936.
Manufacturer: Ernst Heinkel A.G.
Type: long-range photographic reconnaissance.
Crew: four (pilot, copilot, observer, radio operator).
Specification: He 116B-0.
Power plant: four Hirth HM 508H eight-cylinder, inverted-Vee, air-cooled engines each developing 240 hp.
Dimensions: span, 72 ft 2 in; length, 46 ft 11 in; height, 10 ft 10 in; wing area, 677 sq ft.
Weights: empty, 8862 lb; loaded, 15,533 lb.
Performance: maximum speed, 178 mph at sea level; cruising speed, 142 mph; climb rate, 4.2 min to 3280 ft; service ceiling, 21,325 ft.
Armament: none.

The long-range potential of the He 116A, which had been built for Lufthansa, suggested to the RLM that the aircraft had some military application. The B version was produced to realize this, but the outcome was disappointing and the aircraft was confined to carrying out photographic and mapping work over Germany and German-held territories. A total of 14 were constructed and eight of these entered Luftwaffe service.

Heinkel He 162 Salamander

Year: 1944.
Manufacturer: Ernst Heinkel A.G.
Type: fighter.
Crew: one.
Specification: He 162A-2.
Power plant: one BMW 003E-2 axial-flow turbojet developing a maximum of 2082 lb static thrust for short periods and 1764 lb for take off.
Dimensions: span, 23 ft 7 in; length, 29 ft 8 in; height, 8 ft 6 in; wing area, 120.56 sq ft.
Weights: empty, 3666 lb; loaded (maximum), 6184 lb.
Performance: maximum speed with normal thrust, 491 mph at sea level, with maximum thrust, 553 mph at sea level; climb rate with normal thrust, 3780 ft per min, with maximum thrust, 4615 ft per min; service ceiling, 39,400 ft.
Armament: two 20 mm MG 151 cannons with 120 rpg.

Below: the Heinkel He 162 was intended to be a mass-produced jet fighter, manned by inexperienced pilots recruited from the ranks of the Hitler Youth.

Above: this preserved Heinkel He 162A-2 served with 2/JG 1 at Leck. After World War II it was tested by the RAE, Farnborough.

The continual pounding of the German war resources by Allied bombers, which created a serious shortage of fuel, raw materials and fully trained aircrew, called for desperate countermeasures. This resulted in the issuing in September 1944 of a specification calling for a lightweight, high-speed interceptor using non-strategic materials, which could be mass produced in dispersed locations. Heinkel responded with the turbojet powered He 162 which became popularly known as the *Volksjäger* (people's fighter). Time from drawing board to first flight was an incredible 90 days and production was in full swing by January 1945. Constructed of wood with a part-metal monocoque fuselage, the aircraft had a blown acrylic canopy which offered little protection in combat to the pilot, who however had the benefit of a simple ejector seat. Production of over 4000 aircraft per month was planned and it was envisioned that their pilots could be culled from the ranks of the Hitler Youth. Both plans were rather grandiose and, not surprisingly, failed to reach fruition, the only unit becoming operational with the aircraft being I(Einsatz) Gruppe/JG 1, which surrendered four days after its formation. Total production was about 800 of which only 275 were completed.

Heinkel He 177 Greif

Year: 1939.
Manufacturer: Ernst Heinkel A.G. and Arado Flugzeugwerke.
Type: heavy bomber/reconnaissance and antishipping aircraft.
Crew: six (pilot, copilot, observer/radio operator, bomb-aimer/nose gunner, dorsal gunner, rear gunner).
Specification: He 177A-5.
Power plant: two Daimler-Benz DB 610 (comprising two DB 605 engines coupled together by a clutch and gearbox driving one propeller) developing 3100 hp.
Dimensions: span, 103 ft 2 in; length, 72 ft 2 in; height, 21 ft; wing area, 1097.92 sq ft.
Weights: empty, 37,038 lb; loaded (maximum), 68,348 lb.
Performance: maximum speed, 303 mph at 20,000 ft; cruising speed, 258 mph at 20,000 ft; climb rate, 10 min to 10,000 ft; service ceiling, 26,250 ft.
Armament: one 7.9 mm MG 81J machine gun in nose, two 20 mm MG 151 cannons in forward ventral gondola and tail, three 13 mm MG 131 machine guns in forward dorsal barbette (two) and aft dorsal turret; bomb load, up to 13,230 lb, or parachute mines, torpedoes, Hs 293 or FX 1400 Fritz X missiles.

Although the Luftwaffe was conceived as a tactical force working in close liaison with the army, the importance of a long-range strategic bomber capable of hitting targets well behind the front line was appreciated by some advocates of air power. Among them was General Walther Wever, who as early as 1934 had proposed the production of what became known as the 'Ural' bomber. His death in June 1936 is generally regarded as sounding the death knell of this type of aircraft.

The only aircraft coming anywhere near to satisfying the requirements of a strategic bomber was the ill-fated He 177 which had a dismal development record and an inauspicious career.

The RLM issued a specification in 1938 for a long-range bomber and Siegfried Günter of Ernst Heinkel A.G. designed what was to become the He 177 to meet this. In order to overcome the problem of obtaining 2000 hp engines, Günter used pairs of Daimler-Benz 601 units coupled together via a clutch and gearbox to drive large VDM four-bladed propellers.

In addition to this novel engine layout, the aircraft also incorporated remotely operated defensive armament as well as other advanced innovations. The RLM also called for the aircraft

Right: Heinkel He 177A-3/R2 bombers of
KG 100 operated over Britain in 1944.
Below right: He 177A-5s of II/KG 40
undertook maritime reconnaissance.

to be capable of performing as a dive bomber
and the problems associated with stressing such
a large aircraft to carry out this role delayed
development as well as causing a performance
penalty. Throughout its career the He 177 was
plagued by engine fires which, because of the
construction and location of fuel and lubricating
systems, usually resulted in the failure of the
main spar.

Initial production batches of A-0s and A-1s
underwent service trials with KG 40 in 1942
and were followed by variants of the same
airframe with different armament. The A-3 was
the first to use DB 610 engines which were
moved forward in a longer nacelle in an attempt
to overcome the earlier cramped installation.
The A-4 was a high-altitude project which was
developed into the He 274, and was followed by
the next major production type which was the
A-5. This machine had shorter undercarriage
legs, revised armament and the Fowler flaps
removed. Although the A-5 was the last variant
to see service there were other proposals one
of which converted the huge bomber into an
interceptor by loading the bomb bay with
rocket tubes slanted to fire upward. The He 177
was also adapted to carry Henschel 293 and
Fritz X missiles, parachute mines, torpedoes,
and was designated as the carrier for Germany's atom bomb. Over 1000 aircraft were
produced, but their operations over England
and on the Eastern Front had little impact on the
final outcome of the war.

Heinkel He 219 Uhu

Year: 1942.
Manufacturer: Ernst Heinkel A.G.
Type: night fighter.
Crew: two (pilot and radar operator).
Specification: He 219A-7/R1.
Power plant: two Daimler-Benz DB 603G 12-
cylinder, liquid-cooled engines each
developing 1900 hp.
Dimensions: span, 60 ft 8 in; length, 51 ft;
height, 13 ft 5 in; wing area, 478.99 sq ft.
Weights: empty, 24,692 lb; loaded, 33,730 lb.
Performance: maximum speed, 416 mph at
22,965 ft; cruising speed, 335 mph; climb rate,
1810 ft per min; service ceiling, 41,660 ft.
Armament: four 30 mm MK 108 cannons, two
in wing roots, two in rear fuselage firing
upward, two 20 mm MG 151 cannons and two
30 mm MK 103 cannons in ventral tray.

Originally designed as a private venture the
He 219 was potentially the best night fighter
developed in World War II but, as was the case

Right: this Heinkel He 219A-2 was fitted with
FuG 220 Lichtenstein SN-2 radar and
ejector seats.
Below: I/NJG 1 began to equip with the
Heinkel He 219 in late 1943 and was the first
unit to receive the type.

with many promising German aircraft, it became the victim of political wheeling and dealing as well as prejudice among those who could have seen it in service long before it was. In the end, it was yet another case of far too few and far too late. Heinkel's original design was for a high-altitude fighter and light bomber, but when the need for a specialist night fighter became evident his project P1060 was resurrected and became the He 219. The heavily armed and highly maneuverable fighter was fitted with compressed-air operated ejector seats and there is at least one recorded incident of a crew saving their lives with these. The success of the aircraft was indicated on the night of 12 June 1943 when Werner Streib flying a preproduction A-0 accounted for five RAF Lancaster bombers in one 30 minute sortie.

The first variant to leave the assembly line in any quantity was the A-5; the A-1, A-3 and A-4 were projects for reconnaissance bombers. The A-5s began to reach the Luftwaffe in 1944 and were fitted with a variety of *Rüstsatz* armament and equipment modifications. Prior to the introduction of this version, Milch had suggested the abandonment of the aircraft in favor of the Ju 88G, which he argued was capable of handling the current RAF night bombers. However he had not allowed for the Mosquito bomber/intruder with which the Junkers fighter was unable to cope. The A-6 was a stripped version of the A-2 and was followed by the A-7, the major production version. Like its predecessors, this variant was also fitted with a variety of *Rüstsatz* armament kits as well as tail warning radar. A total of 268 aircraft were delivered to the Luftwaffe and served with I/NJG 1, III/NJG 5, II & IV/NJG 1 and NJGr 10 *Nachtjagdstaffel Norwegen*.

Heinkel He 280

Year: 1941.
Manufacturer: Ernst Heinkel A.G.
Type: fighter.
Crew: one.
Specification: He 280 V6.
Power plant: two Junkers Jumo 004A Orkan axial-flow turbojets each rated at 1852 lb static thrust.
Dimensions: span, 39 ft 4 in; length, 33 ft 5 in; height, 10 ft 6 in; wing area, 231.50 sq ft.
Weights: empty, 7073 lb; loaded, 11,475 lb.
Performance: maximum speed, 467 mph at sea level; 508 mph at 19,685 ft; climb rate, 4170 ft per min; service ceiling, 37,390 ft.
Armament: three 20 mm MG 151 cannons in nose.

The potential of the turbojet-powered fighter was completely disregarded by those in authority at the RLM, so the achievement by Hienkel of flying the world's first twin-jet fighter which

Below: the Heinkel He 280 V7 first flew as a glider on 19 April 1943

had been designed as such from the start created little interest. Preoccupied by the quick victory gained by *Blitzkrieg*, which was the fashion of the day when the He 280 first flew, little need was seen for such an advanced fighter. Heinkel persisted with his claims but even after arranging a mock dogfight with a Fw 190 which the He 280 won easily, there was no sign of a development order being placed. Eight aircraft were built and used in a variety of test flights which contributed a great deal to turbojet-powered aircraft research.

Henschel Hs 123

Year: 1935.
Manufacturer: Henschel Flugzeugwerke A.G.
Type: dive bomber/ground support aircraft.
Crew: one.
Specification: Hs 123A-1.
Power plant: one BMW 132Dc nine-cylinder, air-cooled radial engine developing 880 hp.
Dimensions: span, 34 ft 5 in; length, 27 ft 4 in; height, 10 ft 6 in; wing area, 267.48 sq ft.
Weights: empty, 3316 lb; loaded, 4888 lb.
Performance: maximum speed, 207 mph at sea level; cruising speed, 197 mph; climb rate, 2950 ft per min; service ceiling, 29,525 ft.
Armament: two 7.9 mm MG 17 machine guns, or two 20 mm MG FF cannons on underwing racks; bomb load, 992 lb.

Entering service in 1936, the Hs 123 was the last operational biplane used by the Luftwaffe apart from some trainers and floatplanes. Its career as a dive bomber was shortlived but it soldiered on in the close support role on the Eastern Front until mid-1944.

Above: the Hs 123 production prototype.
Below: this Henschel Hs 123 carries the Infantry Assault badge.

Left: this Henschel Hs 126A-1 served with Aufklärungsgruppe 21 on tactical reconnaissance duties over the Eastern Front. From mid-1942 it was gradually phased out of service in favour of the Focke-Wulf Fw 189.

Henschel Hs 126

Year: 1936.
Manufacturer: Henschel Flugzeugwerke A.G.
Type: tactical reconnaissance and army cooperation.
Crew: two (pilot, observer/gunner).
Specification: Hs 126B-1.
Power plant: one BMW-Bramo Fafnir 323A-1 or Q-1 nine-cylinder, air-cooled radial engine developing 850 hp.
Dimensions: span, 47 ft 7 in; length, 35 ft 7 in; height, 12 ft 3 in; wing area, 340.14 sq ft.
Weights: empty, 4480 lb; loaded (maximum), 7209 lb.
Performance: maximum speed, 193 mph at sea level, 209 mph at 19,680 ft; climb rate, 3.5 min to 2000 ft; service ceiling, 27,000 ft.
Armament: one 7.9 mm MG 17 machine gun fixed to fire forward, one 7.9 mm MG 15 on flexible mount in rear cockpit; maximum bomb load, 331 lb (if not carrying camera pack).

The A-1 series entered Luftwaffe service in mid-1938 and the Hs 126 proved to be a well-liked and efficient reconnaissance machine with a good short-field performance. It equipped 80 percent of the tactical reconnaissance units and served on all fronts until gradually being phased out in favor of the Fw 189. The B series, with more advanced BMW-Fafnir engines, had an improved altitude performance and better STOL characteristics. A total of 810 aircraft were delivered and, in addition to their designed role, also performed training, communications, night harassment and glider-tug duties.

Henschel Hs 129

Year: 1939.
Manufacturer: Henschel Flugzeugwerke A.G.
Type: close support and anti-tank aircraft.
Crew: one.
Specification: Hs 129B-2.
Power plant: two Gnome-Rhône 14M 4/5 14-cylinder, air-cooled radial engines each developing 700 hp.
Dimensions: span, 46 ft 7 in; length, 32 ft; height, 10 ft 8 in; wing area, 312.15 sq ft.
Weights: empty, 8400 lb; loaded (maximum), 11,574 lb.
Performance: maximum speed (clean), 253 mph at 12,570 ft; cruising speed, 196 mph at 9845 ft; climb rate (clean), 1595 ft per min; service ceiling, 29,530 ft.
Armament: six 7.9 mm MG 17 machine guns, two 20 mm MG 151 cannons, one 30 mm MK 101 cannon; bomb load, 771 lb.

Designed by Dipl Ing Friedrich Nicolaus the Hs 129 was a small ground support aircraft, which tended to suffer from power plant troubles throughout its service life. The original A series was grossly underpowered and Nicolaus proposed a complete redesign. This was not accepted, due to the delays it would cause, so a greatly modified and reengined B series was produced. The aircraft was very heavily armored and had an extremely small and cramped cockpit. Armament was very powerful and the machine could be fitted with a variety of gun packs which included a 37 mm BK 3.7, and a 75 mm BK 7.5 which fired a 26 lb shell. A total of 870 were produced and they saw extensive service on the Eastern Front.

Junkers F.13

Year: 1919.
Manufacturer: Junkers Flugzeugwerke A.G.
Type: transport.
Crew: two (pilot, observer) plus four passengers.
Specification: F.13.
Power plant: Junkers L 5 engine developing 280 hp.
Dimensions: span, 58 ft 3 in; length, 34 ft 5 in; wing area, 473.62 sq ft.
Weights: empty, 3263 lb; loaded, 5512 lb.
Performance: cruising speed, 106 mph; service ceiling, 16,732 ft.
Armament: none.

The F.13 was an important aircraft since it paved the way for the all-metal cantilever monoplane and introduced practical air transport to many parts of the world. It was operated in Finland during the Winter War of 1939–40, by which time it was grossly out-of-date. A total of 322 were produced and they contributed a great deal to the foundations of military air transport.

Junkers W.34

Year: 1926.
Manufacturer: Junkers Flugzeugwerke A.G.
Type: transport/communications aircraft.
Crew: two (pilot, observer) plus six passengers or cargo.
Specification: W.34h.
Power plant: BMW 132 nine-cylinder, air-cooled radial engine developing 660 hp.
Dimensions: span, 58 ft 3 in; length, 33 ft 8 in; height, 11 ft 7 in; wing area, 462.85 sq ft.
Weights: empty, 3748 lb; loaded, 7055 lb.
Performance: maximum speed, 165 mph; cruising speed, 145 mph; climb rate, 3.2 min to 3280 ft; service ceiling, 20,670 ft.
Armament: none.

Below left: this Henschel Hs 126B-2 flew in North Africa with 2(H)/14.
Below: a Henschel Hs 129B-2 of Schlachtgeschwader 2 in Russia.

Above: the single-engined Junkers W 34 shared many of the larger Ju 52's design features. A wheeled undercarriage could be replaced by skis, or floats as shown in this illustration.

Seeing world-wide service in the 1920s and 1930s, the W.34 was a logical progression from the F.13 and served extensively with the Luftwaffe and its allies during World War II. The aircraft performed a variety of tasks including casualty evacuation, communications, training and for a short period light bombing. Production ended in 1934, after 1991 examples had been built.

Right: groundcrew start the BMW 132 engines of a Junkers Ju 52 during a Russian winter. This aircraft is a Ju 52/3m g6e sub-type.
Below: this Junkers Ju 52 is preserved by a private collector in Britain. Ju 52s remain in Swiss Air Force service in the 1980s.

Above: the Ju 52 was to Germany what the C-47 was to the Allies. A Ju 52/3m g6e (See) is shown fitted with twin floats.

Junkers Ju 52

Year: 1930
Manufacturer: Junkers Flugzeugwerke A.G.
Type: medium bomber/transport.
Crew: four (pilot, observer, radio operator, engineer/gunner), plus 18 passengers or cargo.
Specification: Ju 52/3m g3e.
Power plant: three BMW 132A-3 nine-cylinder, air-cooled radial engines each developing 725 hp.
Dimensions: span, 96 ft; length, 62 ft. height, 18 ft 2 in; wing area, 1189.41 sq ft.
Weights: empty, 12,610 lb; loaded (maximum), 23,146 lb.
Performance: maximum speed, 165 mph at sea level; cruising speed, 130 mph; climb rate, 17.5 min to 9840 ft; service ceiling, 19,360 ft.
Armament: two 7.9 mm MG 15 machine guns, one each in open dorsal position and ventral 'dustbin'; bomb load, 1102 lb.

First flown as a single-engined transport, in which form it saw no military service, the Ju 52 must rank alongside the DC 3 as the world's most famous transport aircraft. It served for over 40 years throughout the world and was the Luftwaffe's mainstay in the transport role throughout the war years. The angular corrugated-skinned aircraft served on every major front and was affectionately known by Luftwaffe personnel as the *Tante Ju* (Auntie Junkers).

Designed by Dipl Ing Ernst Zindel, the first trimotor Ju 52 was designated Ju 52/3m and was in fact the seventh Ju 52 airframe converted to this configuration. In 1933 it was issued to the *Luftfahrtkommissariat* as a *Behelfskampfflugzeug* (auxiliary bomber), an interim measure pending the arrival of the Do 11. When the Dornier aircraft failed to live up to its expectations the Ju 52 assumed a much more important role and became standard equipment for the first bomber squadrons of the new German Air Force.

The Ju 52/3m g3e was a conversion of the basic transport aircraft which had been serving with Lufthansa and by the end of 1935 equipped two thirds of the *Staffeln* of the then existing five *Kampfgruppen*. This aircraft was joined by the Ju 52/3m g4e which was the same basic airframe but fitted with different internal equipment and a tail wheel instead of a skid. The first bombing mission of the Spanish Civil War was

carried out by the Ju 52 on 14 August, 1936.

The g5e was produced with an interchangeable undercarriage enabling the aircraft to be fitted with wheels, floats or skis, and the g6e, which was produced in parallel, had simplified radio equipment and only a wheeled undercarriage, although later some were float equipped. In 1941 the g7e with a larger loading door, and autopilot was introduced, being followed by the g8e which had the same size loading door but an additional loading hatch in the cabin roof, as well as a 13 mm MG 131 in the dorsal position. The g9e with a BMW 132Z engine and glider towing equipment followed in 1942 and a few g12es with 800 hp BMW 132L were produced in the same year. The last production variant was the g14e which had increased defensive armament and armor protection for the pilot. A total of 4850 of all variants was produced and many continued to serve throughout the world long after the end of World War II.

Junkers Ju 86

Year: 1934.
Manufacturer: Junkers Flugzeugwerke A.G. Subcontracted to Henschel and built under license in Sweden by SAAB.
Type: medium bomber.
Crew: four (pilot, observer, radio operator/bomb aimer, gunner).
Specification: Ju 86D-1.
Power plant: two Junkers Jumo 205C-4 six-cylinder, vertically-opposed, diesel engines each developing 600 hp.
Dimensions: span, 73 ft 10 in; length, 58 ft 7 in; height, 16 ft 7 in; wing area, 882.64 sq ft.
Weights: empty, 11,354 lb; loaded (maximum), 18,078 lb.
Performance: maximum speed, 186 mph at sea level; cruising speed, 171 mph at 3280 ft; maximum range with auxiliary tanks, 1240 miles; service ceiling, 19,360 ft.
Armament: three 7.9 mm MG 15 in nose, dorsal and ventral positions; bomb load, 2204 lb.

One of the bombers which was used during the clandestine build up of the Luftwaffe, the Ju 86 was obsolete by the start of World War II and, apart from service in the Polish campaign, saw little use in its designed role. The D version saw service in Spain where it proved very vulnerable and was quickly replaced by the radial-engined E version. Aircraft built in Sweden were powered by Bristol Pegasus engines and carried the K suffix. Perhaps its greatest claim to fame was its use in the R and P versions as a very high altitude reconnaissance aircraft, in which form it operated over the Soviet Union, British Isles and in the Mediterranean theater.

Below: a Junkers Ju 86A-1 of Kampfgeschwader 253 flies on air exercises in 1937. Note that the ventral gun position is extended. The aircraft in the background is a Junkers Ju 86D-1.
Bottom: this Junkers Ju 86E-2 was damaged in a landing accident while serving with a training unit based in Czechoslovakia early in World War II.

Junkers Ju 87A B, R, D, G

Year: 1938.
Manufacturer: Junkers Flugzeug- und
Motorenwerke. Subcontracted to Weser
Flugzeugbau and SNCASO, France
Type: dive bomber.
Crew: two (pilot, gunner)
Specification: Ju 87B-1.
Power plant: one Junkers Jumo 211Da 12-
cylinder, liquid-cooled engine developing
1200 hp.
Dimensions: span, 45 ft 3 in; length, 36 ft 5 in;
height, 13 ft 2 in; wing area, 343.37 sq ft.
Weights: empty, 5980 lb; loaded (maximum),
9560 lb.
Performance: maximum speed, 211 mph at
sea level; cruising speed, 175 mph at 15,090 ft;
climb rate, 2 min to 3280 ft; service ceiling,
26,250 ft.
Armament: two 7.9 mm MG 17 machine guns
fixed to fire forward, one 7.9 mm MG 15
machine gun on flexible mount in rear
cockpit; bomb load, 1102 lb.

Left: a Junkers Ju 87D-2 operating on the Eastern Front with I/StG 2. *Above:* the Ju 87G-1 was fitted with two 37 mm *Flak* 18 cannons.

Junkers Ju 87 A B, R, D, G

Year: 1940.
Manufacturer: Junkers Flugzerug- und *a* Motorenwerke. Subcontracted to Weser Flugzeugbau and SNCASO France.
Type: dive bomber.
Crew: two (pilot, gunner).
Specification: Ju 87D-1.
Power plant: one Junkers Jumo 211J-1 12-cylinder, liquid-cooled engine rated at 1400 hp.
Dimensions: span, 45 ft 3 in; length, 37 ft 9 in height, 12 ft 9 in; wing area, 343.37 sq ft.
Weights: empty, 8598 lb; loaded (maximum), 14,550 lb.
Performance: maximum speed, 255 mph at 13,500 ft; cruising speed, 198 mph at 16,700 ft; climb rate, 19.8 min to 16,400 ft; service ceiling, 23,905 ft.
Armament: two 7.9 mm MG 17 machine guns fixed to fire forward; twin 7.9 mm MG 81z machine gun on flexible mount in rear cockpit; bomb load, 3968 lb.

Arguably the most famous, or perhaps infamous, German aircraft of World War II, the Ju 87 is often known by the appellation Stuka, an abbreviation of *Sturzkampfflugzeug*, a term applying to all dive bombers. The Ju 87 made its maiden flight in 1935 powered by a Rolls-Royce Kestrel engine.

When operating under ideal conditions of total air superiority, the Ju 87 was a formidable

Far left: the Junkers Ju 87R was modified from the Ju 87B to increase internal fuel and to allow drop tanks to be carried thus greatly extending the dive bomber's range.
Left: the Junkers Ju 87's characteristic wheel spats were often removed to facilitate operation from mud or snow covered airfields. This aircraft is a Ju 87D-1 of Stukageschwader 77.
Below left: a Ju 87B-2 of I/StG 1 flies over Poland in 1939.

support weapon, but its success in Poland, France and the Low Countries blinded some of its advocates to its shortcomings. The aircraft met its match when faced with stern fighter opposition and Ju 87 units were decimated during the Battle of Britain. Despite its increasing obsolescence, the aircraft continued to serve in the Middle East, North Africa, the Balkans, over Malta and on the Eastern front, where it achieved its most outstanding successes in the antitank configuration. The B version with its spatted undercarriage and Jumo engine was the first quantity production version for the Luftwaffe and was prominent in the opening campaigns of the war. The B-1 was followed by the B-2 which had ejector exhausts, hydraulically-operated cooling gills and a broader bladed propeller. This model was fitted with a variety of *Umrüst* conversion sets, denoted by U suffixes to the basic type number, an example being the Ju 87B-2/U4 which had skis in place of its conventional undercarriage. The C version was a proposal for a seaborne Ju 87 with folding wings for the aircraft carrier *Graf Zeppelin* and did not proceed past the prototype stage. The R was basically a B with facilities for fitting external wing tanks, as well as having increased internal fuel capacity.

The D version was aerodynamically improved with a refined engine cowling and improved cockpit line. Again, a variety of armament and conversion sets produced minor and major changes to the basic D variants. The G was produced from the D airframe and was initially envisioned as an antitank weapon. The G-1 was in fact a conversion of a D-3 with a pair of 37 mm Flak 18 (BK 3.7) cannons under the wings. The H was a dual control trainer with suffix numbers corresponding with the D series from which they were converted.

Over 5700 Ju 87s of all marks were produced and there can be no doubting their contribution to the Luftwaffe's war effort, but there can also be no hiding the fact that it was basically an outmoded concept and should have been phased out of service long before it was.

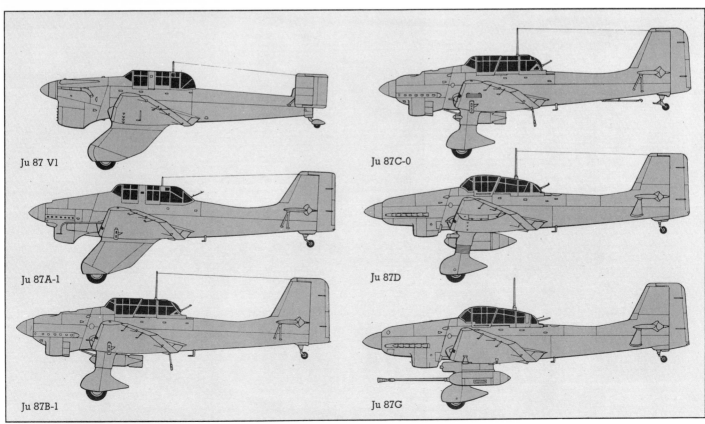

Ju 87 V1

Ju 87C-0

Ju 87A-1

Ju 87D

Ju 87B-1

Ju 87G

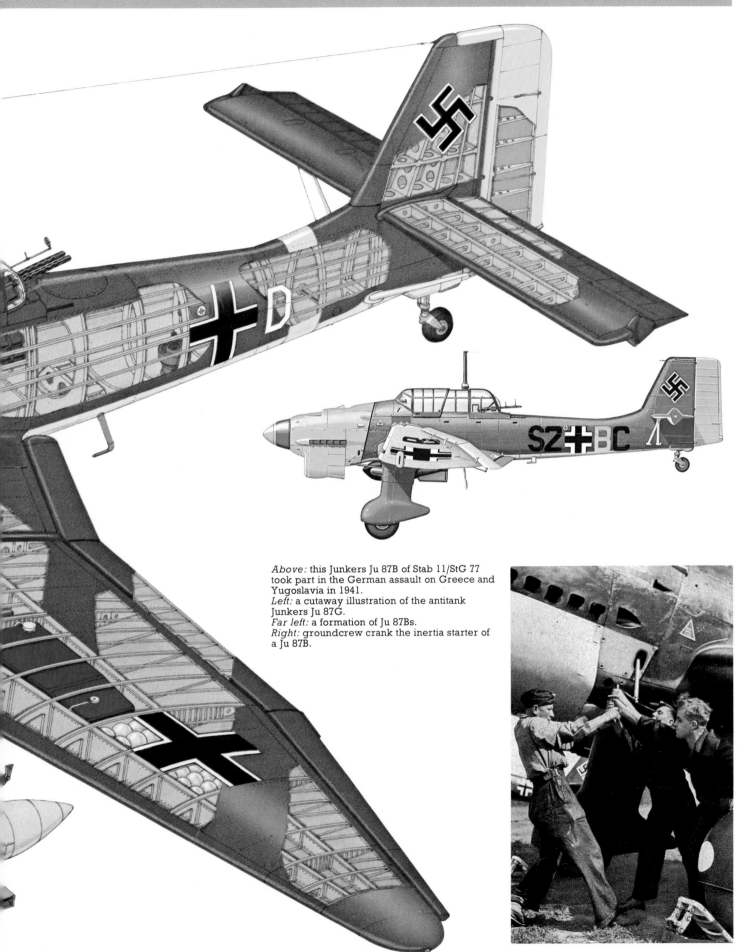

Above: this Junkers Ju 87B of Stab 11/StG 77 took part in the German assault on Greece and Yugoslavia in 1941.
Left: a cutaway illustration of the antitank Junkers Ju 87G.
Far left: a formation of Ju 87Bs.
Right: groundcrew crank the inertia starter of a Ju 87B.

Junkers Ju 88 Series

Year: 1936.
Manufacturer: Junkers Flugzeug- und
Motorenwerke A.G. Subcontractors, A.T.G.,
Opel, Volkswagen and various other groups.
Type: medium bomber, dive bomber and
night fighter.
Crew: four (pilot, observer/bomb aimer,
radio operator/gunner, engineer/gunner).
Specification: Ju 88A-4.
Power plant: two Junkers Jumo 211J-1 or J-2
12-cylinder, liquid-cooled engines each
developing 1350 hp.
Dimensions: span, 65 ft 7 in; length, 47 ft 3 in;
height, 15 ft 11 in; wing area, 586.63 sq ft.
Weights: empty, 21,737 lb; loaded
(maximum), 30,865 lb.
Performance: maximum speed, 292 mph at
17,390 ft; cruising speed, 230 mph; climb rate,
23 min to 17,716 ft; service ceiling, 26,900 ft.
Armament: three 7.9 mm MG 81 machine
guns, one firing forward on fixed or flexible
mount, two firing aft from rear of cockpit; two
13 mm MG 131 machine guns, one firing
forward on flexible mount, one firing aft below
fuselage from gondola; alternatively seven
7.9 mm MG 81 machine guns, three firing
forward from fixed or flexible mounts, two
firing aft from rear of cockpit and two firing aft
below fuselage from gondola; bomb load,
7935 lb.

Junkers Ju 88 Series

Year: 1942.
Manufacturer: Junkers Flugzeug- und Motorenwerke A.G. Subcontractors, A.T.G., Opel, Volkswagen and various other groups.
Type: medium bomber, dive bomber and night fighter.
Crew: three (pilot, observer/gunner, radar operator).
Specification: Ju 88C-6c.
Power plant: two Junkers Jumo 211J-1 or J-2 12-cylinder, liquid-cooled engines each developing 1350 hp.
Dimensions: span, 65 ft 7 in; length, 47 ft 1 in; height, 16 ft 7 in; wing area, 586.63 sq ft.
Weights: empty, 19,973 lb; loaded, 27,225 lb.
Performance: maximum speed, 307 mph at 17,390 ft; cruising speed, 279 mph; climb rate, 12.7 min to 19,685 ft; service ceiling, 32,480 ft.
Armament: three 20 mm MG FF/M cannons, three 7.9 mm MG 17 machine guns all firing forward, two 20 mm MG 151 cannons fixed firing upwards, and one aft firing 13 mm MG 131 machine gun.
Specification: Ju 88S-1.
Year: 1943.
Type: medium bomber.
Crew: three (pilot, observer, radio operator/gunner).
Power plant: two BMW 801G-2 14-cylinder, air-cooled radial engines each developing 1730 hp.
Dimensions: span, 65 ft 7 in; length, 48 ft 2 in; height, 15 ft 8 in; wing area, 586.63 sq ft.
Weights: empty (equipped), 18,250 lb; loaded (maximum), 30,400 lb.
Performance: maximum speed, 340 mph at 26,250 ft; cruising speed, 328 mph at 18,000 ft; maximum endurance, 3 hr 25 min; service ceiling, 38,000 ft.
Armament: one 13 mm MG 131 machine gun on flexible mount in rear of cockpit; bomb load, 4410 lb.
Specification: Ju 88G-7b.
Year: 1944.
Type: night fighter.
Crew: four (pilot, observer, radar operator/gunner, gunner).
Power plant: two Junkers Jumo 213E 12-cylinder, liquid-cooled engines each developing 1725 hp.
Dimensions: span, 65 ft 7 in; length, 47 ft 8 in; height, 15 ft 11 in; wing area, 586.63 sq ft.
Weights: empty (equipped), 28,900 lb; loaded (maximum), 32,350 lb.
Performance: maximum speed, 270 mph at sea level; 402 mph at 29,800 ft; endurance, 3.72 hrs at economical power; climb rate, 1665 ft per min; service ceiling, 32,800 ft.
Armament: six 20 mm MG 151 cannons, four firing forward, two firing obliquely upward, one 13 mm MG 131 machine gun on flexible mount in rear of cockpit.

The Junkers Ju 88 made its maiden flight in 1936 and ranks as one of the classic aircraft to emerge from World War II. Entering service with the Luftwaffe in 1939 in the bomber role, the aircraft first saw action with KG 30 (formerly KG 25 formed from Erprobungskommando 88) on 26 September 1939 when A-0 preproduction aircraft attacked the British Fleet in the Firth of Forth.

From this small beginning the Ju 88 flourished to serve on every front and in almost every role including bomber, night fighter, reconnaissance, torpedo bomber, dive bomber, intruder, ground support, mine layer and finally as the lower half of the Mistel flying bomb.

A total of 15,000 Ju 88s was produced, of which over 9000 were bomber variants, more than all other bomber types combined. It was still in production at the end of the war and was highly regarded by the Allies.

A summary of the main types follows:

Ju 88 V1	Prototype with Daimler-Benz DB 600A engines.
Ju 88 A-0	Preproduction model, 10 were built.
Ju 88 A-1	Initial production model with 60 ft 4 in wing span.
Ju 88 A-2	As A-1 but with rocket-assisted takeoff.
Ju 88 A-3	Dual-controlled trainer.
Ju 88 A-4	Most numerous and widely used variant. Wing span increased to 65 ft 7 in with metal-clad ailerons and strengthened undercarriage.
Ju 88 A-5	Development version of A-4 which it in fact preceded.
Ju 88 A-6	Similar to A-5, but fitted with full-span balloon fender and 132 lb counterbalance weight in tail.
Ju 88 A-7	Dual control trainer version of A-4.
Ju 88 A-8	Similar to A-4, but with balloon cable cutters in leading edges.
Ju 88 A-9 A-10 A-11	Designations of A-1/Trop, A-5/Trop and A-4/Trop built from the outset with tropical modifications for desert operations.
Ju 88 A-12	Dual control trainer with wider cockpit, no gondola or dive brakes.
Ju 88 A-13	Ground attack variant with heavy armament and additional protective armor.
Ju 88 A-14	Antishipping version of A-4 with 20 mm MG FF cannon in ventral gondola.
Ju 88 A-15	Increased bomb bay capacity with bulged doors to carry 6600 lb load.
Ju 88 A-16	Dual control trainer version of A-14.
Ju 88 A-17	Final A series model to be produced. A torpedo bomber with the ETC 500 bomb racks replaced by two PVC racks each capable of carrying an LT F5B torpedo.
Ju 88 B-0	Ten B-0 models were completed,

Far left: a Junkers Ju 88A-14 is bombed up on a Tunisian airfield in 1943. Note the 20 mm MG/FF cannon in the ventral gondola which characterized this sub-variant.
Left: the Junkers Ju 88A-6/U carried FuG 200 Hohentweil radar for long range maritime reconnaissance duties.
Above: this Ju 88D-1 carries the goose emblem of 1(F)/121, the first long-range reconnaissance unit to fly the Ju 88D.
Below: this Junkers Ju 88A-14 served with Kampfgeschwader 30. The Ju 88A-14 sub-variant was essentially a refined version of the widely-used A-4 with increased armor protection.
Below right: the versatile Junkers Ju 88 served in many roles and many theaters. This Ju 88A-4 belonged to Aufklärungsgruppe 122 and served on the Eastern Front.

Left: for service in North Africa Junkers Ju 88s were fitted with sand filters, sun blinds and desert survival equipment for the crews.
Above: the Ju 88's bomb aiming position was sited in the glazed nose.
Below: a Junkers Ju 88D reconnaissance aircraft of 1(F)/121.

Left: this Junkers Ju 88A-4, which carries the fuselage code letters of the Luftwaffe reconnaissance unit Aufklärungsgruppe 122, is now preserved by the United States Air Force Museum at Wright-Patterson Air Force Base, Ohio.

they were fitted with a deeper, fully glazed cockpit on an A-4 airframe. Production was not undertaken and completed aircraft were used in trials and eventually for the development of the Ju 188.

Ju 88 C-0	Early A-1s converted to perform the heavy fighter role.
Ju 88 C-1	Proposed model with BMW 801MA engines. Not produced.
Ju 88 C-2	First production model fitted with one 20 mm MG FF cannon and three 7.9 mm MG 17 machine guns.
Ju 88 C-3	Experimental BMW powered aircraft. Not produced.
Ju 88 C-4	First C version to be built from the start as a fighter. Based on the A-4 airframe with the longer span of that version.
Ju 88 C-5	BMW 801 engined version, which had no ventral gondola but a belly weapons pack. Only 10 were produced before a bottleneck in engine supply caused abandonment.
Ju 88 C-6	First C series to be produced in quantity replacing C-4 after only 100 of the latter had been built. The 6a was a day fighter and the 6b a night fighter.
Ju 88 C-7	Produced in three versions the a, b, and c. The first two having bomb-load capacity as well as fighter armament and no ventral gondolas. The 7c was an experimental BMW-powered version with no bomb carrying capacity.
Ju 88 D-0	Based on the A-4 with extra fuel capacity in place of forward bomb bay and no dive brakes. Used for reconnaissance.
Ju 88 D-1	Proposed variant with Jumo 211 J-1 or 2 engines.
Ju 88 D-2	Reconnaissance equivalent of A-5 with Jumo 211B-1 or H-1 engines.
Ju 88 D-3	Tropicalized version of D-1.
Ju 88 D-4	Redesignated Ju 88 D-2/Trop.
Ju 88 D-5	Three-camera version of D-2.
Ju 88 G-1	Improved version of the C series fighter with redesigned angular tail unit and BMW 801 air-cooled radials.
Ju 88 G-2	Not used.
Ju 88 G-4	A progressive development of the G-1 using avionics which had been installed piecemeal in the earlier model.
Ju 88 G-6	The 6a model was basically a G-4 with BMW 801 G engines. The G-6b had FuG 350 Naxos Z equipment and BMW 801G engines, and the G-6c was fitted with Jumo 213A liquid-cooled engines.
Ju 88 G-7	Final production version of the Ju 88 series night fighters. The -7a was equipped with forward search and tail warning radar, and powered by Jumo 213E engines with water-methanol boost. The -7b had FuG 228 Lichtenstein SN-3 radar which was changed as a result of Allied jamming to FuG 218 Neptun VR, and the -7c had FuG 240 Berlin N-1a radar.
Ju 88 H-1	Based on the combination of a D-1 and G-1, using the wings of the latter and fuselage and tail assembly of the former. Fitted with FuG 200 Hohentwiel radar and a trio of Rb cameras.
Ju 88 H-2	Radar replaced by a battery of six 20 mm MG FF cannons. Both H versions produced in limited quantity and used on long-range Atlantic patrols.
Ju 88 P-1	Based on the ubiquitous A-4 and fitted with a 75 mm PAK 40 cannon.
Ju 88 P-2	Similar to P-1 but fitted with two 37 mm BK 3.7 (Flak 38) cannon, intended for the antitank role but used unsuccessfully as an interceptor.
Ju 88 P-3	Similar to P-2 but with increased crew armor.
Ju 88 P-4	Final P version with reduced armament which consisted of a single 50 mm BK 5 cannon.
Ju 88 S-1	High-speed bomber based on A-4 with BMW 801G engines.
Ju 88 S-2	Improved version of S-1 with BMW 801TJ engines and exhaust-driven turbosuperchargers.
Ju 88 S-3	Final S variant with Jumo 213A engines and nitrous oxide GM 1 boost.
Ju 88 T	High-speed reconnaissance versions designated T-1 and T-3 based on S-1 and S-3.

Below: the crew prepares to board a Junkers Ju 188A-2 bomber prior to an operational mission. Note the forward-firing 20 mm cannon, manned by the bombardier and a similar weapon in the electro-hydraulic dorsal turret.

Junkers Ju 188

Year: 1942.
Manufacturer: Junkers Flugzeug- und Motorenwerke A.G.
Type: medium bomber.
Crew: four (pilot, observer/bomb aimer, radio operator/gunner, radar operator/gunner).
Specification: Ju 188E-1.
Power plant: two BMW 801D-2, 14-cylinder, air-cooled radial engines each developing 1700 hp.
Dimensions: span, 72 ft 2 in; length, 49 ft; height, 14 ft 7 in; wing area, 602.78 sq ft.
Weights: empty equipped, 21,737 lb; loaded, 31,989 lb.
Performance: maximum speed, 310 mph at 19,685 ft; cruising speed, 233 mph at 16,400 ft; climb rate, 17.6 min to 20,000 ft; service ceiling, 30,665 ft.
Armament: one 20 mm MG 151 cannon in nose, two 13 mm MG 131 machine guns one in dorsal turret one in rear of cockpit, twin 7.9 mm MG 81z machine guns firing aft below fuselage; maximum bomb load, 6615 lb.

A private venture development of the Ju 88, 1036 Ju 188s had been taken on charge by the Luftwaffe by the end of the war. Produced in BMW and Jumo engined versions in A, F, G and H series the Ju 188 saw service in Europe, the Mediterranean, Arctic and Eastern Front. The E model was used in the pathfinder role during the 1944 bombing campaign against England.

Junkers Ju 252

Year: 1941.
Manufacturer: Junkers Flugzeug- und Motorenwerke A.G.
Type: general purpose transport.
Crew: three (pilot, observer, radio-operator).
Specification: Ju 252A-1.
Power plant: three Junkers Jumo 211F 12-cylinder, liquid-cooled, inverted-Vee engines each rated at 1340 hp.
Dimensions: span, 111 ft 10 in; length, 82 ft 4 in; height, 18 ft 10 in; wing area, 1,319.65 sq ft.
Weights: empty, 28,880 lb; loaded (maximum), 52,911 lb.
Performance: maximum speed, 272 mph at 19,030 ft; cruising speed, 208 mph; climb rate, 4.3 min to 3280 ft; service ceiling, 20,670 ft.
Armament: one 13 mm MG 131 machine gun in dorsal turret, two 7.9 mm MG 15 machine guns firing from beam positions.

Intended as a replacement for the Ju 52, production of the Ju 252 never reached large-scale proportions as priority was given to the proven Ju 52 and combat aircraft. Twenty-five machines were completed and served in transport, communications, casualty evacuation and the agent-dropping roles with the Luftwaffe.

Junkers Ju 287

Year: 1944.
Manufacturer: Junkers Flugzeug- und Motorenwerke A.G.
Type: heavy bomber.
Crew: three (pilot, observer, radio operator).
Specification: Ju 287 V1.
Power plant: four Junkers Jumo 004B-1 Orkan axial flow turbojets each developing 1984 lb static thrust.
Dimensions: span, 66 ft; length, 60 ft; wing area, 656.60 sq ft.
Weights: empty, 27,557 lb; loaded, 44,092 lb.
Performance: maximum speed, 347 mph at 19,685 ft; cruising speed, 318 mph at 22,965 ft; service ceiling, 35,425 ft.
Armament: none.

One of the more unconventional German aircraft which actually reached flight testing in the form of an aerodynamic test bed. The distinctive swept-forward wings represented a novel approach to the problems of high-speed flight. Preproduction and production versions, the A-0 and A-1, were to be fitted with six BMW turbojets but none was completed before the war ended. The Ju 287 B-1 reverted to four engines.

Junkers Ju 288

Year: 1941.
Manufacturer: Junkers Flugzeug- und Motorenwerke A.G.
Type: medium bomber.
Crew: three (pilot, observer/bomb aimer, radio operator/gunner).
Specification: Ju 288 A.
Power plant: two Junkers Jumo 222A-1/B-1 24-cylinder, liquid-cooled, multibank radial engines each developing 2500 hp.
Dimensions: span, 60 ft; length, 52 ft 2 in; wing area, 581.25 sq ft.
Weights: normal loaded, 33,850 lb; loaded (maximum), 38,900 lb.
Performance: maximum speed, 416 mph at 19,685 ft; range at 338 mph with maximum fuel load, 3,720 miles, with maximum bomb load, 2235 miles; service ceiling, 30,500 ft.
Armament: two 13 mm MG 131 machine guns in remotely-controlled barbettes, one forward dorsal and one aft ventral; bomb load, 6614 lb.

A relatively little-known German bomber which could have achieved considerable success if it had been put into full-scale production. Designed by Junkers to meet the so-called Bomber B specification, the Ju 288 was already in an advanced design stage when details of the specification were released to Arado, Dornier and Focke-Wulf. The high speed and heavy armament coupled with a long range, made the Ju 288 variants formidable projects. However, a shortage of strategic materials and a fear that production would adversely affect current production types eventually led to its abandonment. Twenty-two examples were built of which 17 were destroyed in crashes.

Junkers Ju 290

Year: 1942.
Manufacturer: Junkers Flugzeug- und Motorenwerke A.G.
Type: long-range maritime reconnaissance/bomber.
Crew: nine or four (pilot, copilot, two observers, radio operator, engineer, three gunners. Pilot, copilot, observer and radio operator in transport role).
Specification: Ju 290A-5.
Power plant: four BMW 801D 14-cylinder, air-cooled radial engines each developing 1700 hp.
Dimensions: span, 137 ft 9 in; length, 94 ft; height, 22 ft 5 in; wing area, 2,191.53 sq ft.
Weights: normal loaded, 90,323 lb; loaded (maximum), 99,140 lb.
Performance: maximum speed, 273 mph at 19,685 ft; cruising speed, 224 mph; maximum range at economical cruise, 3820 miles; climb rate, 9.8 min to 6090 ft; service ceiling, 19,685 ft.
Armament: seven 20 mm MG 151 cannon located, two in dorsal turrets, two in lateral aft positions, one in tail, one in nose of ventral gondola, one in glazed nose, and one 13 mm MG 131 machine gun in tail of ventral gondola; bomb load, 6615 lb, or Henschel Hs 293, Hs 294 or FX 1400 Fritz-X missiles.

The Ju 290 was a development of the Ju 90 which in turn was converted from the original Junkers proposal for the so called Ural Bomber, the Ju 89. The A-0 and A-1 were built as transport aircraft and taken over by the Luftwaffe straight from the production line. The A-2 through to the A-5 were maritime reconnaissance aircraft and the A-6 a 50 seat VIP Transport for Hitler's personal transport flight. The A-8 to A-9 were reconnaissance bombers and the B-1, B-2, high-altitude bomber variants of the A-7. A total of 65 was produced.

Below: the Junkers Ju 288 V103 was the production prototype for the Ju 288C series. In June 1943 the Ju 288 programme was cancelled by the Reichsluftfahrtministereum (German air ministry).

Junkers Ju 352 Herkules

Year: 1943.
Manufacturer: Junkers Flugzeug- und Motorenwerke.
Type: general-purpose transport.
Crew: four (pilot, copilot, observer, radio operator/gunner).
Specification: Ju 325A-1.
Power plant: three BMW-Bramo 323R-2 nine-cylinder, air-cooled radial engines each developing 1200 hp.
Dimensions: span, 112 ft 3 in; length, 80 ft 8 in; height, 18 ft 10 in; wing area, 1379.93 sq ft.
Weights: empty equipped, 29,700 lb; loaded (maximum), 43,200 lb.
Performance: maximum speed, 230 mph at 16,565 ft; cruising speed, 186 mph; maximum range at economical cruise, 1860 miles; climb rate, 3.2 min to 3280 ft; service ceiling, 19,685 ft.
Armament: one 20 mm MG 151 cannon in hydraulically-operated dorsal turret.

The shortage of strategic materials and the shortage of Jumo 211 engines which were needed for combat aircraft forced the RLM to look to alternatives for aircraft used in non-combatant roles. One result was the redesign of the Ju 252 which culminated in the Ju 352. Construction was of mixed metal and wood, the whole wing structure being made of the latter material. The A-1 began to enter service in 1944, serving on special duty missions as well as supply and transport duties. The proposed B-1 and B-2 models powered with BMW 801 engines and with additional defensive armament were not produced. A total of 45 A-0 and A-1 airframes was completed.

Junkers Ju 388

Year: 1943.
Manufacturer: Junkers Flugzeug- und Motorenwerke A.G.
Type: photographic reconnaissance, night and all-weather interceptor.
Crew: three or four (pilot, observer, radar operator, gunner).
Specification: Ju 388L-1.
Power plant: two BMW 801TJ 14-cylinder, air-cooled radial engines each developing 1890 hp.
Dimensions: span, 72 ft 2 in; length, 49 ft 10 in; height, 14 ft 3 in; wing area, 602.78 sq ft.
Weights: normal loaded, 30,450 lb; loaded (maximum), 32,350 lb.
Performance: maximum speed, 383 mph at 40,300 ft; maximum range at economical cruise with long-range tank, 2160 miles; climb rate, 30 min to 36,100 ft; service ceiling, 44,100 ft.
Armament: one remotely-operated barbette carrying two 13 mm MG 131 machine guns.

In order to achieve greater speed and altitude without the disruption caused by the introduction of a completely new design, the RLM selected several aircraft for further development and among these was the Ju 188S and T. The result was the Ju 388 which reached the Luftwaffe only in the high-altitude reconnaissance variant, the L-1. Other versions were the J and K, which were bomber and night-fighter models respectively. The L carried a crew of three in a pressurized cabin and its turbo-supercharged engines gave it a superlative performance above 35,000 ft. The J stayed in development after all but aircraft in the 'emergency fighter' program had been cancelled, but it never reached production status.

Junkers Ju 390

Year: 1943.
Manufacturer: Junkers Flugzeug- und Motorenwerke A.G.
Type: heavy bomber, reconnaissance and transport.
Crew: not known.
Specification: Ju 390 A-1.
Power plant: six BMW 801E 14-cylinder, air-cooled radial engines each developing 1970 hp.
Dimensions: span, 165 ft 1 in; length, 112 ft 2 in; height, 22 ft 7 in; wing area, 2,729.73 sq ft.
Weights: empty (equipped), 81,350 lb; loaded (maximum), 166,450 lb.
Performance: maximum speed, 314 mph at 20,340 ft; cruising speed, 222 mph at 8200 ft; maximum range at economical cruise, 6030 miles.
Armament: eight 13 mm MG 131 machine guns in nose and tail turrets, eight 20 mm MG 151 cannon two each in fore and aft dorsal turrets, two in remote-controlled ventral barbette, and two firing aft from lateral positions; bomb load, 3968 lbs in each of four wing-mounted carriers, or four Hs 293, Hs 294 or FX 1400 missiles.

Above: initial production models of the Klemm L 25 were powered by 45 hp Salmson AD9 engines. The type was license-built in Britain before World War II and saw service with both the RAF and Luftwaffe.

The Ju 390 was a proposed stretched version of the Ju 290 which never reached production status, only two prototypes being produced, one of which made a 32-hour test flight to within 12 miles of the coast of the United States near New York.

Klemm L 25

Year: 1927.
Manufacturer: Klemm Leichtflugzeugbau G.mbH.
Type: trainer/liaison.
Crew: two (pilot and pupil).
Specification: L 25D.
Power plant: Hirth HM 60 R air-cooled radial engine developing 80 hp.
Dimensions: span, 42 ft 8 in; length, 24 ft 7 in; height, 6 ft 9 in; wing area, 215 sq ft.
Weights: empty, 926 lb; loaded, 1587 lb.
Performance: maximum speed, 99 mph at sea level; cruising speed, 87 mph; climb rate, 5.75 min to 3280 ft; service ceiling, 15,748 ft.
Armament: none.

A lightweight trainer built extensively in several versions over a 12 year period. A total of 600 was produced by Klemm and a further 134 under license in England. Fitted with floats, skis and wheels, the aircraft saw service with the Luftwaffe during World War II. Some British versions were impressed into RAF service.

Below: the Junkers Ju 388L-1 was fitted with a wooden ventral pannier, which housed an auxiliary fuel tank and reconnaissance cameras. Only a handful of Ju 388s entered service in the reconnaissance role during the closing weeks of World War II.

Above: this Klemm Kl 35D training aeroplane carries the badge of A/B Schule 71, a Luftwaffe flying training school located at Prossnitz in Moravia.

Klemm KI 31 and KI 35

Year: 1933.
Manufacturer: Klemm Leichtflugzeugbau G.mbH.
Type: liaison.
Crew: one (pilot plus three passengers, Kl 31; pilot and pupil/passenger Kl, 35).
Specification: Kl 35D.
Power plant: one Hirth HM 60 R air-cooled, radial engine developing 80 hp.
Dimensions: span, 34 ft 2 in; length, 24 ft 7 in; height, 6 ft 9 in; wing area, 163.61 sq ft.
Weights: Empty, 1014 lb; loaded, 1654 lb.
Performance: maximum speed, 132 mph at sea level; cruising speed, 118 mph; climb rate, 6 min to 3280 ft; service ceiling, 14,272 ft.
Armament: none.

The Kl 31 and 32 were four-seat cabin monoplanes used for liaison duties and the Kl 35 was a trainer which was extensively exported and built under license in Sweden. The Kl 35D saw considerable service with Luftwaffe training schools.

Messerschmitt Bf 108 Taifun

Year: 1934.
Manufacturer: Bayerische Flugzeugwerke A.G.
Type: liaison and communications.
Crew: one (pilot) plus three passengers.
Specification: Bf 108B.
Power plant: one Argus As 10C eight-cylinder, inverted-Vee, air-cooled engine developing 240 hp.
Dimensions: span, 34 ft 10 in; length, 27 ft 2 in; height, 6 ft 10 in; wing area, 176.46 sq ft.
Weights: empty, 1896 lb; loaded, 3086 lb.
Performance: maximum speed, 186 mph at sea level; cruising speed, 165 mph; climb rate, 1180 ft per min; service ceiling, 16,400 ft.
Armament: none.

An advanced design cabin monoplane with many innovations including automatic leading-edge slots and leading-edge hinged control surfaces with no dynamic balancing. The Bf 108 served extensively with the Luftwaffe in the communications role and continued in production after the war in France. A total of 887 was produced in Germany and some examples were still in flying condition 40 years after the flight of the prototype.

Top: a Messerschmitt Bf 109G-2 fighter aircraft of 4/Jagdgeschwader 54 operates from the waterlogged Siverskaya airfield in the northern sector of the Eastern Front during the late summer of 1942.
Above: Messerschmitt Bf 109G-5 Gustavs operate from an airfield in Italy in the summer of 1943.
Left: a Messerschmitt Bf 108 Taifun light communications aircraft pictured while serving in North Africa in 1941.
Below: a Messerschmitt Bf 109E-1 is parked on a French airfield in 1940. The fighter carries the 'Pik As' (ace of spades) emblem of Jagdgeschwader 53. Most Luftwaffe fighter units received the Bf 109F in 1941.

Messerschmitt Bf 109 Series

Year: 1938.
Manufacturer: Bayerische Flugzeugwerke, later Messerschmitt A.G. Subcontracted to various organizations and built under license by Dornier-Werke, Hispano-Aviación and Avia.
Type: fighter.
Crew: one.
Specification: Bf 109E-3.
Power plant: one Daimler-Benz DB 601A a 12-cylinder, inverted-Vee, liquid-cooled engine developing 1175 hp.
Dimensions: span, 32 ft 4 in; length, 28 ft 4 in; height, 8 ft 2 in; wing area, 176.53 sq ft.
Weights: empty, 4189 lb; loaded, 5523 lb.
Performance: maximum speed, 293 mph at sea level; 348 mph at 14,560 ft; cruising speed, 202 mph at 3280 ft; climb rate, 3280 ft per min; service ceiling, 34,450 ft.
Armament: two 20 mm MG FF cannon in wings, two 7.9 mm MG 17 machine guns in upper cowling and engine mounted 20 mm MG FF (not fitted in service).
Year: 1940.
Manufacturer: Bayerische Flugzeugwerke, later Messerschmitt A.G. Subcontracted to various organizations and built under license by Dornier-Werke, Hispano-Aviación and Avia.
Type: fighter.
Crew: one.
Specification: Bf 109 F-4.
Power plant: one Daimler-Benz DB 601E-1 12-cylinder, inverted-Vee, liquid-cooled engine developing 1350 hp.
Dimensions: span, 32 ft 6 in; length, 29 ft; height, 8 ft 6 in; wing area, 174.38 sq ft.
Weights: empty, 5269 lb; loaded (maximum), 6872 lb.
Performance: maximum speed, 334 mph at sea level, 388 mph at 21,325 ft; cruising speed, 310 mph; climb rate, 4290 ft per min; service ceiling, 39,370 ft.
Armament: one 20 mm MG 151 cannon firing through propeller hub, two 7.9 mm MG 17 machine guns in upper cowling.
Year: 1941.
Manufacturer: Bayerische Flugzeugwerke, later Messerschmitt A.G. Subcontracted to various organizations and built under license by Dornier-Werke, Hispano-Aviación and Avia.
Type: fighter.
Crew: one.
Specification: Bf 109G-6.
Power plant: one Daimler-Benz DB 605 AM 12-cylinder, inverted-Vee, liquid-cooled engine developing 1475 hp.
Dimensions: span, 32 ft 6 in; length, 29 ft; height, 8 ft 2 in; wing area, 174.36 sq ft.
Weights: empty, 5893 lb; loaded (maximum), 7491 lb.
Performance: maximum speed, 340 mph at sea level, 386 mph at 22,640 ft; cruising speed, 315 mph; climb rate, 2.9 min to 9840 ft; service ceiling, 37,890 ft.
Armament: one 30 mm MK 108 or 20 mm MG 151 cannon and two 13 mm MG 131 machine guns.

Built in greater number (30,500) than any other warplane of World War II, apart from the Soviet Il-2, the ubiquitous Bf 109 fighter was synonymous with German air power and a classic of its time.
Designed by Willi Messerschmitt, who was at that time a director of Bayerische Flugzeug-werke, from which is derived the Bf prefix, the Bf 109 first flew in 1935 and after competition with the Ar 80, Fw 159 and He 112, was chosen to equip the *Jagdgeschwader* of the expanding Luftwaffe. Messerschmitt had been unofficially advised that his inexperience in designing high-speed aircraft was likely to be a contri-

buting factor to his machine not being chosen, but this was an excuse made by Milch – who strongly believed it – since he and Messersch-mitt shared a dislike for each other.
The political infighting, which at one time looked as though it would bring an end to the Bf 109 in favor of the He 112, ended when officialdom realized that the neat low-wing monoplane was very similar to the Super-marine Spitfire fighter then being ordered into quantity production in England, which became the German fighter's main antagonist.
Early versions of the aircraft fought in con-siderable numbers in Spain during the Civil War and, by the time war clouds gathered over Europe in 1939, the E version was already in service in some numbers.
The angular cowling and distinctive tapered spinner of the E disappeared on the F, which many claim to be the most esthetically pleasing of the series. In the early stages of its career, the F was disliked by many pilots who considered it to be underarmed and less maneuverable than the E. The armament was revised but already escalating weights were making the aircraft more difficult to handle, a problem that increased greatly with the G. The Gustav as it was known, was a formidable aircraft in terms of armament, but it presented considerable problems to pilots who had to be constantly alert to its idiosyncrasies. The G was built in greater quantity than any other model, over 70 percent of the total production being of this version.
The aircraft was subjected to many proposed roles including a carrier-borne fighter desig-nated the T, a very high altitude machine (the H) and a unique long-range version with twin fuselages, the Z. As well as being used in the normal interceptor role, the Bf 109 was also used as a fighter bomber, night fighter and for ground support. Throughout its production the various design changes resulted in con-siderable differences in outline shape, cul-minating in the tall-finned late G and K models. It would be true to say that the aircraft was really stretched beyond its original design envelope and in many ways the final versions bore little resemblance to the machines from which they originated. It could be argued that Messerschmitt would have been better advised to have had a follow-up on the drawing board. However, such was the state of the German war effort that to abandon a design that could be changed to meet a variety of circumstances in favor of a new one with all its associated development problems would have disrupted production to an unacceptable degree.
The main variants of the basic airframe are listed below, but it should be kept in mind that these, like most other German aircraft, could be equipped with many factory or field modifi-cations.

Below: this view of a Messerschmitt Bf 109G-6 shows the underwing mounted MG 151 cannons.

Above: a cutaway view of the Messerschmitt Bf 109E-4 is marked as the fighter flown by Oblt Franz von Werra of JG 3, which was shot down over Kent in September 1940.

Far left: this Messerschmitt Bf 109E-3 is preserved in Britain at the Battle of Britain Museum, Hendon.
Left: this Messerschmitt Bf 109G-2 was captured in the Middle East in 1942 and shipped to the UK in 1944.

W. Nr. 1480

Below: this is the same Bf 109G-2 as pictured above left. It is here painted in Luftwaffe desert camouflage. The Galland hood is incorrect for this model, but a framed canopy has since been fitted.

Messerschmitt Bf 109 Series

Type	Engine	Armament	Remarks
Bf 109B-1	Jumo 210D	three MG 17 machine guns	
Bf 109B-2	Jumo 210E/G	three MG 17 machine guns	
Bf 109C-1	Jumo 210G	four MG 17 machine guns	
Bf 109C-2	Jumo 210G	five MG 17 machine guns	
Bf 109C-3	Jumo 210G	four MG 17 machine guns one MG FF cannon	
Bf 109D-1	DB 600A	two MG 17 machine guns one MG FF cannon	
Bf 109D-2	DB 600A	four MG 17 machine guns	
Bf 109E-1	DB 601A	two MG 17 machine guns two MG FF cannon	E-1/B was a fighter-bomber version
Bf 109E-3	DB 601 Aa	two MG 17 machine guns two MG FF cannon	
Bf 109E-4	DB 601Aa	two MG 17 machine guns two MG FF cannon	E-4/B was a fighter-bomber version
Bf 109E-5	DB 601Aa	two MG 17 machine guns	
Bf 109E-6	DB 601N	two MG 17 machine guns	
Bf 109E-7	DB 601N	two MG 17 machine guns two MG FF cannon	E-7/U2 was a fighter-bomber version
Bf 109E-8	DB 601E	two MG 17 machine guns two MG FF cannon	
Bf 109E-9	DB 601E	two MG 17 machine guns	
Bf 109T	DB 601Aa	two MG 17 machine guns	Proposed carrier fighter
Bf 109F-1	DB 601N	two MG 17 machine guns one MG FF cannon	
Bf 109F-2	DB 601N	two MG 17 machine guns one MG 151 15 mm cannon	
Bf 109F-2/ Trop	DB 601N	As F-2	Tropicalized version of F-2
Bf 109F-3	DB 601E	As F-2	Used 87 octane B4 fuel
Bf 109F-4	DB 601E	two MG 17 machine guns one MG 151 20 mm cannon	Larger caliber cannon with less ammunition F-4/B was a bomber version
Bf 109F-5	DB 601E	two MG 17 machine guns	Cannon removed and aircraft fitted with vertical camera
Bf 109F-6	DB 601E	None	Reconnaissance version with interchangeable camera bay
Bf 109G-1	DB 605A	two MG 17 machine guns one MG 151 20 mm cannon	Also produced as G-1/Trop
Bf 109G-2	DB 605A	four MG 17 machine guns	
Bf 109G-3	DB 605A	two MG 17 machine guns one MG 151 20 mm cannon	Fitted with FuG 16z radio
Bf 109G-4	DB 605A	two MG 17 machine guns	As G-2 but with Fug 16z
Bf 109G-5	DB 605D	two MG 131 machine guns one MG 151 20 mm cannon	
Bf 109G-6	DB 605AM	two MG 131 machine guns three MG 151 20 mm cannons	

The G series was designed from the outset to accept many different *Rustsatze* conversions sets and therefore appeared with a variety of suffix codes after the main designation. The G was also equipped with various modified DB 605 engines, including the AS, ASB, ASM and ASD. It was also used in the fighter-bomber role and could be fitted with long-range tanks.

Bf 109G-8	DB 605A-1 or 605AS	one MK 108 30 mm cannon or one MG 151 20 mm cannon	Long-range reconnaissance version with single camera
Bf 109G-10	DB 605D	two MG 131 machine guns one MK 108 30 mm cannon	R/1 had central ETC rack and R/2 had MG 131s removed and replaced by a single camera
Bf 109G-12	DB 605A	one MK 108 30 mm cannon	Proposed two-seat trainer
Bf 109G-14	DB 605AM	two MG 131 machine guns one MG 151 20 mm cannon	
Bf 109G-16	DB 605D	two MG 131 machine guns three MG 151 20 mm cannons	Fitted with armored oil coolers and radiator, also center-line bomb rack
Bf 109K-4	DB 605 ASCM or DCM	one MK 108 or 103 30 mm cannon and two MG 131 machine guns	K-4 was essentially a pressurized version of K-2
Bf 109K-6	DB 605DCM	two MG 131 machine guns one MK 108 30 mm cannon or two MK 103 30 mm cannons	Carried two MK 103 cannon in wing gondolas and MG 131 in cowling
Bf 109K-14	DB 605L	two MG 131 machine guns one MK 108 30 mm cannon	Fitted with the long awaited two-stage supercharged engine. Very few reached operational status

Gross weight of the prototype Bf 109 was 4195 lb, while that of the K-6 was 7495 lb; some of the heavier armed G-6 series turned the scales at over 8000 lbs, so these figures emphasize the considerable changes, as well as the soundness of the basic airframe design.

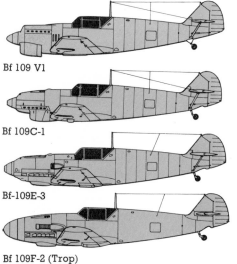

Top: this Messerschmitt Bf 109E-4 was flown by Adolf Galland, an outstanding German fighter leader, during the Battle of Britain. Galland commanded III/JG 26 and later became General of the fighter arm.
Above: this Bf 109F-4 (Trop) was the mount of Hauptmann Hans-Joachim Marseille, a remarkably successful ace who fought with Jagdgeschwader 27 in North Africa.

Bf 109 V1

Bf 109C-1

Bf-109E-3

Bf 109F-2 (Trop)

Bf 109G-6

Bf 109K-6

Messerschmitt Bf 110 Series

Year: 1936.
Manufacturer: Bayerische Flugzeugwerke later Messerschmitt A.G. Subcontracted to various organizations throughout Germany.
Type: long-range, heavy, all weather and night fighter.
Crew: two or three (pilot, observer, gunner, or radar operator/gunner).
Specification: Bf 110C-1.
Power plant: two Daimler-Benz DB 601A-1 12-cylinder, liquid-cooled, inverted-Vee engines each developing 1100 hp.
Dimensions: span, 53 ft 4 in; length, 39 ft 7 in; height, 13 ft 6 in; wing area, 413.33 sq ft.
Weights: empty, 9755 lb; loaded (maximum), 14,880 lb.
Performance: maximum speed, 295 mph at sea level, 336 mph at 19,685 ft; cruising speed, 304 mph at 16,400 ft; climb rate, 2165 ft per min; service ceiling, 32,810 ft.
Armament: two 20 mm MG FF cannon and four 7.9 mm MG 17 machine guns in nose, one 7.9 mm MG 15 machine gun on flexible mount in rear of cockpit.
Specification: Bf 110F-2.
Year: 1940.
Power plant: two Daimler-Benz DB 601F 12-cylinder, liquid-cooled, inverted-Vee engines each developing 1350 hp.
Dimensions: span, 53 ft 4 in; length, 39 ft 7 in; height, 13 ft 6 in; wing area, 413.33 sq ft.
Weights: empty, 12,346 lb; loaded (maximum), 15,873 lb.
Performance: maximum speed, 310 mph at sea level, 352 mph at 17,700 ft; cruising speed, 311 mph at 14,760 ft; climb rate, 9.2 min to 19,685 ft; service ceiling, 35,760 ft.
Armament: two 20 mm MG FF cannon and four 7.9 mm MG 17 machine guns in nose, one 7.9 mm MG 15 machine gun on flexible mount in rear of cockpit.
Specification: Bf 110G-4c/R3.
Year: 1942.
Power plant: two Daimler-Benz DB 605B-1 12-cylinder, inverted-Vee, liquid-cooled engines each developing 1475 hp.
Dimensions: span, 53 ft 4 in; length, 42 ft 10 in; height, 13 ft 8 in; wing area, 413.33 sq ft.
Weights: empty, 11,220 lb; loaded (maximum), 21,800 lb.
Performance: maximum speed, 311 mph at sea level, 342 mph at 22,900 ft; cruising speed, 317 mph at 19,685 ft; climb rate, 2170 ft per min; service ceiling, 36,090 ft.
Armament: two 30 mm MK 108 cannon and two 20 mm MG 151 cannon firing forward and one 7.9 mm MG 81Z twin machine gun on flexible mount in rear of cockpit.

Planned to act as a heavily armed escort for long-range bombers, making up in firepower for its lack of maneuverability, the concept of the Bf 110 was sound, always presupposing that a degree of air superiority had been achieved. The initial success of the aircraft appeared to

vindicate its role in the early campaigns of World War II, but when faced with well-handled single-seat fighters its shortcomings became evident and during the Battle of Britain it could only operate with its own fighter escort. Despite the criticism it has received at the hands of postwar historians, the Bf 110 eventually achieved considerable success in the night fighter role and it is in this capacity that it found its forte.

Top: a pair of Messerschmitt Bf 110E-1/U1 night fighters of 7/NJG 4 fly over France. This sub-variant carried the *Spanner-Anlage* infra-red sensor.
Above: groundcrew work on the cameras of a Messerschmitt Bf 110C-5 reconnaissance aircraft in the Desert.
Below: this Messerschmitt Bf 110G-4/R1 of 6/NJG 6 landed in error at Dubendorf, Switzerland, in 1944.

Above: a Messerschmitt Bf 110E-1/U1 night fighter of 7 Staffel of Nachtjagdgeschwader 4, 1941.

Above left: groundcrew load an Rb 50/30 camera onto a Bf 110C-5. The forward-firing armament was reduced to four MG 17 machine guns.
Above: this Messerschmitt Bf 110C-3 *Zerstörer* carries the shark mouth marking of II/ZG 76.
Left: this view of a Bf 110G-4 night fighter clearly shows the aerials of the Lichtenstein C-1 radar.

Developed through a range of Jumo and Daimler-Benz engines, plus a wide variety of armament, including the provision of bomb racks, as well as the fitting of cameras, the aircraft served the Luftwaffe well in practically every theater carrying out a wide range of duties which included air-sea rescue protection and liaison work.

Production was scheduled to end in 1942, but the failure of the proposed replacement Me 210 and 410, resulted in it being reinstated and modified well beyond its original design.

The last production model, the Bf 110G, was produced in greater quantities than any other variant. Although it became rather sluggish when loaded with radar and heavy armament, the G series night fighters still provided a steady gun platform and took a heavy toll of RAF night bombers. A total of 6050 of all types was produced, the last 45 being delivered during the closing weeks of the war.

Messerschmitt Me 163 Komet

Year: 1941.
Manufacturer: Messerschmitt A.G.
Type: fighter.
Crew: one.
Specification: Me 163B-1a.
Power plant: one Walter HWK 509A-2 rocket motor developing a maximum thrust of 3750 lb.
Dimensions: span, 30 ft 7 in; length, 19 ft 2 in; height, 9 ft 1 in; wing area, 199.13 sq ft.
Weights: empty, 4200 lb; loaded (maximum), 9500 lb.
Performance: maximum speed, 515 mph at sea level, 596 mph at 9840 ft; climb rate, 16,000 ft per min; service ceiling, 39,500 ft.
Armament: two 20 mm MG 151 or two 30 mm MK 108 cannon.

One of the most revolutionary aircraft to enter service in World War II, the Me 163 was developed from the researches into tailless designs by Dr Alexander Lippisch. Starting life as an experimental glider in 1938, development of the Me 163 was transferred to Messerschmitt's top secret Section L in late 1939. First flown in the spring of 1941 as a glider, the aircraft proved to have excellent handling qualities and that summer it was delivered to Peenemünde for the fitting of its rocket engine.

Although the aircraft handled well under power and in fact was pushed to speeds well in excess of the then world air-speed record, problems were continually encountered with its highly volatile fuel, as well as its rudimentary landing skid. The Me 163 was an aircraft in which everything had to be precisely right especially during landings, when any over-correction or tendency to yaw could cause a fatal swing on touchdown, resulting in a somersault and explosion of gases in the fuel tanks.

These were hardly the right ingredients for a combat aircraft likely to be handled by pilots of varying skills, but development and production were rushed ahead with the result that the Me 163 entered service in June 1944. The rapid climb and acceleration of the aircraft made it a formidable adversary, but it was vulnerable during the landing approach, when it proved easy prey to marauding Allied fighters. The impact it made against USAAF day bombers was minimal, but if viewed in relative terms, its historical contribution to air warfare is considerable.

Below: the Messerschmitt Me 163B rocket fighter was operationally tested by EKdo 16 in the summer of 1944.

Above: the Messerschmitt Me 410A-1/U2 was a *Zerstörer* conversion of the basic A-1 fast bomber.

The C version was equipped with a retractable tailwheel, had a longer fuselage and increased span as well as a more powerful engine. It formed the basis of development for the improved Me 263 of which only one example was completed. Some 400 Me 163s were built in Germany and it was also being produced in Japan when the war ended.

Messerschmitt Me 210

Year: 1939.
Manufacturer: Messerschmitt A.G.
Type: heavy fighter.
Crew: two (pilot and observer).
Specification: Me 210A-1.
Power plant: two Daimler-Benz DB 601F 12-cylinder, liquid-cooled, inverted-Vee engines each developing 1350 hp.
Dimensions: span, 53 ft 7 in; length, 39 ft 9 in; height, 14 ft; wing area, 389.66 sq ft.
Weights: empty, 15,586 lb; loaded (maximum), 21,397 lb.
Performance: maximum speed, 288 mph at sea level, 350 mph at 17,820 ft; climb rate, 7.5 min to 13,120 ft; service ceiling, 29,200 ft.
Armament: two 20 mm MG 151 cannon and two 7.9 mm MG 17 machine guns firing forward, two 13 mm MG 131 machine guns in fuselage – mounted remotely operated barbettes firing aft.

Messerschmitt Me 410 Hornisse

Year: 1942.
Manufacturer: Messerschmitt A.G.
Type: heavy fighter, reconnaissance and light bomber.
Crew: two (pilot, observer).
Specification: Me 410A-1/U2.
Power plant: two Daimler-Benz DB 603A twelve-cylinder, liquid-cooled, inverted-Vee engines each developing 1850 hp.
Dimensions: span, 53 ft 8 in; length, 41 ft; height, 14 ft; wing area, 389.69 sq ft.
Weights: empty, 16,574 lb; loaded, 21,276 lb.
Performance: maximum speed, 315 mph at sea level, 388 mph at 21,980 ft; cruising speed, 365 mph; climb rate, 10.60 sec to 22,000 ft; service ceiling, 32,810 ft.
Armament: four 20 mm MG 151 cannon, two 7.9 mm MG 17 machine guns firing forward, and two 13 mm MG 131 in remotely-controlled barbettes firing aft.
Specification: Me 410B-1.
Year: 1943.
Power plant: two Daimler-Benz DB 603G 12-cylinder, inverted-Vee, liquid-cooled engines each developing 1900 hp.
Dimensions: span, 53 ft 8 in; length, 41 ft; height, 14 ft; wing area, 389.69 sq ft.
Weights: empty, 17,598 lb; loaded, 24,772 lb.
Performance: maximum speed, 362 mph at 13,125 ft, 391 mph at 26,575 ft; cruising speed, 362 mph; climb rate, 22.5 min to 26,250 ft; service ceiling, approximately 31,000 ft.
Armament: two 20 mm MG 151 cannon, two 7.9 mm MG 17 machine guns firing forward, and two 13 mm MG 131 in remotely-controlled barbettes firing aft; bomb load, 2205 lb.

Intended as a successor to the Bf 110 and incorporating many of the features used in that aircraft's design and structure, the Me 210 proved to be a dismal failure. Its only saving grace was that it sired the slightly more successful Me 410. First flown in September 1939 and ordered into quantity production from the drawing board, the aircraft proved to be unstable and subject to structural failure. Service evaluation which commenced in 1941 quickly highlighted its many failures and after many accidents a commission which had been established to investigate the aircraft, recommended that all production be stopped and the Bf 110 reinstated. As well as representing a considerable financial loss to the company, this fiasco resulted in lost production and pressure

Above: the Me 410 was a somewhat better aircraft than its predecessor, the Me 210, but even so was not a complete success. The aircraft illustrated is a Messerschmitt Me 410A-3, a specialized reconnaissance variant.

for Willi Messerschmitt to resign from his position as chairman and managing director.

Despite these problems, development work continued on the Me 210 and the stability problem was overcome. Automatic slots were fitted to the wing leading edges and the entire rear fuselage was redesigned. A proposal to develop the aircraft into the Me 310 high-altitude fighter bomber was dropped in favor of the less radical Me 410.

The Me 210s which reached the Luftwaffe were used on the Eastern Front and in the Mediterranean as well as in limited operations over the United Kingdom in the fighter bomber and reconnaissance roles.

The Me 410 achieved considerably more success and over 1160 were produced (production of the 210 was approximately 550). The aircraft was used as a fighter, intruder, reconnaissance aircraft, torpedo bomber and light bomber, some versions being equipped with Hohentweil search radar. Although neither aircraft can be considered successful they were equipped with a tremendous number of optional armament packs, as well as a variety of other equipment, the permutations possible being in excess of 140.

Messerschmitt Me 261

Year: 1941.
Manufacturer: Messerschmitt A.G.
Type: long-range reconnaissance.
Crew: five (pilot, copilot, observer, radio operator, engineer).
Specification: Me 261 V-3.
Power plant: two Daimler-Benz DB 601A-1/B-1 24-cylinder, liquid-cooled engines each developing 3100 hp.
Dimensions: span, 88 ft 2 in; length, 54 ft 9 in; height, 15 ft 6 in; wing area, 818.06 sq ft.
Weights: no data available.
Performance: maximum speed, 305 mph at sea level, 385 mph at 9820 ft; cruising speed, 248 mph; service ceiling, 27,100 ft.
Armament: none.

Initially conceived as a long-range record-breaking aircraft to carry the Olympic Flame

from Berlin to Tokyo, the Me 261 captured the imagination of Adolf Hitler who followed its development with close interest. Unofficially dubbed *Adolfine* the aircraft never achieved production status, only three prototypes being produced. The third of these was used by the *Aüfklarungsgruppe des Oberbefehlshabers der Luftwaffe,* for long-range reconnaissance missions in 1943.

Messerschmitt Me 262

Year: 1942.
Manufacturer: Messerschmitt A.G.
Type: fighter.
Crew: one.
Specification: Me 262A-1a.
Power plant: two Junkers Jumo 004B-1, -2 or -3 axial-flow turbojets each rated at 1980 lb static thrust.
Dimensions: span, 41 ft; length, 34 ft 9 in; height, 12 ft 7 in; wing area, 234 sq ft.
Weights: empty, 8378 lb; loaded, 14,101 lb.
Performance: maximum speed, 514 mph at sea level, 540 mph at 19,685 ft; range, 525 miles; climb rate, 3937 ft per min at 19,685 ft; time to 29,560 ft, 13.1 mins; service ceiling, 37,565 ft.
Armament: four 30 mm MK 108 cannons in nose.

Postwar evidence has proved that many of the claims put forward as reasons for delays in the service debut of the Me 262 were unfounded. It is true that there was pressure to change the configuration of the aircraft to that of a bomber, a role which it did in fact carry out, but the main reasons for its late arrival with the Luftwaffe were associated with its engines. First flown with piston engines in April 1941, the Me 262 was conceived in 1938 when Messerschmitt was asked to carry out a design study for a turbojet-powered aircraft.

A fairly long gestation period culminated in production models reaching the Luftwaffe in July 1944, by which time production far exceeded that of similar Allied fighters. The speed, maneuverability and firepower of the aircraft certainly created problems for the Allies and there can be no doubt that, if the teething troubles had been cured earlier, the aircraft could well have restored Germany to the position of air supremacy that it had enjoyed in 1939/40. Even so, it is doubtful if this would have changed the ultimate outcome of the war, although it may well have prolonged it.

The following is a resume of the main production and proposed versions:

Me 262A-1a	Initial production model
Me 262A-1a/U1	Armament supplemented by two 20 mm MG 151 cannons
Me 262A-1a/U3	Armament reduced to two 30 mm cannons and camera bay added
Me 262A-1b	As 1a but fitted with racks for 24 55 mm R4M rockets
Me 262A-2a	Fighter bomber as 1a but with 1102 lb bomb load
Me 262A-2a/U1	Proposed dive bomber with two 30 mm MK 108 cannons
Me 262A-2a/U2	Modified 2a with glazed nose and Lotfe 7H bomb-sight. No armament
Me 262A-3	Proposed ground-attack aircraft
Me 262A-5a	Reconnaissance version with drop tanks and A-1/U3 armament
Me 262B-1a	Dual-control trainer. Armament as A-1a
Me 262B-1a/U1	Two-seat night fighter with FuG 218 and Naxos FuG 350. Armament as A-1a
Me 262B-2a	Modified version of B-1a with 30 mm MK 108 Schräge Musik
Me 262C-1a	Proposed version with rocket motor in tail
Me 262C-2b	BMW 003A engines and BMW 718 rocket motors. One built
Me 262C-3	Project only with Walter rocket booster

Total production is often quoted as 1100 but the records of Dept 6, Quartermaster General, Luftwaffe, indicate that 1294 were taken on charge. Despite its tactical misuse, the Me 262 was a fine airplane and the first operational jet to serve in quantity with any air force.

Right: the fighter-bomber version of the Messerschmitt Me 262 was named *Sturmvogel* (stormbird).
Below: this Me 262 was shipped to the United States for evaluation.

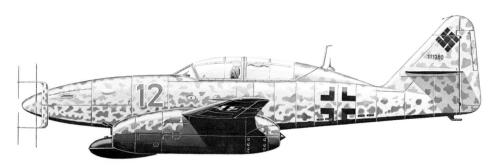

Left: the only Luftwaffe unit to operate the Messerschmitt Me 262B-1a/U1 night fighter was Kommando Welter (later 10/ NJG 11), which flew in defence of Berlin from February 1945.
Below left: this Messerschmitt Me 262A-2a served with 2 Staffel of Kampfgeschwader 51. It was evaluated in Britain after World War II and has been preserved in the markings of its original unit.
Bottom: the Me 262B-1a/U1 was a conversion of the two-seat trainer model. This aircraft is displayed at Willow Grove Naval Air Station, Pa.

Messerschmitt Me 323 Gigant

Year: 1941.
Manufacturer: Messerschmitt A.G.
Type: general-purpose transport.
Crew: up to seven (pilot, observer, engineer, radio operator and 3 gunners).
Specification: Me 323E-2.
Power plant: six Gnome-Rhône 14N 48/49 14-cylinder, air-cooled radial engines each developing 1140 hp.
Dimensions: span, 180 ft 5 in; length, 93 ft 6 in; height, 31 ft 6 in; wing area, 3229.17 sq ft.
Weights: empty, 64,066 lb; loaded (maximum), 99,210 lb.
Performance: maximum speed at weight of 72,580 lb, 150 mph at 4920 ft; cruising speed, 130 mph at 4920 ft; range, 810 miles at 13,120 ft; climb rate, 866 ft per min; service ceiling, 14,760 ft.
Armament: two 20 mm MG 151 cannon in wing turrets, seven 13 mm MG 131 and up to eight 7.9 mm MG 15 machine guns all firing from various blister, beam and flight deck positions.

The Me 323 was a powered version of the Me 321 glider which entered service in 1942. Operated in the Mediterranean, and Eastern Fronts in tactical-support roles and evacuation. It proved very vulnerable to fighter attack despite its heavy armament. Total production was 211, 201 of which were taken on charge.

Above: the Me 323 Gigant was a powered version of the Me 321 glider, the Messerschmitt Me 323 V2 being pictured.

Siebel Fh 104 Hallore

Year: 1937.
Manufacturer: Siebel Flugzeugwerke K.G.
Type: communications and liaison.
Crew: one (pilot) plus four passengers.
Specification: Fh 104A.
Power plant: two Hirth HM 508C air-cooled, inverted-Vee engines each developing 280 hp.
Dimensions: span, 39 ft 7 in; length, 31 ft 2 in; height, 8 ft 8 in; wing area, 240.04 sq ft.
Weights: empty, 3330 lb; loaded, 5180 lb.
Performance: maximum speed, 217 mph at sea level; cruising speed, 194 mph; climb rate, 1.5 min to 3280 ft; service ceiling, 21,653 ft.
Armament: none.

Designed by Hans Klemm and originally designated Kl 104, production of the Fh 104 was transferred to Siebel who took over Klemm's factory at Halle. A total of 48 was produced and the type served as VIP transport and in the communications role with the Luftwaffe.

Siebel Si 201

Year: 1938.
Manufacturer: Siebel Flugzeugwerke K.G.
Type: airborne observation post and army cooperation.
Crew: two (pilot and observer).
Specification: Si 201 V1.
Power plant: one Argus As 10C eight-cylinder, inverted-Vee, air-cooled engine developing 240 hp.
Dimensions: span, 45 ft 11 in; length, 34 ft 1 in; height, 11 ft 2 in; wing area, 333.68 sq ft.
Weights: empty, 2469 lb; loaded, 3175 lb.
Performance: maximum speed, 115 mph at sea level; cruising speed, 93 mph; climb rate, 827 ft per min; service ceiling, 18,050 ft.
Armament: none.

Designed in 1935 to meet the requirements for a short takeoff and landing aircraft, the Si 201 faced many development problems and did not fly until 1938, by which time the Fi 156 was already in production. Its performance was disappointing and the project was abandoned.

Siebel Si 204

Year: 1941.
Manufacturer: Siebel Flugzeugwerke K.G.
Type: communications and trainer.
Crew: two (pilot and observer) plus eight passengers.
Specification: Si 204A.
Power plant: two Argus As 410 12-cylinder inverted-Vee, air-cooled engines each developing 360 hp.
Dimensions: span, 70 ft; length, 42 ft 8 in; height, 13 ft 11 in; wing area, 495.10 sq ft.
Weights: empty, 7628 lb; loaded, 11,023 lb.
Performance: maximum speed, 200 mph at 9842 ft; cruising speed, 186 mph; climb rate, 846 ft per min; service ceiling, 20,997 ft.
Armament: none.

Developed from the smaller Si 104, the 204 had an all-metal stressed-skin structure and was the Luftwaffe's leading light transport and trainer. Together with the 600 hp Argus As 411 engined D version, the aircraft was also used to train radio, radar and navigation aircrew as well as to provide instrument training for pilots. In the communications and transport roles it also doubled as a freighter and ambulance aircraft. A few D versions were pressed into service in the night ground-attack role. Most production was carried out in France by SNCAC and over 1500 were delivered. Production continued postwar in Czechoslovakia under the designation C-103.

Mistel Composite Aircraft

Launching one aircraft from another was not a new idea when it was suggested to the RLM in 1941. Many experiments had been carried out in the United States and the Soviet Union whereby, in most cases, fighters were mounted as parasites on airships and bomber aircraft to provide some form of protective cover. Similarly, the use of time-expired bombers packed with explosives and guided to their targets, either by radio control or a pilot who aimed the aircraft before abandoning it, was tried by the Italians and Americans with S.M. 79s and B-17s. The German conception was a combination of both methods, whereby a bomber was attached to a fighter whose pilot flew the combination to the target area, released the explosive-packed bomber at its target and returned to base.

The war situation in 1941 was such that it was considered hardly worth following up the proposal since, to all intents and purposes, Germany looked to be approaching victory. However, by 1943 the situation had dramatically changed and any method of carrying the fight to the enemy was worth pursuing. Experiments by DFS, in which a 230 glider was flown beneath a light aircraft, proved the feasability of the scheme, and work was started on combining a Ju 88 and a Bf 109.

In addition to carrying an explosive load, the bomber also acted as a tanker aircraft, the carrier drawing fuel from it before initiating the release procedure. The first operational Mistel had the crew compartment replaced by a 7716 lb warhead attached to which was a long-impact fuse. This went into service with 2/KG 101. Its first attack was against Allied invasion shipping in the Seine Bay on the night of 24/25 June 1944. Attacks were also carried out against shipping in the English Channel and eventually, without success, against Scapa Flow, when three combinations crashed en route and the other two failed to find the target.

II/KG 200, formed from III/KG 66 became the main Mistel unit receiving 100 aircraft, mainly Mistel 2, in 1945. The Mistel 3 utilized new Ju 88s rather than refurbished aircraft and by the end of hostilities a total of some 250 combinations had been delivered. Heavy losses and tactical use against military targets lessened the impact of the weapon which did not materially affect Germany's ultimate defeat.

The main Mistel types were:

Mistel S 1	Ju 88A-4 and Bf 109 F
Mistel S 2	Ju 88G-1 and Fw 190A-8
Mistel S 3a	Ju 88A-6 and Fw 190A-6
Mistel 1	Ju 88A-4 and Bf 109F
Mistel 2	Ju 88G-1 and Fw 190A-6
Mistel 3c	Ju 88G-10 or H-4 and Fw 190A-8

Below: this Siebel Si 204D crash-landed during its service with the Czech air force after World War II.

Part Three
POST

Above: the Lockheed F-104G Starfighter has earned a degree of notoriety in German service. This aircraft flies with the Bundesmarine's MFG 1.

WAR

Republic F-84F Thunderstreak/RF-84F Thunderflash

Year: 1956.
Manufacturer: Republic Aviation Corporation, United States.
Type: fighter, fighter-bomber (F-84F), fighter-reconnaissance (RF-84F).
Crew: one.
Specification: F-84F (Details for RF-84F in parentheses)
Power plant: one Wright J65-W-3 Sapphire turbojet rated at 7220 lb st (J65-W-7 rated at 7800 lb st).
Dimensions: span, 33 ft 7 in; length, 43 ft 5 in (47 ft 8 in); height, 15 ft; wing area, 325 sq ft (347 sq ft).
Weights: empty, 13,645 lb (14,014 lb); loaded, 25,226 lb (25,390 lb).
Performance: maximum speed, 658 mph at sea level (629 mph at sl); 608 mph at 35,000 ft (582 mph at 35,000 ft); cruising speed, 539 mph (542 mph); combat ceiling, 42,250 ft (36,900 ft); service ceiling, 36,150 ft (39,390 ft); climb rate, 7.8 min to 35,000 ft (15.8 min to 35,000 ft).
Armament: six 0.50 in machine guns in nose (four 0.50 in machine guns in wings); external ordnance, 6000 lb.

Above: this RF-84F Thunderflash served with Aufklärungsgeschwader 51.

During the late 1940s the funding of new aircraft projects was limited by the pressures of economic recovery and the already widespread allocations to the latest developments in aerodynamics and engine technology. As a means of offering a relatively cheap swept-wing fighter to the USAF, Republic decided to adapt their already successful straight-wing F-84 Thunderjet to have swept flying surfaces. This project evolved as the YF-96A and first flew in June 1950. It was the outbreak of the Korean War which spurred further development and adoption of the license-built Sapphire engine and further design changes led to the YF-84F Thunderstreak. The first production machine flew in November 1952, with deliveries to the

Below: six Luftwaffe fighter-bomber wings flew the Republic F-84F Thunderstreak. This example carries the markings of JBG 34, which was based at Memmingen. The Thunderstreaks were retired in 1967.

USAF starting in 1954. In all 2711 were built, of which some 1300 went to NATO forces, with 450 to the Luftwaffe. By adapting the Thunderstreak to have wing-root engine intakes and a new camera nose, the RF-84F Thunderflash reconnaissance aircraft was evolved; production totalled 718 aircraft, of which 386 went to foreign air forces including 108 to the Luftwaffe. In Luftwaffe service, the F-84F Thunderstreak equipped six operational fighter-bomber wings (JBG31 – 36) with service introduction and continuation training undertaken by various *Waffenschule* (notably WS-30 and WS-10). F-84Fs served operationally from 1958 – 67, when several examples were transferred to Greece and Turkey. The RF-84F equipped two photo-reconnaissance wings (*Aufklarungsgeschwader* 51 and 52), with training by WS-50, and this type served from 1959-65.

Piaggio P.149D

Year: 1957.
Manufacturer: Piaggio & C., S.p.A. (Italy), and under license by Focke-Wulf GmbH (Germany).
Type: basic trainer.
Crew: two.
Specification: P.149D.
Power plant: one (Piaggio-built) Lycoming GO-480-BIA6 six-cylinder horizontally-opposed, air-cooled engine rated at 275 hp.
Dimensions: span, 36 ft 6 in; length, 28 ft 9 in; height, 9 ft 6 in; wing area, 203 sq ft.
Weights: empty, 2557 lb; loaded (maximum), 3704 lb; maximum aerobatic, 3190 lb.
Performance: maximum speed, 192 mph at sea level, 177 mph at 6560 ft; cruising speed, 168 mph at 7500 ft; initial climb rate, 980 ft per min; service ceiling, 19,800 ft; maximum range, 680 miles.
Armament: nil.

Above: this Piaggio P. 149D was built under license by Focke-Wulf and was serving with *Waffenschule* 50 in 1967. Most trainers of this type were withdrawn from use in the 1970s, but some 40 remain in service.

The Piaggio P.149 was a four-seat touring air-craft developed from the P.148 two-seat primary trainer, which first flew on 19 June 1953. From this was developed the two-seat P.149D military trainer which was selected by the new Luftwaffe in 1955 and one example was delivered to Germany for evaluation in 1956. The parent company was scheduled to supply 76 machines and a further 300 would be built under license by Focke-Wulf in Germany. These quantities were respectively reduced to 72 and 194 machines. Initial deliveries from Piaggio commenced in May 1957 and 16 were supplied in

component form for Focke-Wulf to assemble (these being included in the quantity from Focke-Wulf).

These first batches were delivered to the *Flugzeugführerschule Section S* (FFS-S) at Memmingen, and later the FFS-C at Diepholz. All the fighter, fighter-bomber, reconnaissance and two of the transport wings received several examples for communications and instrument rating purposes, as well as the three main flying training schools (WS-10, 30 and 50). Many of the remaining nonoperational units used them, and although most of the aircraft were withdrawn from service in the early 1970s, by 1980 some 40 were still serving with the more-recently formed *Jagdbombergeschwader* (JBG) 49 at Furstenfeldbruck, their proposed replacement by the RFB Fantrainer having been deferred.

Sikorsky H-34 (S-58) Choctaw

Year: 1957.
Manufacturer: Sikorsky Aircraft.
Type: utility helicopter.
Crew: two, plus up to 14 passengers.
Specification: H-34G Choctaw.
Power plant: one Wright R-1820-84 air-cooled radial engine rated at 1525 hp.
Dimensions: rotor diameter, 56 ft; length (fuselage), 46 ft 9 in; height, 15 ft 11 in.
Weights: empty, 7480 lb; loaded (maximum), 12,650 lb.
Performance: maximum speed, 132 mph; cruising speed, 97 mph; service ceiling, 9524 ft; maximum climb rate at sea level, 1100 ft per min; range, 247 miles.
Armament: nil.

Developed from the successful S-55 series of helicopters, the S-58 first flew on 8 March 1954 and soon entered large-scale production for the United States services, also finding a ready export market and widespread civilian use. The type was built under license in France by Sud Aviation and in Great Britain by Westland Helicopters in a turbine-powered version known as the Wessex. An initial batch of 26 H-34s commenced delivery to Germany in 1957, 21 for the Heeresflieger and five going to the Luftwaffe's *Flugzeugführerschule* (FFS) at Memmingen for crew training. This was followed by a second batch of 25 machines, again mainly for the Heeresflieger, but with five for the Bundesmarine. The final delivery of 94 Choctaws (H-34G and J versions) under MAP funding were all ex-US Navy machines; of these 19 went to the Bundesmarine's *Marinefliegergeschwader* (MFG) 5 at Kiel-Holtenau for SAR, ASW and communications duties, and 24 were diverted direct to Israel without seeing German service. The remainder were delivered to the Heeresflieger, which used the type as a heavy lift and assault helicopter, serving with Heeres-

Below: the Sikorsky H-34 served with all three German services. This H-34G belonged to the Heeresflieger's operational training unit HFS(L) 102, based at Buckeburg. The army was the major user of the H-34.

Aerospatiale SA315 & SA318 Alouette II

Year: 1958.
Manufacturer: Aerospatiale, France.
Type: light observation and utility helicopter.
Crew: four to five.
Specification: SA318 Alouette-Astazou.
Power plant: one Turbomeca Astazou II shaft turbine rated at 530 shp.
Dimensions: rotor diameter, 33 ft 6 in; length (fuselage), 32 ft; height, 9 ft.
Weights: empty, 1961 lb; loaded (maximum), 3630 lb.
Performance: maximum speed at sea level, 127 mph; cruising speed at sea level, 112 mph; maximum range, 447 miles; service ceiling, 10,800 ft.
Armament: nil.

Designed and built by Sud Aviation (later incorporated into Aerospatiale) the SE 3130 Alouette II first flew on 12 March 1955 and in 1958 set up five new helicopter records as well as becoming the first turbine-powered helicopter in the world to receive an American FAA Certificate of Airworthiness. Large-scale production was undertaken, with many exports. The designation was later changed to SA315, and a new model, known as the SA318 Alouette-Astazou, also entered production. This had several performance improvements over the earlier Artouste-powered model. The Heeresflieger ordered both versions in quantity with totals of 247 SA315s and at least 54 SA318s, the earlier versions being delivered between 1958-64, deliveries of the latter version commenced in 1968 and were necessitated largely through attrition of the earlier machines. The majority of Alouettes were delivered to 12 squadrons (HFS-1 to HFS-12), four of these attached to each

of the three *Korps*. In addition each *Korps* has its own spearhead battalion (HFB100, 200 and 300) and its own liaison squadron (HFVS101, 102 and 103), all equipped with Alouettes. It was to the spearhead battalions that most of the SA318s were delivered. Many other machines serve with the army weapons school (HFWS), repair squadrons (HFIS), various operational-training units (HFS(L)), and some were also used by the FFS-S section of the joint services *Flugzeugführerschule*. Both variants of the Alouette remain in widespread service and their replacement by the Bölkow MBB 105C and other new types is not expected to be completed until 1986.

Nord-VFW N.2501D Noratlas

Year: 1958.
Manufacturer: Nord-Aviation, France and Flugzeugbau Nord GmbH (later VFW), Germany.
Type: medium range general purpose transport.
Crew: five.
Specification: N.2501D Noratlas.
Power plant: two Bristol/SNECMA Hercules 738 or 758 14-cylinder, air-cooled radial engines, each rated at 2040 hp.
Dimensions: span, 106 ft 7 in; length, 72 ft 1 in; height, 19 ft 8 in; wing area, 1088.9 sq ft.
Weights: empty, 28,765 lb; loaded (maximum), 47,850 lb.
Performance: maximum speed, 273 mph; cruising speed, 201 mph at 4920 ft; climb rate, 1230 ft per min at sea level; service ceiling, 24,600 ft.
Armament: nil.

Designed to meet a 1947 specification issued by the French Armée de l'Air for a new transport aircraft, the prototype Nord N.2500 Noratlas first flew on 10 September 1949, powered by 1600 hp SNECMA-built Gnome-Rhône 14R radials. Seriously underpowered, the second prototype had Bristol Hercules engines. These proved successful and remained the standard power plant for the production version, the N.2501. The Noratlas was already established in French service, when in 1956 a batch of 25 machines was ordered for the new Luftwaffe. At the same time, an agreement for license production was entered into between the parent company in France and the new German consortium Nord Flugzeugbau for 112 mach-

ines. This was later increased to 128 and in 1962 increased yet again to 158, though in the end the total number received was 173 (including the initial 25 from France).

In German service the Noratlas was designated N.2501D and first deliveries went to the *Flugzeugführerschule-S* (FFS-S) transport training flight at Neubiberg and *Lufttransportgeschwader* (LTG) 62 at Köln/Wahn. Further aircraft equipped LTG61 and 63 at Neubiberg and Celle respectively, with a few going to other units such as WS-50 and the experimental establishment at Manching. In 1963 two Nord N.2508 Noratlas were supplied for testing systems in the Transall C.160, one being used by ESt61 and the other stored. This variant was powered by two 2500 hp Pratt & Whitney R-2800 CB-17 radial engines, with wingtip-mounted Turboméca Marboré turbojets. The Noratlas was replaced in service by the Transall and most were phased out of service by 1972, several going to the Greek Air Force and civilian users.

Armstrong Whitworth Sea Hawk 100/101

Year: 1958.
Manufacturer: Armstrong Whitworth Aircraft Ltd, UK, under license from Hawker Aircraft Ltd.
Type: strike fighter (Mk. 100) and long-range reconnaissance and all-weather fighter (Mk. 101).
Crew: one.
Specification: Sea Hawk FGA 100.
Power plant: one Rolls-Royce Nene 103 (R.N.6) turbojet rated at 5400 lb st.
Dimensions: span, 39 ft; length, 40 ft 3 in; height, 9 ft 9 in; wing area, 278 sq ft.
Weights: empty, 9560 lb; normal loaded, 13,785 lb; loaded (maximum), 15,990 lb.
Performance: maximum speed, 599 mph at sea level, 587 mph at 20,000 ft, 560 mph at 36,000 ft; initial climb rate, 5700 ft per min; service ceiling, 44,500 ft.
Armament: four 20 mm Hispano cannon in nose; bomb load, approximately 1600 lb offensive stores underwing.

Originally designed as a fighter intended for RAF use, the Hawker P.1040 prototype first flew

Below: a Nord N.2501D Noratlas of LTG 63 approaches the runway.

Above: an Armstrong-Whitworth Sea Hawk Mark 101 of the Bundesmarine's MFG 2 based at Schleswig and later at Eggebeck. This version was used for radar reconnaissance. Although the German Sea Hawk's were land-based, they retained the folding wings of the Fleet Air Arm's Sea Hawks, which operated from aircraft carriers.

on 2 September 1947. Two other prototypes were built to naval specifications and the type was adopted by the Admiralty as the Sea Hawk. Six variants were built, primarily for the Royal Navy, and production of the type ended with the FGA 6 in 1956. Meanwhile, the newly created Bundesmarine had been seeking a new strike and long-range reconnaissance shipboard fighter for the Marineflieger. Although this service possessed no carriers, ability to operate from other NATO countries carriers was desired. Some months after production for the Royal Navy had finished, the Dutch Navy placed an order for the type, closely followed on 20 February 1967 by an order for 68 machines for the Bundesmarine. Production was evenly divided between two versions, the Mk 100 and Mk 101; the former optimized for the strike role and very similar to the Royal Navy FGA 6, while the Mk 101 was modified for radar reconnaissance and carried the EKCO Type 34 radar in a pod under the port wing. Both versions also had UHF radio and featured a distinctive enlarged vertical fin and rudder. Following crew training on the first 12 machines at Lossiemouth in mid-1958, *Marinefliegergeschwader* (MFG) 1 and 2 at Schleswig and at Eggebeck flew them until 1964.

Right: A Canadair Sabre Mk 6 in the colourful markings of Jagdgeschwader 71 'Richthofen'. Three Luftwaffe fighter wings operated this Canadian-built variant of the Sabre.

Above: Jagdgeschwader 72 equipped with the Sabre in 1959 and this Mark 6 was pictured in 1966.
Left: the Luftwaffe took delivery of 88 Fiat-built North American F-86K Sabre all-weather fighters. The nose-mounted radar and cannon armament distinguished this version from the day fighter Sabre variants.

Canadair CL-13A & B Sabre (North American F-86E)

Year: 1958.
Manufacturer: Canadair Ltd under license from North American Aviation Inc.
Type: day fighter.
Crew: one.
Specification: CL-13B Sabre 6.
Power plant: Avro Orenda 14 turbojet rated at 7275 lb st.
Dimensions: span, 37 ft 1 in; length, 37 ft 6 in; height, 14 ft 7 in; wing area, 302 sq ft.
Weights: empty, 10,850 lb; loaded, 17,315 lb.
Performance: maximum speed, 710 mph at sea level, 680 mph at 36,000 ft; climb rate, 40,000 ft in 6 min; combat radius, 363 miles.
Armament: six 0.50 in Browning machine guns in nose.

North American (Fiat-built) F-86K Sabre

Year: 1961.
Manufacturer: North American Aviation Inc and Fiat, Italy.
Type: all-weather fighter.
Crew: one.
Specification: F-86K (NA-232 Batch).
Power plant: one General Electric J47-GE-17B turbojet with afterburner, rated at 5425 lb static thrust, 7500 lb with afterburning.
Dimensions: span, 37 ft 1 in; length, 40 ft 11 in; height, 15 ft; wing area, 287.9 sq ft.
Weights: empty, 13,367 lb; loaded, 16,252 lb.
Performance: maximum speed, 692 mph at sea level, 612 mph at 40,000 ft; climb rate, 1 min to 12,000 ft, 7.3 min to 40,000 ft; combat ceiling, 47,700 ft; service ceiling, 49,600 ft; combat radius, 272 miles.
Armament: four 20 mm M-24A-1 cannons in nose; two GAR-8 Sidewinder AAMs (some aircraft only).

Making its first flight on 1 October 1947, the prototype XP-86 paved the way for what was to prove one of the most successful combat aircraft of all time. It was the Western world's first combat type capable of supersonic speeds and during the 1950s it formed the backbone of the USAF and many other major and minor air arms. It is perhaps best remembered for its role in the Korean War. In 1949 the Royal Canadian Air Force urgently required a modern fighter and with sufficient quantities to warrant license production, Canadair Ltd produced the basic F-86E variant for the RCAF, under the designation CL-13 Sabre 2 and 4. Many of these variants were supplied to other air forces, notably the USAF, RAF, Greece and Turkey. Later on, many ex-RAF machines were supplied to Italy and Yugoslavia.

With the introduction of the Canadian Orenda 10 engine into the airframe, the CL-13A Sabre 5 was produced, some 75 out of the total of 370 built going to the Luftwaffe where the type was used by *Waffenschule*-10 for converting aircrew to the two-operational versions of the Sabre that were to enter service. These were the CL-13B Sabre 6, 225 of which were delivered, and the F-86K all-weather fighter built under license by Fiat in Italy, though of the 88 delivered to the Luftwaffe not all were used. The Sabre 6 was delivered to WS-50 and most served with the three operational fighter wings, *Jagdgeschwader* 71, 72 and 73, and a few with *Erprobungsstelle* 61. The F-86K was a variant of the distinctive-looking F-86D 'Sabre Dog' all-weather fighter, in which the all-missile armament of the latter was replaced by a revised nose, housing four 20 mm cannons and simpler radar-coupled fire-control system. The Luftwaffe machines were from the final production batches, some having later mark wings with an extended span of 39 ft 1 in. The F-86K was used operationally only by JG74. Sabres served with the Luftwaffe from 1958 until 1965.

Lockheed F-104F, F-104G, RF-104G, TF-104G Starfighter

Year: 1961.
Manufacturers: Lockheed Aircraft Corporation, and European/NATO consortium.
Type: single-seat fighter-bomber, reconnaissance fighter, two-seat combat trainer (F-104F, TF-104G).
Crew: one (F-104G, RF-104G); two (F-104F, TF-104G).
Specification: F-104G.
Power plant: one General Electric J79-GE-11A turbojet rated at 10,000 lb static thrust, 15,800 lb st with afterburning.
Dimensions: span, 21 ft 11 in; length, 54 ft 9 in; height, 13 ft 6 in; wing area, 196.1 sq ft.
Weights: empty, 14,300 lb; loaded (maximum), 25,027 lb.
Performance: maximum speed (clean), 1550 mph at 40,000 ft, maximum low level speed, 915 mph; climb rate, 1.5 min to 35,000 ft; 6.5 min to 49,200 ft; combat ceiling, 55,000 ft.
Armament: one 20 mm M-61 Vulcan rotary-barrel cannon (F-104G only); Sidewinder AAMs and approximately 4000 lb external ordnance.

Designed in the early 1950s as an advanced interceptor for the USAF, the prototype XF-104 first flew in 1954 and was popularly referred to as the 'missile with a man in it.' Some 277 production machines were delivered to the USAF,

Above right: the Lockheed TF-104G was a two-seat conversion trainer version of the Starfighter. This aircraft was serving with JBG 33 at Buchel.
Above far right: JBG 36 flew F-104Gs from Rheine-Hopsten.
Right: this aircraft is a German-owned TF-104G, which trains Luftwaffe pilots in the United States at Luke AFB, Az.

Above: this TF-104G Starfighter flew with JBG 33 from Buchel in 1975.

comprising F-104A and C single-seat models and F-104B and D two-seat trainers. During the mid-1950s several NATO countries, Germany and Canada included, were looking for an advanced fighter and fighter-bomber aircraft with which to replace their large numbers of rapidly aging fighters during the 1960s. Germany, after studying the options available, chose a developed version of the Starfighter that would be optimized for a multimission role. Other countries followed suit, with Canada opting for a similar development but optimized for the strike-fighter role. The result was the F-104G Super Starfighter and to facilitate production for the European countries concerned, the NATO Starfighter Management Office (NASMO) was created. Production was centered in four European countries (Germany, Holland, Belgium and Italy), as well as Canada and USA. All the F-104F models were built by Lockheed, some being delivered to Germany pending introduction of the TF-104G. Under the program, the number of aircraft built exceeded 1700 of all versions, of which Germany received the following variants: Luftwaffe F-104G 503, Bundesmarine F-104G 119, Luftwaffe RF-104G 100, Bundesmarine RF-104G 27, Luftwaffe TF-104G 131, Bundesmarine TF-104G 6, F-104F 30 (all Luftwaffe). Following training problems in Germany, many single- and two-seat F-104s of the Luftwaffe were based at Luke AFB, Arizona, for this purpose. These machines carried USAF markings and came under USAF control. Operational units of the Luftwaffe that received the Starfighter are: *Jagdbombergeschwader* (Fighter-Bomber Wings) 31–34 &

36, with F-104Gs; *Aufklarungsgeschwader* (Reconnaissance Wings) 51 & 52, with RF-104Gs; *Jagdgeschwader* (Fighter Wings) 71 & 74 with F-104Gs. Most F-104F and TF-104Gs were operated by Waffenschule 10 in Germany and the 4510th Combat Crew Training Wing in the United States, with some distributed to the operational wings. In Bundesmarine service, *Marinefliegergeschwader* 1 (MFG1) operates the F-104G and TF-104G, while MFG2 equipped with the F-104G, RF-104G and TF-104G.

Fiat G.91R, G.91T

Year: 1961.
Manufacturer: Fiat, Italy, with license production in Germany.
Type: lightweight fighter-reconnaissance fighter-bomber and trainer.
Crew: one (G.91R), two (G.91T).
Specification: G.91R-3.
Power plant: one Bristol Siddeley Orpheus 803 turbojet rated at 5000 lb static thrust.
Dimensions: span, 28 ft 1 in; length, 33 ft 9 in; height, 13 ft 1 in; wing area, 176.7 sq ft.
Weights: empty, 7405 lb; loaded, 12,500 lb.
Performance: maximum speed, 668 mph at sea level, 675 mph at 5000 ft, 637 mph at 20,000 ft; climb rate, 1 min to 6000 ft, 4.5 min to 13,120 ft, 6 min 40 sec to 24,420 ft; service ceiling, 43,000 ft.
Armament: two 30 mm DEFA cannons in nose; various underwing ordnance loads.

Designed to meet a NATO requirement of 1953 which called for a lightweight high-performance battlefield strike aircraft capable of rough field operation, Fiat proposed their G.91 in competition with designs from seven other European

manufacturers. The G.91 won this competition, although Fiat had already decided in any event to proceed with development and production of 27 G.91As for the Italian Air Force. The G.91R series incorporated a modified nose, housing reconnaissance cameras, and the G.91T was a two-seat variant for advanced training. In 1958 the Luftwaffe became interested in the type and 50 G.91R-3s were ordered from Fiat; agreements were reached for the G.91R-3 to be license produced in Germany by Dornier. Fifty G.91R-4s were also delivered to the Luftwaffe following the cancellation of orders by Greece and Turkey and these served only in the training role, mainly with *Waffenschule* 50. G.91Ts were also delivered from Fiat and built by Dornier, so that by 1973 the Luftwaffe had taken delivery of some 345 G.91R-3s and 66 G.91Ts and these were used operationally by *Jagdbombergeschwader* 41 & 42 (later renamed *Leichtenkampfgeschwader* 41 & 42), and LKG43 and LKG44. (*Aufklarungsgeschwader* 53 and 54 were originally equipped but these two units were retitled LKG44 and LKG43 respectively in 1966). Numerically a major type in the Luftwaffe inventory, the G.91 will remain in service until supplanted by the Alpha Jet.

Above right: a Fiat G.91R-3 built by Dornier, which served with Waffenschule 50, the operational training unit for this aircraft type.
Right: a two-seat Fiat G.91T-1 serving with the communications and instrument rating flight of LKG 41 at Husum.
Below: one of Waffenschule 50's Fiat G.91T-1 trainers about to touch down. The rear cockpit canopy is bulged to improve the instructor's view.

Below: a pair of Fiat G.91R-3 light fighter-bombers take off. They are serving with LKT 41 at Husum.

Above: Breguet Atlantics serve with the Bundesmarine's MFG 3 'Graf Zeppelin' at Nordholz. Their primary role is ASW, but four have been converted for ELINT duties.

Breguet 1150 Atlantic

Year: 1966.
Manufacturer: Breguet Aviation, France, with subcontract in Germany, Holland and Belgium.
Type: long-range maritime patrol aircraft.
Crew: twelve.
Specification: Breguet 1150.
Power plant: two Rolls-Royce (Hispano-Suiza built) Tyne R.Ty.20 Mk.21 turboprop engines each rated at 6105 shp.
Dimensions: span, 119 ft 1 in; length, 104 ft 1 in; height, 37 ft 2 in; wing area, 1,291.67 sq ft.
Weights: empty, 52,800 lb; maximum loaded 95,900 lb.
Performance: maximum speed, 363 mph at 19,685 ft; maximum cruise speed, 342 mph at 26,250 ft; maximum endurance cruise speed, 199 mph; maximum range, 4150 miles; climb rate, 2450 ft per min.
Armament: bomb load, various combinations of standard NATO torpedoes, depth charges and bombs in internal bay; also air-to-surface missiles.

Designed to meet a NATO requirement of 1958 for a Lockheed Neptune replacement, Breguet's successful entry was chosen and two prototypes of the Atlantic ordered in 1959, the first flying on 21 October 1961. Production of the Atlantic was truly international, with the governments of five countries (France, Germany, Holland, Belgium and United States) involved in the procurement program. The main production plants of Breguet and Sud Aviation (France), Fokker (Holland), Dornier (Germany) and Avions Fairey, SABCA and Fabrique Nationale (Belgium) forming a consortium headed by Breguet for building the airframes. In addition, production of the Rolls-Royce Tyne engines by Hispano (later SNECMA) in France involved MAN in Germany and FN in Belgium. Ordered by the naval air arms of Germany, Holland, France and Italy within NATO, the Bundesmarine received 20 examples, which all went to *Marinefliegergeschwader* 3 based at Nordholz. The machines have been progressively updated; four have been modified as Elint aircraft, while the other 19 in service (one having been lost) are being modified by Dornier to have improved search radars, electronic surveillance measures and navigation systems.

Above and below: the Heeresflieger's standard light transport helicopter is the Dornier-built Bell UH-1D Iroquois. The pictured aircraft served with LHFTR 10 at Celle.
Right: this UH-1D served with HTG 64 at Ahlhorn in 1980. Since then a reorganization of the Luftwaffe's transport element has resulted in three Lufttransportgeschwader operating a mixed force of Transall C.160 transports and UH-1D helicopters.

Bell/Dornier UH-1D Iroquois; Bell Model 212

Year: 1968.
Manufacturer: Bell Helicopter Company, United States, and Dornier-Werke GmbH, Germany.
Type: utility helicopter.
Crew: two, plus up to 13 troops.
Specification: UH-1D.
Power plant: one Lycoming T53-L-11 (or -13) shaft turbine rated at 1100 (1400) shp.
Dimensions: rotor diameter, 48 ft 3 in; length, 41 ft 7 in; height, 14 ft 2 in.
Weights: empty, 5060 lb; normal loaded, 9460 lb.
Performance: maximum speed (loaded), 138 mph; cruising speed, 126 mph; service ceiling, 15,763 ft; normal range, 357 miles.
Armament: nil.

Winner of a US Army competition in 1955 for a new battlefield utility helicopter, the Bell Model 204 first flew in prototype form as the XH-40 on 22 October 1956, and subsequently received the US Army designation UH-1. Produced in large numbers for that and other services over the years, the type was progressively improved, and the Model 205/UH-1D variant first flew on 16 August 1961. Germany acquired two aircraft from the United States for evaluation by Est61 at Manching, these being followed by four more ex-USAF machines, which were assembled by Dornier. A large number of UH-1Ds was required by the Luftwaffe and Heeresflieger and license production of the type by Dornier commenced in 1968, with final deliveries in 1971. A total of 344 machines was delivered, with 204 going to the Heeresflieger and 140 to the Luftwaffe. Also part of the contract was a total of 16 for police border-patrol duties (these being civil registered); the original proposal for 27 machines for the Bundesmarine was cancelled. In Luftwaffe service the main user is *Luft-transportgeschwader* (LTG) 61 based at Landsberg, with detachments at numerous operational airfields; other users are the FBS at Koln-Bonn, HFS at Fassberg and HRVStl, 2 and 3 at Ahlhorn in the SAR role. With the Heeresflieger most of the UH-1Ds are attached to a *Korps Kommando*, of which there are three, under the designations *Leichtestransportregimenten* (LHFTR) 10, 20 and 30, respectively based at Celle, Roth-Nurnberg and Fritzlar. Three Bell Model 212s were also acquired, these serving with the Italian operated Decimomannu base flight in Sardinia on SAR duties.

Transall C.160A, C.160D

Year: 1968.
Manufacturer: Transall (VFW-Fokker and
MBB in Germany, Aerospatiale in France).
Type: STOL tactical transport.
Crew: four, plus accommodation for 93 troops,
or 81 paratroopers, or 62 stretcher cases plus
four attendants.
Specification: C.160D.
Power plant: two Rolls-Royce Tyne R. Ty.20
Mk 22 turboprop engines, each rated at
5665 shp (6100 eshp) with water/methanol
injection.
Dimensions: span, 131 ft 2 in; length,
105 ft 3 in; height, 38 ft 5 in; wing area,
1722.7 sq ft.
Weights: empty, 61,843 lb; normal loaded,
97,440 lb; maximum take off 108,250 lb;
maximum payload 35,280 lb.
Performance: maximum speed, 333 mph at
14,760 ft; economical cruising speed, 308 mph
at 26,250 ft; takeoff run at maximum weight,
2600 ft; maximum range with maximum
payload and reserves, 730 miles; maximum
range with maximum fuel and 17,640 lb
payload, 3010 miles.

The C.160 was designed to meet the different
requirements of two air forces: the Luftwaffe for
a medium-range tactical transport with STOL
capability for operations in the European
Theater and the Armée de l'Air, which needed
a long-range medium-size economical transport capable of meeting its several overseas
commitments. Both air forces also required a
replacement for the Noratlas transports and,
despite some political difficulties in the early
stages, and the problems of setting up production in Germany and France as well as various
subcontracts placed in other countries, the
resulting machine has proved very successful.
Following the creation of Transall (*Transporter
Allianz*) in 1959, three prototypes were built, the
first of these flying on 25 February 1963 and the
second and third on 25 May 1963 and 19 February
1964 respectively. Meanwhile six preproduction
aircraft were ordered, these being delivered to the French Air Force for joint service
development flying in 1965. In 1964 a production contract was placed by the two governments for 160 aircraft, 110 of these for the
Luftwaffe as C.160Ds, the remaining 50 as
C.160Fs for France. The first German machine
was delivered in June 1967 and later that year
Germany wanted to reduce its order by 20
machines. The French protested, and the Luftwaffe took delivery of all 110, though later 19
aircraft were sold to Turkey. Entering service
with *Lufttransportgeschwader* (LTG) 63 in 1968,

Left: the Heeresflieger's Sikorsky CH-53G heavy lift helicopters were built by VFW-Fokker. This example served with MHFTR 15 at Rheine.

and LTG 61 in 1971, now respectively based at Hohn and Landsberg, these two units form the heavy tactical transport element of the Luftwaffe's transport fleet, with training undertaken by LTG 62 based at Wunsdorf

Sikorsky/VFW-Fokker CH-53G (S-65)

Year: 1969.
Manufacturer: Sikorsky Aircraft, United States and VFW-Fokker GmbH, Germany, under license.
Type: heavy transport helicopter.
Crew: three, plus up to 38 troops.
Specification: VFW CH-53G.
Power plant: two General Electric T64-GE-7 shaft turbines each rated at (max) 3940 shp.
Dimensions: rotor diameter, 72 ft 3 in; length (fuselage), 67 ft 2 in; height, 24 ft 11 in.
Weights: empty, 24,000 lb; maximum takeoff 42,000 lb; payload 18,000 lb.
Performance: maximum speed, 196 mph; cruise speed 173 mph; maximum climb rate, 2180 ft per min; service ceiling, 21,000 ft; range, 540 miles.
Armament: nil.

Designed to meet US Marine Corps requirements for a heavy assault and transport helicopter, the S-65/H-53 prototype first flew on 14 October 1964 and since then a variety of versions have been produced in large numbers for many users. During the 1960s the Bundeswehr looked for a suitable replacement for its limited-capacity H-34 Choctaws and H-21 Shawnees and, following a decision to reequip with the CH-53G, 133 of the type were ordered in 1968 to be built under license by VFW-Fokker, with Dornier and Messerschmitt-Bolkow-Blohm acting as major subcontractors. The first of these flew on 11 October 1971, but in the meantime two additional machines had been purchased direct from the United States in 1969 and these were delivered to *Erprobungsstelle* 61. In 1972, the production order was cut to 110 machines and initial deliveries were made to ESt61 and the *Heeresfliegerwaffenschule* (HFWS). From March 1973, machines progressively equipped the three medium transport regiments, MHFTR 15, 25 and 35, respectively attached to I, II and III *Korps* and each unit operating two *Staffeln* of 16 aircraft. Deliveries were completed in 1975.

Left: the Transall C.160 replaced the Noratlas as the Luftwaffe's tactical transport from 1967. A late production C.160D is shown.
Below: each CH-53G equipped transport regiment of the Heeresflieger can carry up to 1000 men in one airlift.

Right: operational conversion training
on the Transall C.160 is carried out at
Wunsdorf by LTG 62.

Below: these Sikorsky CH-53G helicopters
serve with MHFTR 15. Note that the
aircraft in the background has its
main rotor and tail boom folded.

Below: the Dornier Do 28D Skyservant serves as a communications aircraft with many Luftwaffe units. This example belongs to AG 51, Bremgarten.

Dornier Do 28D-2 Skyservant

Year: 1970.
Manufacturer: Dornier-Werke GmbH.
Type: light STOL utility aircraft.
Crew: one or two, plus up to 13 passengers.
Specification: Do 28D-2.
Power plant: two Lycoming IGSO-540-A1E six-cylinder, horizontally opposed, air-cooled engines each rated at 380 hp.
Dimensions: span, 50 ft 11 in; length, 37 ft; height, 12 ft 9 in; wing area, 308 sq ft.
Weights: empty, 4818 lb; maximum takeoff, 8140 lb.
Performance: maximum speed, 199 mph at 10,000 ft; cruising speed, 143 mph; maximum range (internal fuel), 1143 miles; initial climb rate, 1180 ft per min; service ceiling, 25,451 ft.
Armament: nil.

The Do 28 series started life as a logical development of the highly successful Do 27, in effect being a twin-engined version of the latter. The prototype first flew on 29 April 1959. One example of the Do 28A-1 was issued to the *Flugbereitschstaffel* (FBS) for VIP duties. The Do 28D was a completely new design and a much larger aircraft, the first of three prototypes flying on 23 February 1966. Like the Do 27, it was intended for both the military and civil markets and has also proved a very successful type. Four Do 28Ds were delivered to the FBS as VIP transports, while production of the military variant (Do28D-2) got underway for the Bundesmarine and Luftwaffe as communications and utility transports. The first 20 machines were delivered to the Bundesmarine's MFG5 at Kiel, replacing Pembrokes. Following Luftwaffe evaluation by ESt61, a total of 105 machines was delivered (including the four originally supplied to the FBS), these serving with all the main *Geschwader* and the *Flugzeugführerschule* at Wunsdorf, replacing most of the older utility types. A few also serve with the *Technische Schule* 1 (TSLw1) at Kaufbeuren for technical-training duties. These machines are often fitted with underwing fuel tanks to extend their range.

Above right: the Luftwaffe's only Do 28A-1 serves as a VIP transport.
Below: this civil registered Do 28D-2 was later delivered to the Bundesmarine.

McDonnell-Douglas RF-4E/F-4F Phantom

Year: 1971.
Manufacturer: McDonnell-Douglas Corporation.
Type: RF-4E: tactical reconnaissance; F-4F: fighter interceptor and strike.
Crew: two.
Specification: RF-4E.
Power plant: two General Electric J79-GE-17 turbojets rated at 11,870 lb static thrust and 17,900 lb with afterburning.
Dimensions: span, 38 ft 5 in; length, 62 ft 10 in; height, 16 ft 3 in; wing area, 530 sq ft.
Weights: empty, 28,000 lb; normal loaded, 46,076 lb; maximum takeoff 57,320 lb.
Performance: maximum speed clean, 910 mph at 1000 ft, 1500 mph at 40,000 ft; service ceiling, 70,000 ft; tactical radius (with tanks), 685 miles; initial climb rate, 28,000 ft per min.
Armament: nil.

Designed to meet 1953 US Navy requirements for a long-range, single-seat fighter with cannon armament, rapid changes in the requirement led to a two-seat, missile-armed fighter which emerged as the XF4H-1 Phantom II in 1958. Ordered in quantity for the USN in its F-4A and B versions, the USMC also placed orders, initially for the RF-4B reconnaissance version. The USAF ordered the F-4C and D versions, plus the RF-4C reconnaissance version (which in fact preceded the RF-4B in design). Experience in the Vietnam War led to another major variant, the F-4E, with a fixed M-61AI Vulcan 20 mm cannon housed under the nose and other new versions were appearing for all three Services as well as for export to many foreign air arms. The impressive record of the Phantom family is well detailed

Right: this McDonnell-Douglas F-4F Phantom serves as a conversion trainer for Luftwaffe crews with the USAF's 35th TFW at George AFB, California. Although they wear USAF insignia, the US based F-4Fs are German owned.
Below: this RF-4E Phantom serves with AG 51 'Immelmann' at Bremgarten.

Top: one of the United States based
McDonnell-Douglas F-4F Phantoms pictured
at George AFB in 1973. Ten of the 175
F-4F Phantoms purchased by Germany were
retained in the United States for training
and a supplementary batch of 10 F-4Es
was bought in 1977.
Above: one of JBG 36's F-4F Phantoms
pictured during the 1978 NATO Tactical Air
Meet at Wildenrath.

elsewhere, one of the major milestones being
production of the 5000th machine in 1978.
Needing a more effective reconnaissance aircraft than the RF-104Gs, the Luftwaffe ordered 88
RF-4Es. The RF-4E version is basically the F-4E
airframe with the RF-4C camera nose. These
replaced the RF-104Gs of AG.51 and 52 from
September 1971 onward, the released Starfighters being converted back to standard
F-104G models for Luftwaffe use. In 1971, the
RF-4Es proving satisfactory, the Luftwaffe purchased 175 more Phantoms, this time for air-
defense duties and the ground-attack role. This
version is the F-4F, a modified F-4E, and in the
former role it entered service with JG71 and
JG74, and the latter role with JBG35 and 36, the
four wings equipping between 1973–76.

Westland Sea King Mk 41

Year: 1974.
Manufacturer: Westland Helicopters Ltd, United Kingdom, under license from Sikorsky, United States.
Type: long-range search-and-rescue helicopter.
Crew: four, plus up to 22 passengers.
Specification: Sea King Mk 41.
Power plant: two Rolls-Royce Gnome H.1400 shaft turbines each rated at 1500 shp.
Dimensions: rotor diameter, 62 ft; length (fuselage), 57 ft 2 in; height, 15 ft 11 in.
Weights: empty, 11,311 lb; maximum loaded, 20,500 lb.
Performance: maximum speed, 144 mph at maximum weight; cruising speed, 132 mph at maximum weight; maximum climb rate, 1770 ft per min at maximum weight; maximum range, 300 miles at maximum weight.
Armament: nil.

The prototype Sikorsky HSS-2 Sea King first flew on 11 March 1959 and entered service as the SH-3A with the US Navy in September 1961. Designed primarily as an antisubmarine warfare helicopter, Sea Kings were built under license in Italy by Agusta for the Italian Navy and by Westland in the United Kingdom for the Royal Navy, the latter being an Anglicized version of the SH-3D and used in the utility role as well as the normal ASW role. The Mk 41 ordered by the Bundesmarine was one of a number of Sea Kings developed and built by Westland especially for the SAR role, normal ASW gear being omitted, but search radar capability is retained if needed. Twenty-two of the type were ordered in 1969, with the first production aircraft going to RNAS Culdrose, England, where the German crews were trained by the Royal Naval Foreign Training Unit between 1972–74. First deliveries to Germany were made in late 1973, the sole user being *Marinefliegergeschwader* (MFG) 5 based at Kiel-Holtenau, with detachments at Sylt, Borkum and Heligoland. A total of 23 machines was in fact built, as one machine was lost prior to delivery and was replaced.

Below: 22 Westland Sea King Mark 41 search and rescue helicopters were bought to equip the Bundesmarine's MFG 5, which is based at Kiel with detachments along West Germany's North Sea coast.
Below right: this MBB 105 was evaluated by ESt 61 before the helicopter was ordered into production.

MBB105M/MBB105P

Year: 1976.
Manufacturer: Messerschmitt-Bölkow-Blohm GmbH.
Type: light observation, liaison and utility helicopter (MBB105M) and antiarmor helicopter (MBB105P).
Crew: two, plus four passengers.
Specification: MBB105M.
Power plant: two Allison 250-C20 shaft turbines each rated at 400 shp.
Dimensions: rotor diameter, 32 ft 3 in; length (fuselage), 28 ft; height, 9 ft 9 in.
Weights: empty, 2447 lb; maximum loaded, 5070 lb.
Performance: maximum speed, 163 mph at sea level; cruising speed, 145 mph at sea level; climb rate, 1771 ft per min; service ceiling, 16,500 ft.
Armament: MBB105P: TOW or HOT guided missiles, 80 mm unguided missiles, machine guns or cannons.

The Bölkow 105 was the first helicopter from this manufacturer to achieve production status, having been preceded by three projects between 1961–66. These were the Bölkow 102 Heli-Trainer, a ground instructional training machine, the Bo 103, tested by *Erprobungsstelle* 61 in 1962, and the Bo 46 experimental heli-

Above: the MBB 105M is replacing the elderly Alouette II in the communications and observation helicopter roles. A total of 227 MBB 105Ms is on order.

copter, three of which were built. The first prototype Bo 105 flew on 16 February 1967, but was later destroyed through resonance problems, and the second machine and all subsequent production machines were fitted with the rigid-rotor system developed by Bölkow. This second machine was also tested by ESt61 in the early 1970s and in 1974 the type was ordered for the Heeresflieger. By 1976 several Bo 105s were serving with ESt61 and the *Versorgungsstaffel* at Celle and main production deliveries of the Bo 105M started in 1978, 227 of this version were on order to fulfil communications and liaison duties. In order to meet the army's requirement PAH-1 for an antiarmor helicopter the Bo 105P is also in service, final deliveries of the 212 on order are scheduled for 1982. Each Army *Korps* will receive a full regiment of 56 Bo 105Ps operating at divisional level in conjunction with the Bo 105Ms to form air-mobile formations, and these will supplant a majority of the Alouettes currently in service. The Bo 105 also serves with the *Heeresfliegerwaffenschule* (HFWS) at Buckeburg, and it is believed this unit assimilated some machines originally destined for Luftwaffe service.

Dornier/Dassault-Breguet Alpha Jet

Year: 1980.
Manufacturer: Dornier GmbH, Germany, Avions Marcel Dassault-Breguet Aviation, France.
Type: tactical strike/trainer.
Crew: one (operational), or two (training).
Specification: Alpha Jet A (Luftwaffe).
Power plant: two SNECMA-Turbomeca Larzac O4-C5 turbofan engines each rated at 2975 lb thrust.
Dimensions: span, 29 ft 11 in; length, 40 ft 4 in; height, 13 ft 9 in; wing area, 188.3 sq ft.
Weights: normal takeoff (clean), 13,227 lb; empty, 6945 lb.
Performance: maximum speed, 576 mph at sea level, 560 mph at 40,000 ft; service ceiling, 45,000 ft; climb rate, 11,200 ft per min; tactical radius at maximum load (hi-lo-hi), 391 miles.
Armament: 27 mm Mauser cannon in ventral pod; external stores, 4850 lb.

During the 1960s both Germany and France were drawing up requirements for a subsonic light strike trainer of relatively simple design to equip the Luftwaffe and Armée de l'Air during the 1970s. In 1968 the German and French governments approved development of such an aircraft as a joint venture. Four prototypes were ordered in February 1972, with Dornier to build the second and fourth machines and Breguet to build the first and third. Alpha Jet 01 made its first flight on 26 October 1973, and 02 made its first flight from Oberpfaffenhofen on 9 January 1974. While the French requirement is primarily for the Alpha Jet to be used as an advanced trainer, the Jaguar fulfilling their strike role, the Luftwaffe's main requirement is for the Alpha Jet to replace the elderly Fiat G.91s in the strike role. For this purpose they will be operated as single seaters, the rear crew compartment housing electronic counter-measures equipment. However of the 175 machines ordered, the first 60 or so will equip *Jagdbombergeschwader* (JBG) 49 at Fürstenfeldbruck, which will be responsible for training pilots for the two operational wings (JBG 41 and 43) as well as for themselves and in addition JBG 49 will also undertake training of Tornado navigators. Following various delays in production, JBG 49 received its first machines in January 1980 and deliveries to the Luftwaffe should be completed in 1983.

Left: one of the development batch of Dornier/Dassault-Breguet Alpha Jets is displayed with a variety of the offensive stores that the type will carry in Luftwaffe service. The German Alpha Jets will be operated as single seaters – unlike the French trainers – with electronic countermeasures equipment in the rear cockpit.
Below: this Alpha Jet serves with JBG 49 at Furstenfeldbruck, the first *Geschwader* to receive this light strike aircraft.

Below: this Alpha Jet is one of the pre-production batch and it was demonstrated at the SBAC display at Farnborough in 1978.

Below: this Panavia Tornado is readied for a test flight. The Tornado first entered service with the Tri-National Tornado Training Establishment at Cottesmore in the UK early in 1981.

Below: an early pre-production Tornado carries the markings of the Bundesmarine's MFG 1, with which it is scheduled to enter service in 1982.

Panavia Tornado (IDS Version)

Year: 1982.
Manufacturer: Panavia (Germany, United Kingdom, Italy).
Type: all-weather inderdictor, strike, close support and reconnaissance.
Crew: two.
Specification: Tornado IDS.
Power plant: two Turbo-Union RB-199-34R-04 turbofan engines each rated at 9000 lb st, 16,000 lb st with afterburning.
Dimensions: span, 45 ft 7 in fully spread; length, 54 ft 9 in; height, 18 ft 8 in; wing area, 322.9 sq ft.
Weights: empty, 28,000 lb; maximum loaded, 58,400 lb.
Performance: maximum speed, 840 mph at 500 ft, 1385 mph at 36,090 ft; tactical radius with external stores (hi-lo-lo-hi), 863 miles, or (lo-lo-lo) 450 miles; takeoff and landing run, approximately 1200 ft.
Armament: two 27 mm Mauser cannon in nose; external ordnance, 16,000 lb.

The Tornado IDS is designed to meet long-term requirements of three NATO allies (West Germany, Great Britain and Italy) for an all-weather, low-level combat aircraft able to operate effectively in the often poor weather conditions and potentially extremely hostile war environment of the European Theater. The Tornado MRCA prototype first flew on 14 August 1974. It is the first European-designed variable-geometry combat type to achieve service status and is built by a consortium of three national companies (Messerschmitt-Bölkow-Blohm GmbH in Germany, British Aerospace and Aeritalia S.p.A. in Italy) under the overall management of Panavia Aircraft GmbH in cooperation with NAMMA (NATO MRCA Management Agency) acting as customer organization. There are nearly 500 companies with over 70,000 employees engaged in the project; Germany and UK each have a 42.5 percent share of the program, while Italy has 15 percent. A total of 809 aircraft is scheduled for service with the three countries, Germany receiving 212 for the Luftwaffe and 112 for the Bundesmarine. The Italian Air Force will receive 100 and the RAF 385, of which 165 will be the F Mk 2 variant ordered only by the RAF. Joint-service aircrew training commenced in July 1980 with the Tri-National Tornado Training Establishment (TTTE) at RAF Cottesmore with machines taken from the first production batch. Aircraft from the second production batch will go to the Bundesmarine from 1982 onward to reequip MFG1 and MFG2 in the naval strike role. Thereafter Tornado will progressively reequip several wings of the Luftwaffe currently operating F-104 Starfighters. These will be used primarily in the fighter-bomber role. The Tornado can carry a wide range of offensive stores and standard for German machines are the Kormoran antiship missile and the German-designed MW-1 multipurpose weapon.

Left: this Tornado carries four Kormoran antishipping missiles. In Bundesmarine service the Tornado will replace Lockheed F-104G Starfighters with MFG 1 and MFG 2. Eventually the Bundesmarine will operate over 100 Tornados from the Jutland peninsula. *Below:* the Luftwaffe will receive a total of 212 Panavia Tornados and the type will operate in the fighter-bomber role with JBG 31, 32, 33 and 34, replacing those units' F-104Gs.

Above: this Boeing 707-320C, named 'Hans Grabe' is one of four such aircraft currently in use. They serve with the Flugbereitschaftstaffel, based at Köln-Bonn, on long range transport and VIP flight duties.
Below: the Luftwaffe has shown interest in the RFB Fantrainer as a replacement for the Piaggio P 149D basic trainer. The Fantrainer's unusual ducted fan propulsion simulates the handling of the turbojet-powered aircraft onto which the trainee will progress.

MINOR TYPES

Above: 18 North American OV-10 Broncos are operated from Lubeck on target towing and gunnery calibration duties.
Above left: this Putzer Elster B flies with the armed services' *Sportflug* club at Memmingen.
Above far left: 46 Northrop T-38A Talons were bought by Germany for advanced flying training in the US.
Below: three Bolkow Bo 46 experimental helicopters were built in 1962–64.

Left: the EWR-Sud VJ 101C experimental VTOL aircraft was intended as the forerunner of VJ 101D mach 2 interceptor. However this project was cancelled in 1965 after only two VJ 101Cs had flown.
Right: the Luftwaffe received a total of 192 Lockheed T-33A trainers from 1956. The type was progressively withdrawn in the early 1970s.
Below: two Sikorsky S-64 Skycranes were evaluated in Germany between 1962 and 1965, but this heavy-lift helicopter was not accepted for service.

Above and below: 16 Hawker Sea Fury
TT 20 targets tugs served at Lubeck
between 1958 and 1975.
Left: two de Havilland Heron light transports
were supplied to the Luftwaffe as VIP
transports in 1957.
Right: five S.O. 1221 Djinn helicopters served
with the Heeresflieger in 1957–61.

Left: the Bundesmarine's MFG 3 was equipped with 15 Fairey Gannet AS 4 anti-submarine aircraft in 1958. A single Gannet T 5 trainer (illustrated) was also delivered.
Right: ten Saro Skeeter light helicopters were delivered to Germany in 1958–59, and they served with both the Bundesmarine and Heeresflieger.
Below: 32 Weserflug-built Boeing-Vertol H-21C Shawnees served with the Heeresflieger and Luftwaffe in 1957–72.

Left: the Bristol Sycamore Mk 52 was used for crash rescue and search and rescue duties by the Luftwaffe and Bundesmarine, 50 being supplied.
Right: 45 Bell 47G-2 helicopters were supplied to the Luftwaffe from 1957. The type remained in service for some 17 years.
Below: several Hunting Percival Pembroke Mk 54s served with the Bundesmarine's MFG 5.
Bottom left: this Grumman HU-16D Albatross undertook SAR duties with MFG 5. Eight Albatrosses were in service between 1956 and 1972.
Bottom right: this Canadian-built North American Harvard Mk 4 served with FFS-A at Landsberg in 1959.

Below: 34 Hunting Pembroke Mk 54 transports were delivered to West Germany between 1957 and 1959, serving with both the Luftwaffe and Bundesmarine.
Left: the Luftwaffe operates four Lockheed C-140 Jetstars as fast VIP transports.
Bottom right: the HFB 320 Hansa has been used by the Luftwaffe since 1967 and it serves as a transport and ECM trainer.

Index

Bibliography

Enzo Angelucci & Paolo Matricardi *World Aircraft* Samson Low.

Christopher Chant *Air Forces of WW1 & WW2* Hamlyn.

The Encyclopedia of Air Warfare Spring Books.

Peter Gray & Owen Thetford *German Aircraft of the First World War* Putnam & Co Ltd.

William Green *The Augsburg Eagle* Macdonald & Janes.

William Green *The Focke-Wulf Fw 190* David & Charles.

William Green *Warplanes of the Third Reich* Macdonald & Janes.

Bill Gunston *The Encyclopedia of the World's Combat Aircraft* Salamander Books.

Paul A Jackson *German Military Aviation 1956–76* Midland Counties Publications Ltd

Francis K Mason *Battle Over Britain* McWhirter Twins.

Bryan Philpott *German Fighters of WW2* Patrick Stephens Ltd.

Bryan Philpott *Luftwaffe Camouflage & Markings* Patrick Stephens Ltd.

Bryan Philpott *World War Two Photo Albums* Patrick Stephens Ltd.

Alfred Price *The Luftwaffe Handbook* Ian Allan.

Alfred Price *Pictorial History of the Luftwaffe* Ian Allan.

Anthony Robinson (editor) *Air Power* Orbis.

Sir Robert Saundby *Early Aviation* Library of the 20th Century.

JR Smith & Antony Kay *German Aircraft of the Second World War* Putnam & Co.

John Stroud *European Transport Aircraft since 1910* Putnam & Co.

John Taylor (editor) *Combat Aircraft of the World* Eburey Press & Michael Joseph.

Elke Weal *Combat Aircraft of World War Two* Arms & Armour Press.

Tony Wood & Bill Gunston *Hitler's Luftwaffe* Salamander Books.

Various aviation magazines including; *Air Pictorial, Flight, Aircraft Illustrated, Aeroplane Monthly, Air International, Scale Models, Modell-Fan, Airfix Magazine, Aviation News, Air Mail* and the journal of the Royal Aeronautical Society.

Acknowledgments

In compiling this book I have been fortunate to have had the help of many people whose contributions I should like to gratefully acknowledge.

I must give my sincere thanks to my old friend Richard Leask Ward who not only helped with photographs but contributed all the text on post war German aircraft; the following also unselfishly provided, photographs, advice and technical details, Chaz Bowyer, Martin Windrow, Alex Imrie, Ken Munson, Julian Edwards, Dave Howley, Larry Beuttner, John Beaman, Paul Jackson, Stuart Leslie who kindly provided many photographs of WW1 aircraft from the Stuart Leslie/Jack Bruce Collection, Ashley D. Annis; M. J. Gething; Alan W. Hall (Aviation News); M. J. Hooks; David H. Kirkman (Flightlines International); Roger Lindsay; Hans Redemann; Elfan ap Rees; Jerry Scutts; John W. R. Taylor; Robin A. Walker, the Bundesarchiv Koblenz and Mike Bailey who contributed the colour artwork. My thanks also go to the many enthusiasts who, over the years, have helped me in one way or another, with my research into German Military Aircraft and operations.

Picture credits

Air Technical Service Command via M Taylor p 129 (bottom)
R Alexander via R Ward p 178 (top)
via AD Annis/R Ward pp 24–25 (top), 26–27, 142–43, 148 (top), 151 (top), 154 (bottom), 164 (top), 176 (top left), 177 (top right), 187 (top right), 188–89
Archiv Schliephake via K Munson/M Taylor p 104 (bottom)
P Bergagnini via R Ward p 166 (top)
Bildstelle via M Taylor p 106–07 (center)
Bison Picture Library pp 85 (bottom), 89 (bottom), 104 (above), 105 (top), 122 (bottom), 123 (bottom), 126 (center), 136 (center)
Bolkow via M Taylor pp 176–77 (main pic)
JW Boyce p 96 (top)
JM Bruce/GS Leslie Collection pp 16, 32 (bottom two), 36 (bottom), 72–73 (main pic)
Bundesarchiv pp 4–5, 21, 22–23, 76–77, 80 (bottom two), 82 (bottom), 83 (bottom), 84 (bottom), 87 (bottom), 88 (center), 89 (both), 91 (above), 93 (top), 98 (top and center), 99 (both), 100 (bottom), 103 (top), 108 (bottom), 110 (both), 112 (top), 113 (all three), 115 (top three), 117 (all four), 118 (top and center), 119 (top), 120 (all four), 121 (top), 124–25 (all), 127, 130 (bottom), 130–31 (both), 131 (both), 134 (top two), 135 (top two), 136 (center right), 138 (top)
Bundes der Vert via Defence p 147 (bottom)
TA Caws via R Ward p 167 (bottom)
CB Collection pp 1, 9 (top), 10–11 (bottom), 18–19, 30 (below), 31 (both), 32 (top), 33 (below), 35 (top two), 37 (both), 38 (top), 39 (bottom), 40–41 (all four), 44 (top), 45 (bottom), 46 (bottom), 47 (both), 48 (both), 52 (both), 58, 59 (all three), 60–61 (main pic), 62 (both), 64–65 (all three), 66–67 (main pic), 68 (top), 70–71 (main pic), 73 (top), 74–75, 106 (bottom), 109 (top)
CB via Herbert Ekhart p 91 (bottom)
Dassault-Breuget via R Ward p 168
Dornier via M Taylor pp 90 (top), 92 (bottom and top), 93 (center)
via SRB Edwards/R Ward p 86 (top left)
Fairey Aviation Ltd via K Munson/R Ward p 184 (top)
G Fischbach via K Munson/R Ward p 182 (right)
Focke-Wulf via M Taylor 103 (bottom)
N Franklin via R Ward p 94 (bottom)
A Hall/Aviation News via R Ward p 180–81 (main pic)
de Havilland via M Taylor p 182 (top left)
Heinkel via R Ward pp 108 (center), 116 (bottom)
M Hooks p 183 (top)
Howley pp 114 (top), 132 (top left), 137 (top)
Imperial War Museum pp 30 (top), 54 (top), 55 (bottom)
via JABE pp 10–11 (top three)
via B Jones p 114 (bottom)
via B Jones/R Ward p 137 (bottom)
via B Jones, LB Hansen/R Ward pp 119 (bottom), 138 (bottom)
via G Kipp/R Lindsay/R Ward pp 151 (bottom), 170 (bottom), 171 (bottom)
P Lastrow via R Ward p 176 (top right)
via P Leaman p 116 (top)
via P Leaman/RL Ward pp 86 (bottom), 87 (top), 90 (bottom), 97 (bottom), 119 (center)
MMB via Michael Taylor p 78 (bottom)
J Meaden pp 8–9 (bottom), 28–29, 33 (top)
Messersxhmitt-Bolkow-Blohm via Defence pp 2–3, 6–7
K Munson pp 55 (top), 151 (center)
K Munson via M Taylor pp 97 (top), 128 (bottom)
via K Munson/R Ward p 186 (top)
HJ Nowarra p 74 (top)
via H Obert/R Ward p 106 (top)
Panavia Gmbh via Defence p 172
B Philpott pp 12–13 (bottom), 36 (top), 38 (center and bottom), 39 (top), 44 (bottom), 46 (center), 49 (center and bottom), 51 (bottom), 53 (all three), 54 (bottom), 56 (bottom), 57 (all three), 61 (top), 63 (top), 67 (bottom), 68–69 (main pic), 69 (top), 85 (top), 100 (center), 128 (top), 132 (top right), 133 (bottom), 135 (bottom), 139 (top), 140 (center and bottom)
H Redeman/R Ward p 165 (bottom)
Reicharchivr p 70 (top)
Rhein-Flugzeubau GmbH via Defence p 174–75 (main pic)
Saunders Roe Ltd via J Taylor/R Ward p 185 (top)
K Sissons via K Munson p 182–83 (main pic)
via M Taylor pp 14–15, 88 (bottom), 95 (bottom), 96 (bottom), 109 (bottom), 180 (top)
M Taylor via Lufthansa Archiv pp 83 (top), 141 (top)
via Z Titz/R Ward pp 79 (main), 130 (top), 105 (bottom), 112 (bottom)
USAF Museum via M Taylor p 101 (bottom)
RA Walker/R Ward pp 145 (top), 146 (bottom), 148 (bottom), 152–53 (bottom), 165 (top), 184–85 (main pic), 186 (bottom left), 187 (bottom right)
via R Ward pp 20–21 (bottom), 81 (bottom), 94 (bottom), 129 (top), 139 (bottom), 141 (bottom), 144 (both), 145 (bottom), 147 (top), 149 (left), 152 (top), 153 (top), 154 (top), 155 (both), 156–57, 159 (bottom), 160–61 (all three), 162–63 (all three), 164 (bottom left), 166 (bottom), 167 (top), 171 (top), 178–79 (main pic), 181 (top), 186–87 (main pic)
G Wegemann via Defence pp 173 (right)
VFW Werkfoto via M Taylor p 104 (top)
R Williams/R Ward p 150 (top)
J Wood via R Ward pp 174 (top), 179 (top)
via P Zastrow/R Lindsay/R Ward pp 159 (top), 169 (right)

The author would like to thank
Anthony Robinson, the editor
David Eldred, the designer
Mike Badrocke for the artwork on pages 34–35 (main pic), 43 (main pic), 50–51 (main pic), 100–01 (main pic), 102, 121 (bottom), 122–23 (main pic), 132–33 (main pic), 134 (bottom)
Mike Bailey for the artwork on pages 46 (top), 54 (center), 56 (center), 80 (top), 80–81 (center), 111, 115 (bottom), 123 (center), 126 (bottom), 135 (top), 136 (top), 140 (top)
Peter Castle for the artwork on pages 34 (left), 35 (center), 43 (top left), 45 (left)
Penny Murphy for preparing the index